African American Cultural Theory and Heritage
Series Editor: William C. Banfield

The Jazz Trope: A Theory of African American Literary and Vernacular Culture, by Alfonso W. Hawkins Jr., 2008.

In the Heart of the Beat: The Poetry of Rap, by Alexs D. Pate, 2009.

George Russell: The Story of an American Composer, by Duncan Heining, 2010.

Cultural Codes: Makings of a Black Music Philosophy, by William C. Banfield, 2010.

Willie Dixon: Preacher of the Blues, by Mitsutoshi Inaba, 2011.

Representing Black Music Culture: Then, Now, and When Again?, by William C. Banfield, 2011.

D1551377

Representing Black Music Culture

Then, Now, and When Again?

William C. Banfield

African American Cultural Theory and Heritage

THE SCARECROW PRESS, INC.
Lanham • Toronto • Plymouth, UK
2011

Published by Scarecrow Press, Inc.
A wholly owned subsidary of The Rowman & Littlefield Publishing Group, Inc.
4501 Forbes Boulevard, Suite 200, Lanham, Maryland 20706
http://www.scarecrowpress.com

Estover Road, Plymouth PL6 7PY, United Kingdom

British Library Cataloguing in Publication Information Available

Library of Congress Cataloging-in-Publication Data

Banfield, William C., 1961–
  Representing black music culture : then, now, and when again? / William C. Banfield.
      p. cm. — (African American cultural theory and heritage)
  Includes index.
  ISBN 978-0-8108-7786-3 (pbk. : alk. paper) — ISBN 978-0-8108-7787-0
(ebook)
   1. Banfield, William C., 1961- 2. African-American composers—Biography.
3. Composers—United States—Biography. 4. African Americans—Music—History
and criticism. I. Title.
  ML410.B2084A3 2011
  780.92—dc22 [B]   2011017278

Printed in the United States of America

For Anne Lou Banfield (1925–2008)

My beautiful, bold, art and education loving mom

She imbued in me a dynamic, a sincerity for the pursuit of clarity,
integrity, and a directed purposefulness she demanded of our family.

Thanks, Mom

In special memory to those musicians/artists/mentors who passed as I was
completing this work: Brazeal Dennard (2010), Wendal Logan (2010),
Hale Smith (2009), George Russell (2009), Horace Boyer (2009), Dr. Ray
Brown (2009), Duvaughn Banfield (2008), John Hope Franklin (2008),
Mark Ledford (2004), Bill Brown (2004), and Dr. Billy Taylor (2010).

We were seeing examples to live by. Thus we fabricated our own heroes and ideals . . . scholars, jazz musicians and scientists, Negro cowboys and soldiers from the Spanish American War. . . . We felt to develop ourselves for the performance of many and diverse roles . . . not only were we to prepare but we were to perform with, may we say Negro American style. . . . Behind each artist there stands a traditional sense of style, a yearning to make everything of quality Negro American; to appropriate it, possess it, re-create it in our own group and individual images.

—Ralph Ellison, age 50, Introduction to the
1964 edition of *Shadow and Act*

The first black solo musician on the scene was the blues singer. . . . These musicians composed their own songs, based, for the first time on secular problems of the black individual.

—Ben Sidran, *Black Talk*

The musician is the document . . . the information itself. The impact of stored information is transmitted not through records or archives, but through the human response to life. And that response is ongoing, in the air, everywhere, an alternative constantly available to those who have ears to hear.

—Ben Sidran, *Black Talk*

Contents

Foreword

Cornel West

William Banfield is one of the last grand Renaissance men in our time. He is a towering artist, exemplary educator, rigorous scholar, courageous freedom fighter, and spiritual genius. To put it bluntly, Brother Banfield represents the best of the richest tradition in the modern world—the Black musical tradition. This tradition expresses and enacts profound experiences of what it means to be human, what it means to be modern, and what it means to be American. Brother Banfield's classic memoir grounds his unique life of public artistry service in the rich soil of Black remembrance and resistance. Like the great W. E. B. Du Bois's second autobiography that tells his life story through the history of the concept of race, Brother Banfield lays bare his own life story through the history of the flow of Black music and musicians. This is a musical book about a musical life that encourages us to keep alive a great musical tradition. Unique voices sit at the center of this tradition—voices that constitute calls to which other voices respond. Call and response, ancestor appreciation, and antagonistic cooperation are central to the achievement of excellence, eloquence, and elegance in the Black musical tradition. The vast variety of voices in this book is a tribute to the very tradition it enacts and embodies. In this way, this distinctive memoir is itself part of the very tradition it preserves and promotes. Like the Sankofa bird, Brother Banfield looks backward in order to move forward.

Yes there is no Black musical tradition without the ugly backdrop of death—the physical death of each of us, the social death of American slavery, the civic death of Jim Crow, the psychic death of self-hatred and the spiritual death of cold-hearted living. Wrestling with forms of death is at the core of this powerful and poignant memoir—especially the death of Brother Banfield's precious mother, Anne L. Banfield. Grappling with death is the ultimate test of one's humanity and maturity. For many of us, music is an indispensable armor in this battle for sanity and dignity. Brother Banfield's memoir gives us clarity and courage in this tear-soaked and blood-stained battle. Like the African griot of old, this book tells our stories so that we can keep on keepin' on—it talks the talk so that we can walk the walk.

Yet too many young people are stumbling—with little sense of history, no musician's culture that transmits high-quality styles, skills, and habits. Brother Banfield writes out of a deep heartache and heartbreak owing to the deplorable state of youth culture. The wholesale commodification and commercialization of contemporary culture and music have so utterly impoverished us that we too often cling to "bling" rather than fight to keep alive the best of what was and is. The recording, video, and radio industries have taken so much of the rich substance out of the music and given us a culture of superficial spectacle. Brother Banfield's own plethora of musical compositions and performances—from classical symphonies to jazz urbane expressions—are his own artistic efforts to connect with us, especially young people. And, needless to say, his visionary leadership at the prestigious Berkley College of Music as founder and director of its pioneering Africana Studies is historic. The quality of the study of Black music is escalating and expanding. But will the quality of Black music itself continue to escalate and expand? Brother Banfield's life exemplifies a vocation and calling to protect and preserve the high quality of Black musical scholarship and Black musical performance. In other words, Black music matters, in part, because Brother Professor Artist William Cedric Banfield matters.

Acknowledgments

I wish to thank the following people who contributed greatly to the creation and completion of this book:

Krystal Banfield, my incredible wife who understands and commands so much of what I do. I love you.

Stephen Ryan, my straightforward and supportive editor, for helping the book make sense and making the layout as elegant as possible. Stephen, I really appreciate all you've done: giving your extra time, working after hours, and providing invaluable advice on so many issues and details. My best.

Jessica McCleary at Scarecrow for always digging in and helping us deliver the best books possible.

Dr. Cornel West, whose big, bright, bold, and culture-loving mind propels me to clarity. Brother West, I thank you for what you do and represent and for all your friendship, support, ears, and wise advice; Amiri Baraka, for writing our intellectual cultural scripts, and being there always in the wings to cheer on the performances the right way; my many students over the years who challenge, charge, and carry my ideas and music.

Thanks to my family: Bruce, Gayle, Tara, Brooke, Duey, Doug, Anne, and Bill Banfield.

Also, thanks to my second family—the many great musicians and artists who provide me with the love, inspiration, and reasons to make art in our needing world.

Introduction

Moving toward Clarity

From left to right, behind couch: My brother Duvaughn, my father William, and my brother Bruce Banfield; On couch, left to right: My sister-in-law Katie Alice Banfield holding my niece Tara Ann, my grandmother Carrie O'Neal, and my mother. That's me in the front. Detroit, 1968.

There were many mornings in those days I would slip downstairs real early to see Mom. You could smell the coffee that had already been brewed and you could hear the smooth pour of the half-and-half cream, but no sugar. The back stairs, that led up from the kitchen two flights and around walls, channeled the aroma that crept under bedroom doors and summoned me. I awakened regularly and crawled away and out of my dreams in an almost mummy stagger, creeping slowly, stumbling down the stairs to see Mom and have a talk. As I reached the kitchen, she had already been there, I would bet, by 5 a.m. But where I would find her was in the dining room, sitting quiet in her favorite chair with lights off.

She would be there, just sipping her coffee. I would always ask her the same "kindly inquisitive" and rhetorical question, "Mom, what are you doing?" The answer was consistent, "I'm having my coffee, baby." That early morning cup of coffee and the silence of the room where she sat queenly came to mean for me reflection and clarity. I am sure of it now, my mother's clarity concoction was her morning coffee and the moments of order that she squeezed away to herself; sitting early way before the day's business began, was how she claimed clarity. In those days, Mom would have had it all already worked out long before my small ashy feet hit the kitchen floor.

I am coming to think that clarity is getting through the world around you, and you inside of yourself working in that world, and the means you are allowed to see clearly through and under the door and windows that also allow you to reach the seats assembled there for you to rest. Understanding yourself, following your faith and your goals, taking time to be caring and reflective, being set in your soul about your identity and who and what you love in this life—that is clarity. I'm pretty sure now that the word and the tones left to reflect what we see and know, are as valuable as anything we leave here standing to represent culture and the story of life as we live.

My job as an artist is to document the culture as I live through and within it. This book talks about what it is to be a Black musician growing up in America. A story rarely told, badly needed, and from which there is much to gain because our stories of people and music light, inspire, and lift. Why Black musicianship and artistry? Because for Black people all over the world, Black music in particular has played a unique and critical role due to the primacy of music in the evolution of our cultural, historical development in the modern world. Black artistry somehow always attached the meaning of life to the measure of how the music was to be valued. That's why representing this is important. And no matter if it's the spirituals in the 1790s, or blues, jazz, gospel, or R & B, rises hip-hop and contemporary Black artistry and its connection to shaping worldview. And there in the brew of this are all these

Mom and me, c. 1966.

poets, dancers, painters, philosophers, teachers, and musicians telling the meaning of the tales and singing the new representative song.

I often think about what I set out to do in 1983 when I graduated from college. We tried to get out there and make some music. We jammed, gigged, recorded, and we inspired folk and wanted to do something with our music. We weren't trying to change the world, but as I look back on it now, what we participated in was life changing. For the next twenty-five years and without really stopping to think about it, I leaped into music as a way to find and define life, and that too has been life changing. And that should not be left standing as some kind of metaphysical magic; it's really much simpler than that.

There's something about doing music if you are fortunate enough to do it for what it is meant to be. Doing art puts in your grasp a language that speaks to the way people are moved inside, emotionally. It's the most natural internal-to-external and then external-to-internal enterprise you can imagine, and yet we have been exposed to this experience with music since our birth. Some are called to be square in the middle of that creative sharing art called music, and you spend your life with this, and all along the way lots of sounds and joys are made and people are moved. That movement of the soul, that joy can be life sustaining and life changing. People are greatly moved by music, really moved. I figured I'd try to have my life shaped by that moving in our world.

What and How This Memoir Represents

What I wanted to write about now, most importantly, was to share what musicians and artists do, how we live our lives, our ideas about the world, and through these connections, musicians to musician, teachers to student, and students out in the world. You come to a certain point where you realize that what you do lifts and is actually helpful to others or your walking can be a map as much as a painting or song can be inspiring. We rarely tell the story of local, hard-working musicians who play every night at a gig, for your dinner music, at your fund-raising function. I wanted to also represent images and stories of "not famous and fabulously gifted people." In this book there are images of us—musicians, artists, seen hanging out and making culture. The exchange of the ideas, brushes of inspiration, encouragement, direction, the mode of teaching from elder to younger, critique and challenge, copying and borrowing—this is how culture, life, and meaning are cemented. People in the arts—writers and musicians—are constantly in the mix with this kind of exchange. We live from this and grow in it. Because of this, artists leave significant impressions of the world, imprints on the world, and are inspired by living in the world. Their measure of those impressions comes through as artist expressions, be it music, dancing, poetry, painting. This memoir is about the life of being an artist, connecting to people in our world, and it is that humanness that this story is about and the contexts where music artistry weaves, transforms, interacts, and touches folks. This is a multidimensional memoir, also consisting of reflective essays by and interviews with artists dealing with being creative in modern America. Part 1 is growing up themes. Moving on to part 2, which is daily working entries from 2004 to 2010, intersecting with artists, events, interviews, and topical essays, some previously published and some appearing for the first time here. In these pages I filled the book with photo snapshots that I, and others, took to show where creative artistry meets the challenges of cultural chaos by imaging a better world as people participate in expressive culture. Additionally, the photos are accompanied by essays, ideas, reflections that always accompany Black music making.

The coolest part about a memoir, unlike a history book, is that people are less likely to tell you what you believe or have lived isn't true, or that your dates are wrong. We live the life we have lived and we can write what we know, and as South African activist Steve Biko said, "I write what I like." Most importantly here we can all share our stories and enjoy them and one another.

In ways, this is a long reflective poem, a sharing among various artists, with stories and sayings about what I see, like, create, dream, and comment on as I am representing culture. Our job as artists is to document the culture. This sharing, too, highlights valued transfer and how art and cultural codes are in fact transmission vehicles. Since 1980 I have kept a detailed daily log—a musical diary of sorts— of participating and growing up in American society. And each particular year included here, from 2004 to the date of this publication, I have been writing, hanging out, making music, traveling, and fussing with these questions about seeing the world as an artist approaching fifty years old in 2011. To a general reader, it's not that music and art are the "everything is special only" view at all, but that art perspectives are one valued way of sensing the world we live in. People should read what musicians say, listen to how dancers move, sing the way painters visualize experience.

Before I share this musician's tale, I had to say something about the cultural climate of the times I grew up. For me as a musician, music provides the most connective tissue of these experiences, and all the friends and family, which somehow for me anyway, fitted into that, because my family and friends expected that I was happy doing what they knew me to be, a musician. Maybe I'm kind of weird in that way, but that's how I remember it. Yeah I skated, dated, played basketball, attended camps, but I gigged since age ten and the lens through which I saw a whole lot, but not everything, was making music. For me now trying to relive what I can remember, it is that soundtrack of both the cultural times and the music that weaved through the time that helps me best describe what I have seen, heard, grooved with, and believed in.

Growing up in the 1970s and maturing through the 1980s to the 2000s was a fast way through time to our current point of modernity. Cultural shifts were swift, technology raced us even faster forward, and the popular culture arenas seemingly allowed us to falsely believe we had created creativity, all by ourselves and at the push of a button. Our popular megaculture seemed to explode with pervasive trends, styles, and support mechanisms that grew multibillion dollar industries that our time has seen.

And the music industry began to sell society this reality as a common culture destiny and stardom—being famous was now an American dream as was being the "American Idol," the "Apprentice," the "Survivor," or the "Last Comic Standing." And how to get there was any way fast, fabulous, and furiously. This is where we live today through approaching cultural chaos in American culture, and it affects the ways we are learning to be creative or noncreative, to live, or walking deadened. It feels like "my group" were the last ones who lived during a musical period in our culture and society where music was valued for what music deeply means. I want to mark and document what that means before we totally forget. We grew up in a time where people valued music as music, not as "beats" or being cute and famous for five minutes.

In the last forty years or so, I saw the rise and fall of popular artists through self-destructive pop life; world cultural upheaval in social movements, wars, and assassinations; new epochal eras defined by political regimes; the falling of evil empires (South African Apartheid); the rise of four major popular music movements (social protest, punk, grunge, and hip-hop); unprecedented merger of popular music, television, media, fashion, film, and technology; terror which now rules world and cultural events; a second wave of great wars post–World War II and Vietnam (Iraq, Afghanistan) that still keep us from peace and sanity; and the rise and the fall of great leaders—failed and faulty ones, too.

Our world globally shakes, is swelled, rumbled, burned, thawed, leaking, and the most troubling, unprecedented and unchecked political and social indecency, apathy, and greed has risen to unbelievable atrocities and absurdities in our modern era.

Before 2001, 9/11 seemed unthinkable, but afterward we attacked our own people with the Katrina levy failures, and piled onto that a greedy deed with unchecked, unsafe, life-suffocating oil spills. Our inhumanity now seems to be a permanent fixture in the future of American modern culture. Music was still a soiled and yet super soundtrack to all this.

These are the Black popular musicians we listened to not so long ago: Stevie Wonder, Jackson 5, Donna Summer, Sister Sledge, Kool and the Gang, L.T.D., Billy Preston, War, Gladys Knight and the Pips, Spinners, Patti LaBelle, Isley Brothers, Al Green, Chic, Barry White, the Four Tops,

Smokey Robinson and the Miracles, Marvin Gaye, the Supremes, Diana Ross, the Temptations, Booker T. and the MG's, Otis Redding, 5th Dimension, Wilson Pickett, B. B. King, Sly and the Family Stone, Jeffrey Osborne, Earth, Wind & Fire, Natalie Cole, Patti Austin, James Ingram, Tina Turner, Atlantic Starr, Peabo Bryson, Roberta Flack, Donny Hathaway, Ohio Players, Aretha Franklin, Lou Rawls, Cheryl Lynn, George Benson, Johnny Taylor, the Dramatics, the Crusaders, Teddy Pendergrass, Minnie Ripperton, the Chi-lites, Bob Marley, the Commodores, Rick James, the Pointer Sisters, Curtis Mayfield, Harold Melvin and the Blue Notes, Bill Withers, Rufus and Chaka Khan, Lionel Ritchie, Ashford and Simpson, Cameo, Whitney Houston, the Emotions, the Brothers Johnson, Gil-Scott Heron, Brian Jackson, the Staple Singers, Isaac Hayes, the O'Jays, Luther Vandross, Parliament Funkadelic, Shalamar, the Whispers, the Dazz Band, the Gap Band. Can you even imagine what I'm getting at is the difference?

As young jazz musicians, we grew up with Black popular music and gospel. Brought all together, radio programs heard and played music in this mix as well. So, yes, and Miles, Earth, Wind & Fire, Weather Report, Luther Vandross, Billie Holiday, Joni Mitchell, James Cleveland, Steely Dan, and Prince were clearly all great music.

Regarding today's generation of popular artists that would be known by most young people, I thought, too, about who I liked and "bumped" to at ages seventeen to twenty. Born in 1961, I danced to Earth, Wind & Fire, Chaka Khan, and Elton John's "Benny and the Jets." Tupac and Queen Latifah were born in 1970. Erykah Badu was born in 1971, and Jill Scott in 1972. D'Angelo, born 1974; André (Benjamin) 2000, born 1975. John Mayer and Kanye West were born 1977. John Legend, born 1978. Alicia Keys and Beyoncé were born 1981. Janelle Monáe, born 1985; Rihanna, born 1988; and my current students were born in 1993.

It is clear to me that today's young people's music percolates with significantly different cultural meanings, and much of that is expected, good, and I get it. Without the advantages of the technological choices and demand configurations that propel everything today, we lived in a "music-making culture" because the industry relied upon musicians making the music, DJs who loved and knew the music, and distribution and marketing outfits that fashioned themselves out of how people liked musical artists which they connected with. No one is naïve and thinks that money was not a part of this, nor a profit incentive that drove business—it's just that what we want to have is music first. Secondly we want to have music and cultural expressions that contribute to our lives and living. Music is supposed to be a meaningful, beautiful experience, energizing, and mind and booty stimulating, but not a menacing, mechanized madness of beats regulated and controlled to sell stuff or engender apathy and selfish pursuits or champion indecent thinking as a way of life.

Nobody ever expected music to be a drink of holy water either, but I came up as a young musician when music was notes played and sung by musicians— that's music. What happened to Black music especially?

Growing up, I became entrapped by the image of a musician, Jimi Hendrix. Now what does a kid, who has my level of potential, see when he looks at today's popular music culture? Let me set this right. I don't have a problem with the music culture being the sole ownership and direction for this generation. What bothers me most is that we have, for the first time in my life, a generation of young people for whom there is no "musicians' culture" being created. If your griots no longer tell the tradition, if that tradition has been completely hijacked by corporate outsiders, how will the people find their centers again? That's the question I ask daily. I was encouraged by my parents to be my naturally creative self, and I fell in love with playing the guitar and following my creative gifting. Years later I became a man reckoning with what to do with that shaping and my creative gifting while living in a time that needed transformation. Our culture had become broken and disillusioned from the abandonment of the 1980s and 1990s (the new era). When I came up as a musician, things were different, actually *very* different, musically and culturally. I am not suggesting we turn back the hands of time, mythologizing those eras and dreaming backward, but some of that "back in the day" we want back.

Let's Represent

I am a Black man. I was born in Detroit, Michigan, in 1961. I was born with creative gifts into the time of great American social changes in the 1960s. I was named William Cedric Banfield. My parents, William J. Banfield (b. 1924) and Anne L. Banfield (1925–2008) brought forth two other sons before me: Duvaughn Douglas (1948–2008) and Bruce Carlton (b. 1951). They were both baby boomers. I was born later, in another era—the 1960s—and so I was different. As a post–civil rights child, I became aware of these changes as I was shaped too by the cultural, sociopolitical strategies, value systems, religious and dance Black rituals, block clubs and family reunions, communal and expressive products evident in my teen years in the 1970s. That's what being Black meant: seeing yourself by being and defining yourself in a wider mind-set for doing and being about things great even, no limitations. My parents helped me believe in this. I lovvvvve the time in which I was born.

Banfield outing. My parents with brother, Duvaughn, and a young Bill seated on my dad's lap, 1963.

Being an Artist

Being in an artistic community is really quite an extraordinary experience. The life you spend connecting and sharing, exchanging and hanging, being in the spray of artistic life and sensibility is as rich as doing music itself. So artists spend lots of time connecting with each other, hanging, because while being admired and beloved, they are outcasts too. Family, friends, loved ones, and society sometimes do not understand nor value what the life of artistry is about, beyond entertainment. Artists are sometimes thought to be "weirdos." Veiled behind the bold, brass-cussing ass, freestyle feistiness, more than not, there lives a sensitive soul whom many times has thought about and felt ideas, poetically placed words, expressions, and meanings that are treasures and valuable. Many times the musicians are wise philosophers, well read (Charlie Parker was said to read regularly quantum physics), master storytellers, precise and insightful historians, and fluid writers. More than a bowling club, basketball team, golfing party, artists are a connected collective of a community of committed arts—laborers who know each other. As well they can tell you about tons of tunes, recording sessions, busted dives, trickster managers, and cheap club owners and "girls or guys on gigs."

To follow the lives of musicians is a real theater of souls, drama, tales, and characters. More importantly than my own ideas about art and culture, this memoir is about a sharing among movement of artists, and ideas among musicians who hang together.

The reason why I and others have pushed so hard at particularly this issue of Black music is that much of the cultural terrain that defines and documents what Black people have been about— yes, while literature is there— our story has been told through our music. Historical studies are about the people and their cultural, social, political, and humanistic reactions to lived conditions. For us, many times those reactions were translated into musical creations. Black narratives in music globally symbolize and exemplify high reaches toward the measure and depth of human integrity and dignity. Long before America could embrace a Black person legally, the global view of Black artistry, with early accounts from the 1890s, embraced the ingenuity, innovation, artistic impact, and genius of the Fisk Jubilee Singers, Sydney Bechet, Louis Armstrong, Bessie Smith, and Paul Robeson. There is no other group of people whose humanity was measured, tested, and defined by their music, and it was this definition which manifested style, approaches, and conceptions of music making that became the quintessential aesthetic foundation for modern American music and popular music as we know it today. Even in the early twentieth century when racist and hateful depictions of Black people were circulated in American popular culture, consciously calling and claiming Blacks as coons and watermelon eaters, bucks and mammies, Black people were making music that better defined the human condition, and that art went onto actually changing the human condition in modernity. Cultural criticism and the history and documentation of ideas of that process are fundamentally critical and crucial.

My Gifted Gang

My cultural and age group bridges the values divide between the baby boomers (those "older people" born in the mid- to late 1940s now in their midsixties and retiring) and the hip-hop generation of today. I believe my generation, the post–civil rights kids (born during the late 1950s and early 1960s) born after the baby boomers and before the Xbox, hip-hop, and gadget generation, is "the gifting one." Yes, I know, everybody claims their generation is *the* one. The difference is though that our group was given the gift of hard fought and well-earned opportunities and more so than any other. We were expected to do something with those gifts and deliver on the promises of the civil rights fights. Secondly, we believed in those gifts and opportunities and raced and kicked through those doors to reign, obtain, sustain, and maintain the American dream.

And we were master achievers in many fields and areas of expertise, and we were ambitious, bright, and busy. We took the opportunities in education, finance and business, sciences, the arts, government, and we walked into a mainstream social culture that for the first time in this society's history was prepared especially for us. Couldn't care worth a pigeon's butt about White people nor what they thought, especially the Detroiters, who are surely the proudest and cockiest Black people in America. Coleman Young, the steps of the Temptations, the fineness of the Supremes, and making Cadillacs made us that way. Yes, my generation is the golden one. We represent. We have been given the values of hard work, "stick-to-it-ness," citizenry, lovers of good music—great music, yes, the greatest music ever created. But my generation also failed the greater work of those promises which is the true mark of generational accomplishment: to transfer values and successful experiences and strategies, onto the next generation.

Young people born in the late 1980s are not, as far as I can tell, megaculturally feeling by 2011 what we had felt so firmly and fervently as accomplishments, what was valued and fought for. Something changed drastically and before I point to the market-forced, insidious, greed-filled industries, we have to look "in-house" to the golden Black generation. That would be my gang. Where we failed is we were so happy to have powerfully arrived, instead of being strengthened for the long haul of resistance of the "man's" tricks, and giving back to the community. We fell into accomplishment and complacency, so much so that we expected that it would be a protective covering for our children. It wasn't.

Anyway, I can tell you, my students don't really care about anything written by Nina Simone or Marvin Gaye or Earth, Wind & Fire, which to them might as well be Cab Calloway's band, clown suits, hopping antics and all. Civil rights to them is what the Emancipation Proclamation was to previous generations. Hell, Tupac and Biggie to them are the new Martin Luther King Jr., Malcolm X, Elvis! Why are they so far removed from much of our history?

Why wasn't that picture of the world, those values weaved into them? But perhaps, why should they value any of this? I'm no old fart, I get it, Beyoncé and Jay-Z, Will Smith and Jada are fine cultural subjects and idols. I'm not blaming parents my age either. I am simply asking questions. Moreover, we have had little to say, little effective protests, boycotts, legislation to defang the industry monster and current market forced commodities that have poisoned our ideals, prescriptions for success and such which have sensitized us and defined many of our current cultural identities. Now I'm no Luddite living on a bark and soybean farm either. I am a twenty-first century journeyer.

But here's the dilemma: We have so much to show for too, but the generation today and to follow lives in a world where they have to work themselves out of the greasy belly of the cultural monster that we allowed to form during our bliss. Their innovations through the tools of modern technology and communication are mind blowing! The innovations of the communication age, our hyper-produced American consumer driven popular culture too, created the spaces for this monster that thrives on a selfish, noncaring, at times criminally coded mentality and cultural, worldview. Sadly, this generation is more closely aligned for survival or suffocation to that problematic acculturation and self-definition. Being a hustler, pimp, player, trump, and apprentice to this madness has too often become the code words not just as style but as daily practice. While disputes over new identities, class values, and generational divides create problems in every era in our society with "great gain, gaps, and gizmos" and lapses in judgment, more recently all this has created is a different divide causing far more palpable social issues among us than I can remember during my own growth into adulthood. The hardened line of Blackness, victimized defeated normalcy ("Yo bro, I'm still in the struggle . . ."), the blinged-out materialist cultural acceptance of success, these cultural codes as I call them, push people into cold casted identity sets which rule all it seems. Now I'm supposed to be "cool," " hard," "hot," "nerd," "dorkie," "a hustler," "pimp," "thug," "a punk," "gangsta," or "gay." Hmmmmm, which market forced identity that is made into a commodity, sold and styled as normative shall you choose? These hardened "ways of being"—institutionalized in songs, TV, and movies, commercialized culture as urban, being Black, having "juice"—have actually driven a stake down into the heart of our humanity, creativity, civility, sensitivity, individuality—our power, our soul, our caring for each other. And if I want to be a Black musician today, what are my options? Rapper, rapper/R & B producer, or a gospel singer?

Keeping the Code

Today's generation might have become trapped in a greedy world my group participated in, but was created and insidiously crafted by greedy, financial regimes which set a mold and ruled for their own profit. My group participated in but didn't reshape the new era with the older values, really. I believed when I turned fifty though I would be an old assed dude, but one who could look other old assed dudes in the face and say, "Y'all know you ain't right." Maybe I would be looking in the mirror at the "y'all" and it would be me looking into my own fogged, failing eyes. Approaching my fiftieth birthday three years out, I don't feel that way at all though. But I did wake up to my reality in this my year of clarity when I turned forty-seven, as we witnessed powerful leaders who continued in those messed up ideals of the 1980s and tricked their nation and the world. We had recently a horrible, horrible president whose worth was $10 million and whose evil second in command was worth more than twice that. These kinds of ugly bad men sided with profiteers and business moguls whose greed ruled their ambitions, and they rigged political, financial systems, corporations to Supreme courts to provide profit and cultural cover for themselves and their constituents. The larger "megaculture" followed suit and continues to sell and sell and sell our souls away for more stuff and we are now all drinking from soiled wells. Wonderfully, during their long awaited political demise came a younger man, born too in 1961, who spoke of significant change. We bathed in this idea, this hope, and it changed and raised at that moment, for a mini-second, our national consciousness, debates, and discourses politically.

I felt inspired, obsessively compelled as an artist to respond in my own ways. I had already figured out that it was important to become focused on addressing a needed transformation through imaging, imagining, teaching, creating, and representing "cultural codes." I speak of "cultural codes" as sets of principles, representations, and practices understood to be embraced by society. This all suggests certain ways of being, thinking, looking, and styling as normative, preferable, and validated. Because codes set patterns for how people think, behave, and define their roles, rationale, worldviews, and value systems, we ought to be thinking about how those codes are defined.

Those cultural codes that defined aspects of thinking and being that moved our culture forward—those I was committed to. I actually had been working on these ideas in music, in teaching, and through my writings for many years, but my year of clarity helped to crystallize my commitments and secure a grasp on my passions.

The summer of my year of clarity in 2008 was oddly clouded and confused, too, because of the death of my champion, my advisor par excellence: my mother. The profundity and absurdity it seemed of losing the very person who gave you life: now what do you do in the living? My father had all these years provided my gender identity as a Black man of value, hardworking, progressive thinking, and success. But it was my mother who was my "think tank partner and sparer," challenging my ideas and encouraging my experiments, and who could be seen at my concerts listening to my music and telling stories to her friends always about what I did to be and become and what my parents were doing to assure the arrivals.

Now I ask you, how do you forge ahead and beyond without the one who wrote you into existence? It's like Billie Holiday singing along endlessly without any accompaniment; the tone, the sentiment is there but sometimes the tones of songs need their sounding sonority. My mother in all I did was my sounding sonority. I asked hard the question, "Will I be a better human and artist without her to check in with?" "Mom, am I doing it the way you'd expect me to do it well?" Six months before this, we lost my big brother to a cancer he wouldn't recognize until death was tapping and singing the blues in his ear. A close friend of mine commented, "Man, your mom poured everything she had and believed into you." Pouring what you have into someone is an act of purposeful giving. This idea of love and giving to one another, our ideas and values, and who we are to one another really means even more to me in the light of that great loss. I reasoned in how I might accept these losses, and that becoming an adult may be easier than being one. But we believe in our values because we live and breathe in them from birth.

My values were given to me by strong parents, a loving family, a connected, deeply spiritual committed and community activated church, and great Black music, teachers, and artists. All this was proven as necessary ingredients because the culture and times that brewed around us was fitting for all this. Less and less of this seems to fit in today.

My parents were race parents. They were married for sixty-two years at the time of my mother's soul going home. As Black people, they believed, like Baldwin, that their sons were living proof that Black people were capable of greatness, strong character, ideas, achievements, and contributors in society. I embraced their hopes and their lessons.

I am finding though that there are groups of us who still think this way because we have become by virtue of the needs of our times, in our culture the twenty-first century "race men and women." The concerns, needs, and processes for addressing the megacultural fallout in the twenty-first century are tremendous. I actually like that term, or idea, as outdated and unlikely as it is. What does this mean to be a race man?

It suggests that one is concerned, dedicated, and focused on addressing and working on the social, cultural, and spiritual well-being and furtherance of Black people. It means you view the history as sacred canon and see the possibility of greatness and achievements in those lines of living, those dances, those Hughes blues verses, and the reality of life in those exaggerated Jacob Lawrence cartoonish expressions, and clashes of identity in Beardon's

Me and my father, William J. Banfield in 1970.

collages. But the race men and women were not reduced to just that. Their work was solidly multicultural. For them it started on the block, in their community, and moved toward embracing the role of human citizenry.

I have friends who say this is absurd and that nothing in our cultural trajectory today looks like this or warrants such representations that apply and mean nothing. For them, nobody cares, really, about this. To them, such a positioning of a racial or cultural uplift is unnecessary and why do they feel this way? First, a cultural apathy exists as well as a lack of responses to these issues from younger people who generally can't see race consciousness, pride, nor cultural clarity as a priority. My wife and I don't have kids, but we are artists and educators and we work with and among all kinds of young people. Maybe if I did have kids I would feel less sharply divided on this, but I speak with my family members and friends with kids, and they keep in hands daggers, dripping with blood from the swipes and stabs they have to take at today's culture as they try to desperately shield and protect (to no effect) their children from the excesses in American popular culture. Secondly, when the heat is on us to be progressive and politically correct, inclusive, being bigger is being multiethnic and seems for a second, to suit all just fine. Well, at the end of the day I am still a Black American man, and as the hip-hoppers say, "You gotta represent."

But even more importantly, being "Black folk concerned" means being people concerned, and people come in multiple stripes, forms and we encounter each other through our various human exchanges. And so, speaking as a "twenty-first century race man" has community, national, and global resonance and reason. A more inclusive question might as well be, what must we do now to become more humane? I truly believe that one of the great challenges and charges of the twenty-first century is guiding people in our society to maintain humanness. How must we become again considerate, compassionate, and civil in our exchanges and ideology? Each day we slip away from what that feels like as normative and nowhere is that apathy more evident than in many of our cultural creations in music, Hollywood films, TV, electronic games and sports, and entertainment endeavors.

There is no shortage of skill sets in rhetoric or ideology that we do well. But where we have fallen short, it seems to me, is in the cultivation of being human again and maintaining this. In this configuration of cultural representation, value transfer is huge. It's how wisdom is shared and maintained within a generation and family to family. It's how cousins learn how to be a loving woman from an aunt who owns a business. It's how uncles teach young Black boys how to dance, talk to a lady, tie a bow tie, golf, shoot a free throw, or paint. My uncle trained me weekly how to paint with precision and patience. Culture is trained and transmitted through value transfer, and these are cultural codes which define how people become and are sustained in that becoming. In this cultural configuration there is too much time spent on getting attention, adulation, praise, and fame. To feel good, be famous, be an "Idol or star," and to bypass focused hard work, discipline, excellence, and the long haul of perfecting your skills, is fast becoming the norm, the center practice and not in the margins at all. Disenchantment, pushing the easy button, and complacency have seemingly replaced competency. We do in fact have a generation of young people who through their large and always giving "megaculture mom and dad" are being taught they can do anything now because they have access to it and can push a button to get what they see they want. Because of corporate greed, the proliferation of unchecked violent popular culture, less substance and fast success prescriptions, megacultural suffocation of gadgets, video games, and consumer junk, weakened family and church structures, and broad and far range social incompetence, younger people are being sold a bad bag of tricks. Someone is writing a bad program and selling it as normative when it's clearly dysfunctional. I see this as us being systematically deprogrammed and cut off from our human centers.

My group laments these current cultural configurations constantly, even choking on its fumes. The questions we ask ourselves are: Do we fit in anymore? How do you make your art, besides the fact that you are older, but where does your expression fit into an environment for which there is no definition publicly for what you do? It's not a crybaby's song, or a need for attention since you are getting older, it's being at a fundamental crossroads of meaning actually.

We have a generation who use many languages at their discretion, music and popular film imagery to shape who they think they may want to be like, because it's cool instead of being shaped by a family, parental, uncle tradition of values and some wise ideas of hard work, long range skill sets and how to live. In terms of younger Black people, well, I see many all the time, talk to them and there is, I'm sorry, a palpable lack of confidence, assurance of how beautiful, intelligent, and potentially powerful they can be because of lack of love in their lives, and a missing aura they take in and walk in that assures them they can "be somebody."

Just watch and observe closely and you can see our young men walking, heads down, wired up, hands flapping, rapping expressively to themselves yet loud enough for passersby to feel their frustration, concentration in verse. The music is warped in their heads and wrapped around their everything and says, "Watch out for me, let me be. I just might not see ya, 'cause you don't never see me." This generation is a "walking hurting." They are depicted, imaged in popular culture as angry, volatile, and the public enemy of the urban terrain, and this affects how a generation sees itself. That's what Mr. Baldwin in his letter to his nephew is getting at, about not believing what White people say is your "constructed demise" (. . . the details and symbols of your life have been deliberately constructed to make you believe what White people say about you. . . .) and being race conscious "in-house" shows them who in their own "crab's barrel" is crawling in the wrong direction. It's as if the generation needs a great good word, ". . . be strong, of good courage. Observe, do not turn from it . . . so that you may prosper wherever you go . . . making your way prosperous . . . and having good success . . . be not dismayed and be not afraid." Like the messages in this old world wisdom literature, who's telling them this today? This is why being a self-conscious race and ethnic champion from "the inside of the family" for the sake of saving, imaging, teaching, and securing achievement in many ways gives me reason, pride, and sufficient justification to work toward these ends. Working toward modeling excellence and achievement, artistic expression, creativity, and love of history and culture for our young people now is critical in our society. And why is this necessary? Because you can't inspire the world of changes by yourself; you have to start by making the place where you live on your block percolate with willing minds, able hands, and love-filled hearts to be ready to do the work. My block ain't ready yet.

So as an artist, I'm not really singing my song until I address the state of our cultural demises. And the question today becomes too, whose call is this to accountability? Mom, dad, community, churches, schools, leaders, government policy, entrepreneurial investment, common people in the streets, our rehabilitation investment in the industrial prison complex, political bloggers, health care system (mental, physical), information technology, infoculture, music, entertainment, sports heroes and sheroes, media megacultural industry? These are the players in this megadialogue. We can only look to models of societal success which are immediate, attractive, valued possibilities and can be seen and sustained visibly. We have to be courageous and innovative as Black folks have always been. There needs to be a repositioning, a balance of visible and real options, values, payoffs presented so that where there is a lack of resources, there is a hike on the values that imbue kids with a desire to seek higher goals that make them independent, self-propelled, creative, innovative. If there are fewer resources at home, there needs to be a higher impacting presence in the schools, churches to fill in the gaps. If there are failing family structures in society, there needs to be a more visible projection of what makes a family functional. We don't need to be shown "more dysfunction" is desirable, normative, or entertaining. We need to encourage younger people to make a better way for their families, friends, and communities. I can only speak as a common person who is a musician and who teaches. In our culture creative arts are powerful images, identity carrying and effective expressions that change people's lives, and sustains those identities and ideas. Creative culture seeks a deeper engagement, impact and makes us—me, you—see and feel a deeper valued world.

I show this story by examining our creative history, heroes and sheroes, and their conventions and commitments to cultivate music, a practice in life that raises values that are markings of our best beat in human potential. Everybody has to be accountable for this kind of retooling. Profit and greed drive our cultural blindness but the drive for greed must be slowed. But all this circles around value transfer, transmission, and sustainable valued information, and these must be the center again of our existence in culture. We have to believe in them again and live out within deeper values and spaces of what constitutes the "good life." The artificially produced plastic set of market values has taken our minds off, it seems, the center (inner depth). We have to reach deeper and around the current cultural chaos, reach our centers again and come up with, as Ossie Davis said, "a new mojo on how to be Black again," and for all, how to be humane again. This is a megacultural formula that we can conjure up, mix, prescribe, and disseminate. I truly believe this is the challenge to retool, and we must take a vow to make good on it. Arts and education that cultivates creativity and reflective thinking are bulwarks against a society seemed destined to fall into upholding problematic values and identities that push us to celebrate and glorify mean-spirited competitiveness, hatred, divisiveness, violence, and indecency as normative. Cultivating our culture is one of the investments in ensuring we are the best we are becoming. The safeguards to social chaos at this point, so close to our edges of incivility, are careful and caring concerns for one another.

So, what does this have to do with an artist's memoir, you say?

For me it has everything to do with an artist's memoir. Everything I am coming to believe about our society, making music, reaching people, and being Black, is being dynamically shaped by these societal trends, movements, and the exchanges we are all having trying to make sense of this deafening and defying tempo of our turbulent yet fascinating times.

As I have written as I'm approaching fifty (ages forty-four to forty-nine), this book is meant to be a living expression, a document of public artistry-service in the twenty-first century, a sharing. But maybe too in my own way it is like Baldwin's "letter of fire" (one of the most powerful illustrations of the care of one generation for another). I too see this as a letter and call to "my gang," my group, the mid-forty-year-olders, post–civil rights kids. This is an artistic, poetic, educator's, philosopher's, writer's, musician's, artist's framing of a "moment of becoming," and possibly raising and mobilizing movements of ideas, reflection, and critical action to touch people to be about something that changes the thinking of the world we inhabit.

More importantly, this moment calls us to mobilize and support a younger group coming into mainstream empowerment right on our heels. I still believe in what that powerful, poetic griot Baldwin spoke of, ". . . our living in the jaws of the teeth of terrifying odds and still achieving unassailable and monumental dignity, and reminding us that we come from a long line of great poets who muse so meaningfully that we cause the dungeons to shake and the 'chains to fall off.'"

I want to be continuing in that kind of representation, role, and reason, as long as I have a tune to write and a song to sing with others.

Salvation for a race, nation, and class must come from within. Freedom is never granted, it is won. Justice is never given, it is exacted. Freedom and justice must be struggled for by the oppressed of all lands and races and the struggle must be continuous, for freedom is never a final act, but a continuing evolving process to higher and higher levels of human, social, economic, political, and religious relationships.

> We want to talk about the richest tradition in the history of modernity, and that has to do with musical tradition(s), from people of African descent who were able to transcend and transfigure their moans and groans into an art form . . . Black Music Matters . . . bringing together those voices that actually connect political engagement and social reflection with music, music, music. *I want to disabuse you of the notion that music is simply a form of stimulation and titillation. It's not about superficial entertainment.* We have to peer back into the Spirituals and listen to those non-literate peasant folks who had to struggle against laws that didn't allow them to read or write, listen to that art! . . . We want to remind the younger generation, that they were not singing for some search for a cheap American dream. They were not looking for some narrow conception of success. No, they were looking for a greatness and a magnanimity and an integrity of self respect, self regard that allowed them to love themselves but to do it in such a way that did not require putting others down. Spiritual maturity, moral wisdom, connecting all folks on the human scale. Any time you talk about the Black music tradition, be it Louis Armstrong, Sarah Vaughan, John Coltrane, Alice Coltrane, we mean beyond superficial classifications.
>
> —Cornel West

PART I

THEN

Me at Cass Tech: High school cool (1976).

CHAPTER ONE

Growing Up as a Musician in Detroit

My musical journey began in the late 1960s at the age of eight when I saw Jimi Hendrix on TV playing his electric guitar. This incredibly gifted musician—who looked like me—created something that sounded extraordinary. He commanded his instrument, he was playing the music his way, and he was in control of his image. Without knowing all the trappings and what went into the Jimi Hendrix "experience," I just knew as an eight-year-old that I had to have a guitar so that I could be like him.

I was always in church singing, playing the piano, doing those Sunday school plays, and reading the scriptures in front of the church. Probably most of the Black musicians from my generation and earlier began in a similar way, nurtured by Black communities rich in cultural activities, many times exclusively in the church. But my parents also went to the symphony, attended plays, and took us to the *Nutcracker Ballet* every year.

My earliest recollection of wanting to mix music up was upon hearing the "Young Peoples Concerts" with the Detroit Symphony in the early seventies. The conductor was Paul Freeman, a Black man. So, I simply thought I could write Jimi Hendrix music for the symphony. It seemed logical to me then, and still does today. My mother told me, "One day that orchestra is going to be playing your music." That day arrived in 1995 when the Detroit Symphony premiered my *Essay for Orchestra* in Detroit's Orchestra Hall. And that conductor, Paul Freeman—some thirty plus years later—conducted and recorded my *Essay for Orchestra* in Chicago during his 2002 symphony season.

So this nurturing and flirtation with multiple strands of Black music culture—from gospel to R & B, from rock and roll to jazz, and from contemporary avant-garde music to writing operas—has been an integral part of my music mapping. I had always seen Black music and culture painted in broad strokes of color, and I always understood that Black—the deepest and richest color—is "best" because it encompasses all.

I grew up in a middle class Black neighborhood in Detroit called Russell Woods, on the city's northwest side. Detroit was a great place—where Black people looked beautiful, Black people worked hard. I grew up on Sturtevant Street, with its beautiful homes and well cut lawns. Kids played in the streets, and ice cream trucks waited for us to come running out after school. We had a park with swings, and we attended art and music festivals. Back then, the neighborhood kids had names like Michael, Stephen, Roy, Wendy, Angie, and Kathy. No Shanequas, Maliks, or Kwames. Protected by trees and the belief that we had arrived safely, my neighborhood was still not far from the streets where people knew struggle and neighborhood decay on a first name, daily basis.

My father was one of the first Black corporate design engineers in the country, and my mother was the public relations director of one of the nation's leading Black newspapers, the *Michigan Chronicle*. For her, media and meaning meant everything, and she passed that value to me. My parents were the first generation of fully vetted Afro-American achievers, and they passed that torch onto us. We had to do something with that. My doing turned out to be melodic.

The parents in Russell Woods expected their children to be *some*bodies and worked for that to happen. My friends and I were four or five years old when Malcolm X was shot in 1965, and we probably heard nothing of it. But in 1968, when we were all about seven or eight, Martin Luther King Jr. was assassinated, and I remember the mood of the country then. But Russell Woods was like living in a bubble, and the kids on Sturtevant Street thought our neighborhood was a mirror of the whole Black world. It wasn't. We were not far from the "hood," and all the hood kids and all the Russell Woods kids went to those same schools. We all knew both sides of the modern Black urban tale. In school, there were no guns, just fists.

Junior high school was a breeze because of the music programs. Those programs in the Detroit public schools made me and my friends who we are today. Music nurtured our growth, helped us to do well. Playing in the bands, singing in the choirs—and later in high school, going to state festivals and slammin' all those suburban schools—made us productive, gave us discipline, and helped forge our artistic integrity. Most of our high school and junior high school teachers were great Black musicians. They were trained, tough, and loving.

My first gig was a sock hop at Birney in 1971, when I was ten years old. Even then I was a young musician, playing in school bands, church camp bands, after school bands, and talent shows with other young musicians. In the early 1970s, we learned music with our cassette tape recorders. There was no reading the music, because there were no charts done of popular radio tunes. Instead, we would "take it off the record." We would tape the song playing on the radio, then transcribe it, learn each part, then chart it by writing it down or doing a horn arrangement. We played over and over until we got the part down. Then we'd get together with the other guys and pull it together. Everybody had to learn their parts.

My best friend, Stephen Newby, was a PK (preacher's kid). He was the captain of the local neighborhood Birney elementary safety patrol, and I was his lieutenant. Our posts spanned the Russell Woods neighborhood down several blocks that reached Birney Elementary, and past Birney to the hoods where the "bad" kids and their families lived. No tracks separated these neighborhoods—just good grass and bad torn up "ghetto" grass, as they called it.

Newby was always getting into trouble with his parents. As the son of a prominent pastor of a traditional Baptist church, Stephen was supposed to help his mom, brothers, and sister with music for the services. I know many others who dreamed of life as a musician while being shaped to be a preacher or church choir director. This was kind of emblematic of traditional Black identity—torn asunder, as Du Bois wrote, fighting within one's insides to keep it all together. The "father" of the blues, W. C. Handy, was also the son of a minister, and his father swore he'd rather see his son dead than as a musician chasing the devil's music!

We found many such struggles in Black peoples' culture, a fight for values from within the community and against an American backdrop which has always been ambiguous as to how it valued African American life, culture, image, and identity. Black people had to do something respectable for their people, *always*.

But we also had our music, and for everybody around there was a lot of music. On AM radio they had pop music, gospel, R & B, rock and roll, and jazz, and it all seemed to flow back and forth, and we had access to it all.

Stephen's folks saw me as a "bad" influence on him, because I was just into pop, jazz, rock, and R & B. Although many, like Stephen, faced suspicious eyes at home, none of us ran away to find ourselves. We didn't dress in black, pierce our bodies, spike or bleach our hair, or cut ourselves for attention. Our distractions in those days seemed so normal. We practiced and played. And played. In some ways, I suppose, we became part of rival "gangs"—competing bands that would play after school for the neighborhood parties, talent shows sponsored by different schools, community houses, and the like. One such rival was Gabriel Dunbar. Today Gabriel and I are friends but, man, back then, I hated him. We were warring guitar players, in warring bands. We'd fight from talent show to talent show, school dance to school dance, and over girls, trying to prove ourselves as "baddest ass" musicians.

On my block, there was one boy—I'll call him Jimmy Watson—whose dad was also a minister. Reverend Watson was one of those fancy storefront business preachers in the community, fashioned diamond down with cane, watches, and cool daddy preacher hats. He drove a big new Cadillac every year, always in and out, and busy with, I guess, church stuff. Jimmy, who wasn't very talented musically, made his own contribution to our group. The kids had formed a band on the street and were playing local talent shows, even a few radio shows, and starting to get some recognition. We were so young then—maybe nine or ten, eleven, twelve—and we needed equipment. While parents supplied the basics, there were certain items—wah-wah pedals, new chords, microphones, new amplifiers—that they didn't have the money for in those days. To keep up with the musical needs, we had to earn enough money from paper routes, selling soap and housewares, sweeping, cleaning, taking out boxes for local store owners, etc. That wasn't always enough, though, so Jimmy came up with a plan. His father's church created several "ministries," which brought in monies that his father stashed safely away in their home. Jimmy's plan was to stage a break-in.

One day after school, Jimmy came home, found his dad's ministry loot, broke a back window, and climbed out through it. Then he pretended to come home and called the police to report the burglary. It worked! Police reports were made and after things simmered down a bit, Jimmy and band had cash in hand!

Nobody took a cab in those days, especially all the way downtown. It just cost too much. But on this day, all of us kids in the band hopped in the cab, dashed downtown to Grinnell's music store, and bought a couple hundred dollars' worth of new chords, wah-wah pedals—the whole bit. Being a good church boy, I told myself I hadn't done anything wrong but accept a few toys, but I still felt uneasy.

Sure enough, a few days later our parents became suspicious of the more consistent rehearsals and the new sounds we were producing. Somebody had squealed. Our moms called a meeting, and the band was summoned to the Sturtevant "high court." I remember it well. Mrs. Potts, a concerned mother who worked for the county judge, presided. She was as sharp as a prosecuting attorney. It was through Mrs. Potts's "court" that Jimmy's scam was found out. She made each of us tell where and how we got all our new equipment. Of course, Jimmy's parents didn't press charges against their son, but the band had to give all the equipment back to the store, and that was the end of the funk for that funk band! But, as far as I can gather, this was the kind of thing that kept us out of more trouble—that and our music.

And of course, our parents kept watchful eyes on all of us—their kids and their kids' friends—staying on top of whatever went down. We took to the bank their investment in our well-being, and we believed we could pull from that deposit and develop ourselves into future "somebodies." I never believed the "it takes a village" theory was something that only came from Africa, since that idea ruled on Sturtevant Street! We didn't need police officers or social workers, because the neighbors on the block—every household—kept watch. That's the way it was.

In our days, Black music streamed from cars, radios, and our basements, and it was the most beautiful thing. My mom's generation had swing, but musicians like Louis Jordan never expressed social consciousness like ours. Our music was—had to be, I guess—a full flowering of all we hoped and lived for. That Black soul stuff was enough to set the world on fire. And, it did. If nothing else, it helped to set us off as musicians, teachers, lawyers, community leaders—some fantastic individuals with all they wanted to be. But what I remember the most was that music. Not only did music give Black people peace of mind, it gave them a piece of land, food, identity, national heritage, community—a way in the world and a song that brought a future. Music is very serious business for Black people all over the world. Indeed, one of our essential codes is musical.

Our schools were set up with music and arts programs, with teachers who the kids idolized. For me, there was Mrs. Yearby, Mr. Pitts, and Mr. Wiggins. They directed the school bands, jazz and pep groups, gave voice and instrumental lessons, and they themselves were musicians who played gigs all over town. Didn't matter that a kid was going to be a scientist or secretary—everybody did music. It was a part of the plan to keep us all creative, and we loved the music. In those days, afterschool sock hops didn't have DJs but local bands, and we would play. Everybody wanted to be like James Brown or Jimi Hendrix or the Jackson 5. We were learning songs—singing, dancing, performing, and making up the steps or routines. We were really a talented bunch of kids.

They say the soundtrack to your life is the music you grew up on. We grew up with a music that was not only a soundtrack but was the soul-connecting source of who we were then, of who we are now. Everyone felt connected through the music, which seemed so normal, so natural. Music and the stories in those songs created a picture from Black people about Black people: a beautiful portrait of our lives—lives which were valuable, which were essential, which created a community of experience. This communal music connected us to each other, flowed from one generation to the next, so Dinah Washington singing "What a Diff'rence a Day Makes!" wasn't that far from Michael Jackson singing "Maybe Tomorrow."

The music in those days expressed essential values, which were wrapped up in the blends of the rhythms and the melodies. Everybody embraced those beliefs, which were sanctified by music. Black music *said* something.

The songs we heard on the radio made folks feel proud to be Black. The musicians who produced that music didn't just reflect that feeling. Their songs were a projection of what Black people held up among us—songs like "A Change Is Gonna Come" by Sam Cooke, "Wake Up Everybody" by Harold Melvin and the Blue Notes, "War" by Edwin Starr, "Higher Ground" by Stevie Wonder, "What's Going On" by Marvin Gaye, "Ball of Confusion" by the Temptations, "Message in Our Music" by the O'Jays, "Yes We Can Can" by the Pointer Sisters, "Fight the Power" by the Isley Brothers and, of course, "Say It Loud—I'm Black and I'm Proud" by James Brown!

The melodies made you feel something inside, and the words reinforced those emotions. The lyrics echoed African proverbs, bible verses, blues lyrics and rhymes, and street sayings like, "Brother man, brother man . . . it's all good, and it is what it is . . . what it be."

CHAPTER TWO

Cass Tech High

Cass Tech High School in Detroit had the world's greatest public music program in the country. Regina Carter, Carla Cook, Geri Allen, Gregg Phillangaines, the great Motown arranger Paul Riser, Ron Carter, Curtis Fuller, and yes, me too—we all came out of Cass Tech. My dad even graduated from there, way back in 1938. That place stood six stories high, occupied a whole city block, and graduated more than a thousand kids a year. In those days and today, even the remodeled school, Cass Tech was near the downtown section. Dead center in an area called the Cass Corridor, surrounded by prostitutes and all sorts of characters, was this big productivity machine called Cass Tech High.

At the start of the century and post–War World I, Cass Tech trained kids to learn technical skills, and it drew the city's best and brightest. These kids came from all sorts of families, both White and Black. But as the years went on, Black families pushed to get their kids into Cass Tech. In a city that has more than 60 percent Black residents, Cass drew a lot of the sharpest Black minds. By the 1970s many Black families wanted their kids to get into top-notch colleges, traditionally Black ones like Spelman and Morehouse, but also the University of Michigan and Harvard. There was great optimism, and Black folks reached out for the great promise of the American dream, something that everybody could see. We were the post–civil rights kids, able to ride into Dodge on that silver Cadillac made in Detroit, baby! There was much hope for so many of us, and we had reason to hope!

Cass Tech gave us this kind of ambition and optimism, with its great teachers and a curriculum that covered everything. We had engineering, chemistry, biology, business, science, performing arts, music, fashion design. I mean, this is wayyy unlike my mom's generation which was offered no more than home ec, sewing, and cooking for the girls. We were armed with choices. Excellence was something most of us kids strived for, and there were rewards for achieving that excellence. Cass had social clubs that stressed positivity: the Spirits, the Ambassadors, the Renaissance Club, and others. Actually, the school was more like a junior college than anything else.

For many of us, perhaps, this place represented a view of what the corporate world, the business-busy world, was like. And Cass Tech was preparing us to conquer that world. It had the kind of energy that produced young people who excelled. There are probably other schools like this all over the country today, and if so, I'd like to hear more about them. But good news about good people doesn't sell newspapers.

Cass Tech was huge, so huge that it had cargo elevators that could carry fifty kids up and down to get to classes. The music program occupied an entire first floor wing. Like many departments in the school, we were isolated, en-

Me, Susan Wilson (piano), Regina Carter (violin), Trent Mitchell (bass), and Michael Caruthers (trombone).

couraged to ferment in our own juices. Many of us came specifically to study music as a technical major. We participated in all sorts of performances—concert and marching, orchestra, choirs, vocal, jazz, harp ensemble, and the school's award-winning symphonic wind band. Many of us had gotten real popular, which meant lots of activity, lots of attention, lots of performances, and of course, the interest of lots of young ladies.

We would produce events after school which we called Jazz Festival Concerts. The rooms were packed with musicians, pre-med students, computer science majors, football players, and chemistry majors. Even the music teachers stayed after school to watch and listen. We prepared for these concerts not only by rehearsing, but by researching the artists whose music we played. We had such a passion for the music, a real pride, and we felt a need to impart that information to our peers. So we opened our concerts with lectures about Mary Lou Williams and Duke Ellington. Billy Strayhorn's niece, Robin Strayhorn, was in our class, so we had some connection to the history.

My buddies—Trent Mitchell, Derry Allen Kelly, and Kenny Scott—and I would go downtown on Saturdays to the public library where they had a room called the Azalia Hackley room, which is still there today. Ms. Hackley was a well-known musician who produced concerts in Detroit early in the century and was beloved by the community. This particular room was a special collections room filled with files of articles, clippings on musicians,

Derry Allen Kelly, Captain Banfield, and Trent Mitchell. Mark's Other Room, Detroit, 1980.

and whoever we were interested in researching: Duke Ellington, Sarah Vaughan, Count Basie.

After we signed in, the librarian would lead us down a corridor, into the belly of the already remote library, to a little room with soft lights. I loved to get lost in that room for hours, because it was so removed from the noise of the streets, and I could think and dream in there. Reading all those clippings was like a voyage to another world. The librarian would say to us: "You all take care of how you handle these materials now. This is your history, you in there, so you be sure to take care of it, so you can learns your ways forward."

The Hackley room stocked all the old reviews, stories, and obituaries of Detroit music. In the 1960s and 1970s, the Motown sound may have domi- nated Detroit music, but in the 1930s, '40s, and '50s, jazz was huge in Detroit. All the local musicians played the jazz clubs, and those clubs were stopovers for the biggest names in the business. Lionel Hampton, Miles Davis, Duke Ellington, and all the cats stopped in there and hung out.

We would research these figures and prepare—I guess you could call them emcee papers—for our concerts, so that we could tell the audience all about the musicians' lives before we played their music. We'd thumb through the articles, read concert reviews and funeral notices, pore over the stories, and even note the clothing advertisements or announcements for the opening of new venues. We photocopied articles and wrote down stats. We imagined a world that seemed far away, one that we could only dream performing in. We tried to picture clubs in New York where Charlie Parker might walk in or where we might overhear a conversation between Mary Lou Williams and Charles Mingus. And we were allowed to listen to those albums. Wow!!

When we held those concerts, it didn't matter that all the kids listen- ing weren't musicians. We felt the need to inspire thought, to reinforce our Black identity through our music. It was our mission to carry on the musical traditions of our people, not only to preserve but also to project the vitality of Black music expression, as others had cared and carried it on to us. One of my compositions, a big band piece called "And What Would You Like to Hear, Little Lady?" was actually something Duke Ellington said to my mother in 1944 when she was a young woman hearing him play in Detroit.

As young as we were, we felt a real responsibility to the music, to carry on the musicianship of those who came before us. We were real musicians in those days, and in our work you could hear the future.

The musician—from Jimi Hendrix to Berry Gordy to a church organ- ist—holds an elevated position in a community's identity, in its cultural coding, and such figures possess a special ability to stir joy, to bring life to their listeners. Influence had always come from the ranks of spiritual leaders and musicians first. The communal identity of Black folks—especially in the atmosphere of repression—was represented by musical figures like Louis Armstrong, Bessie Smith, and Duke Ellington. These men and women were "spokespersons" for the race and were accorded respect and admiration. And whether we recognized this, whether we spoke to each other about it or not, when we gave those concerts and shared the information about the musicians who came before us, we became spokespersons for our generation.

We not only played the music, but we had high expectations for what that music meant. We all believed that we could go beyond and achieve what we needed, and we pushed ourselves to excel. The music delivered us, but it demanded we take care of it, too.

Cass Tech not only influenced me as a musician, but as an educator as well. Producing those concerts stirred an interest in teaching the meanings of the music by sharing its history with others.

In the tenth grade I started a group, the Concept Jazz Orchestra. I was only sixteen and even back then, my hometown newspaper dubbed me "Little Quincy." This was a seventeen-piece jazz band that I booked with performances in some major clubs. A great group of young musicians participated.

Mark Ledford (on trumpet) and me at Mark's Other Room, Detroit, 1980.

Our pianist, Vernon Fails, later went on to play for and write a good number of Anita Baker's late 1980s hits. Regina Carter, our little sister, was already making a name for herself, playing in a group called Brainstorm that opened for Michael Jackson. Kim Jordan went on to be the music director for Gil Scott-Heron. From this young Detroit experience, a whole group of us went to Boston to attend the New England Conservatory and Berklee School of Music. Thinking back on it now, we were a remarkable flock of young musicians poised for doing something of note. That flock included: Regina Carter, Carla Cook, Kenny Scott, Derry Allen Kelly, Mark Mitchell, Stephen Newby, Mark Ledford, Jeff Stanton, Gabriel Dunbar, Phenisher Harris, Valencia Edner, Janet Williams, Kim Jordan, Michael Caruthers, Vernon Fails, Susan Wilson, Stephen Millen, me, and many others.

In 1978, at age seventeen, I received a fellowship grant to study music abroad. Of course, I chose the guitar capital, Mexico. It was there that this Detroit boy began to see the world from larger spaces and places. I studied guitar at the Federation of Musicians in Acapulco, performed concerts there, and lived the culture. For the first time, I saw and hung out with Black people who looked just like me but who were very different, spoke different languages, and were mixed with more than just my African American and Native American bloods. These folks were Spanish, West African, Chinese, French—the whole mix! But true to its universality, music was a common chord and community builder.

I went to college and spent my professional training time in Boston learning to be a musician, totally believing that my preparation was a further tuning up to meet the world with the "right song." I graduated in the eighties, and that's the world those in Black music may have died and lost our soul.

CHAPTER THREE

Boston (1979–1988)

I settled into my college music studies in Boston, and there is no doubt in my mind that this was the most important music college town, ever. So many extraordinary musicians and movements were developing there. I would be willing to bet that there have not been too many other places and times more potent for the development of so many young musicians—other than, of course, Harlem in the 1920s, the Bopper's New York during the late forties, and Chicago's creative nurturing of the AACM. They are history now, but clubs like Pooh's Pub, Michael's, Wally's, 1369, Riley's, and the Willow Club cooked nightly.

All the great jazz masters were still living and teaching there during this period. Alan Dawson, Jaki Byard, Mick Goodrick, Miroslav Vitous, William Thomas McKinley, Ran Blake, and George Russell were a few. Boston was the training ground and then they were off to New York. Some were being picked up by G.R.P. records with Wynton Marsalis (though not studying in Boston at this time, he was a constant presence) and his brother Branford with Columbia. And of course at that time Art Blakey was still a drop off point for a number of cats we knew then.

My earliest memory of a major artist who came to perform in Boston was Patrice Rushen. Patrice was the Janet Jackson of our day. For us, she was one of the most famous and influential musicians. To this day, she is one of the most respected musicians, particularly on the popular music scene in Los Angeles, where much of the heartbeat of the industry lies. We knew her not only as a hit song maker ("Forget Me Nots"—remade by Will Smith for

Bobby McFerrin and Patrice Rushen.

"Men in Black," which brought Ms. Rushen great new honors—and some cash, I'm sure), but also as a great jazz pianist. I still have the ticket from a concert at the Berklee Performance Center, Boston, April 11, 1980. She opened up for Gil Scott-Heron, and I remember being so blown away by her performance. During intermission I went up to the balcony to look down on the stage, and standing right there was Patrice Rushen! I couldn't believe it. I very shyly introduced myself, and she asked me what I wanted to do with my music. I was so stunned that I probably said something stupid like, "I want to be just like you, Ms. Rushen." She encouraged me.

Some fifteen years later, when I was a professor of music and African American studies at Indiana University, I received a call from Patrice. She was interested in getting my help to circulate her name and works among concert music circles that I was involved in. Consequently I invited Patrice to perform at the university and talk about her work in the industry. Her willingness to participate is just one example of the importance of musicians sharing with each other, passing on torches, and fostering participation, so that the cultivation of traditions can be maintained. Since then, we have collaborated on several projects.

Just a cursory flashback recalls so many young musicians training at the same time in Boston. My first gig in Boston was with Smitty Smith, later the drummer for *The Tonight Show* band with Jay Leno. I vividly remember my attempts to pay rent as a street musician, playing my guitar in Copley Square, Boston Commons, train stations, and Harvard Square singing with Lynne Fiddmont, who went on to sing with Stevie Wonder. My first band in Boston (1980–1983) had Najee playing E flat sax, flute, and soprano sax, and he subsequently went onto become one of the most important sax voices in smooth jazz, *before* Kenny G. My pianist was Rachel Niccolazzo, now known as Rachel Z. Her roommate, Regina Carter, is the preeminent jazz violinist of this generation.

Our camps were divided between the two schools, Berklee College of Music and New England Conservatory, but we all gigged together. Two other well-established jazz greats emerged from my class of 1983: my roommate and dear friend Nelson Rangell and clarinetist/composer Don Byron. My first composition at the New England Conservatory (NEC) was called "Don Lee," composed for Don Byron.

There was an apartment building on the corner of Westover and Hemingway Street. I promised, when I got a chance in later years, that I would be the first to tell the story of 96 Hemingway. This apartment will be remembered as the place that housed some of the greatest young jazz musicians from this period. Visiting that house was like going to the musicians' club of Boston: Donald (Duck) Harrison, Walter Beasley, Mark Ledford, Victor Bailey, Jean Touissant, Clyde Hunt, Dwayne Cook Broadnax, Gene Jackson, and Jeff "Twain" Watts. And the list grows longer still of all those studying, gigging, and hanging out together in Boston at that time: The Marsalis brothers (Wynton, Branford, Delfeayo), Kevin Eubanks, Terry Lyne Carrington, Greg Osby, Curtis Williams, Cindy Blackman, Bobby Broom, Carla Cook, Lenora Helm, Monte Croft, Cyrus Chestnut, Damon Duewhite, Cecilia Smith, Lynne Fiddmont, Rachelle (Barnes) Farrell, James Williams, Jerry Atkins, Tommy Campbell, Billy Kilson, Mike Stern, Jeff Berlin—and I know I'm missing a few dozen more. This was just the jazz lions set. At the same time, Tracy Chapman was making a name for herself in folk music circles.

In the teen pop market, Maurice Starr's crew set off a mega movement that the Backstreet Boys, *NSYNC, and all the other copy boy bands can't touch: New Edition. These young men were actually high school students, and one of them was in my music class. In 1981, not yet twenty, I had been hired (illegally I bet) as a full-time music teacher in the Boston public school system at Madison Park High, Roland Hayes Division of music in Roxbury, the "hood." New Edition—which included Ricky Bell, Michael Bivins, Ronnie Devoe, Ralph Tresvant, and Bobby Brown—as well as their white counterparts, the multimega dollar group New Kids on the Block, were all in

Donald Harrison and Greg Osby.

Boston developing their acts. Both groups developed in the hoods of Roxbury/Dorchester Mass and were trained by pre–Puff Daddy mogul, Maurice Starr, who, by the way, was a great musician.

NEC was a place where jazz and classical music were taught side by side due to the extraordinary vision of composer and historian Gunther Schuller. Third Stream (the combination of classical and jazz conventions) ideology ran thick at NEC, and all my teachers spoke multiple languages. My composition teachers were George Russell (Lydian Chromatic Concept) and William Thomas McKinley. Mick Goodrick was my guitar teacher. Through an exchange program with Tufts University, I also met the man who introduced me to the idea of being a composer, T. J. Anderson. It was T. J. who hipped me to the academic avant-garde of twelve tone, aleatoric, and modern ideas of mixed media, multiple performance platforms, non-notated scoring, etc. Also he was the first serious Black composer I had ever met. He changed my life and planted the seed for the next directions which were to shape my thinking, music, and activities.

At twenty-two I had received a bachelor's degree in music from NEC, and I was a full-time music teacher. I continued making music, playing gigs, and establishing ties. It was out of these contacts with musicians that I was inspired to think about music from a broader scope: music making (performing, composing and arranging, publishing, recording, and producing), education, and the music industry. Because I was already booking recording dates and producing my mixed bag of works (jazz, funk with string quartets and vocals), I consequently decided to form my own recording company.

With a $4,000 liquidated stock-savings gift from my parents, BMagic Records was born. I was the president of my own record company, complete with a small staff, a roster of artists, and a deal with NDN distributors out of New York. We had a running contract with the Port Authority train and bus station in New York. We were hired by a friend who worked there to bring groups from Boston to play in the station. A couple of my in-house producers and I generated money by producing demos for high school kids who wanted to be "recording stars." Everybody wanted to record a New Edition–like demo or a rap demo, since rap was just hitting. We honestly thought rap was the stupidest thing ever and wondered where was that mess going to take anybody? We were clueless! The company was going well, so after graduation I decided to quit my teaching post and run BMagic full-time.

In Boston during this time there was more money and public funding available for educational partnerships. So I began to write grant proposals to fund the record company, which subsequently grew into Young Artists Development Inc. (YADI). My good buddy, Stephen Newby, came east to study

A BMagic single from 1983.

jazz composition at the University of Mass at Amherst. Stephen and I would form a series of artistic partnerships that would help us develop as musicians and best friends. Drawing on Stephen's undergraduate music education major, we decided to start a school.

We raised some thirty thousand dollars from 1985 to 1987 and moved into the Boston Community Music School. My thinking at the time was that the school would be able to generate more interest in the philanthropic community and subsequently channel those funds into my recording company. When money ran out, we operated YADI in the basement of my church, Union United Methodist on Columbus Avenue. We created an afterschool community arts education/performing school and ensemble. We taught classes in music history, popular music production, voice and ensemble coaching. It was a great effort of which I was extremely proud.

My years of teaching in public school made it evident that the crossroads of music and reaching younger people was part of my calling. In 1985, I decided that I needed to train in theology and philosophy to better understand where all this was taking me. Knowing nothing about aesthetics or philosophy, I applied to Boston University's School of Theology, minoring in composition studies. I immediately fell into another world, intellectualizing about meanings. I wrote concept papers on the history of religion, epistemology, ontology, aesthetics, Paul Tillich, Karl Barth, and systematic theology!

While working on my master's, I was also a room service waiter at the Hyatt in Cambridge (I turned this into a vehicle to do a music showcase in the hotel's restaurant) and substitute teaching. Stephen came down from Amherst and we would run YADI on the weekends. During this time I met a group of very brilliant aspiring preachers and future philosophers at Harvard Divinity School (including Anthony Pinn and Allan Callahan who are now professors of Religious Studies at Macalester College in St. Paul). I was allowed to study there because all the schools of divinity in Boston provided cross-school registration through the Boston Theological Institute. My theology and preaching courses were done at Harvard and my church history and advanced composition courses were done at Boston University. My final master's thesis was the study of Richard Wagner's operas, arguing the case of a "theological music" based on the idea of a European super-artist heroism model and the stage as a moral institution.

In 1988 I took a group of musicians (through a Boston University–sponsored program) to Dakar, Senegal, West Africa. Stephen Newby and jazz vocalist Carla Cook were on this trip as well. Being there confirmed for all of us the functionality of music in traditional West African culture, as we attempted to understand the cultural, historical, and practical teaching/performing applications. The performances and teachings from the West African master musicians confirmed our understanding of Black American African roots in our musical traditions: Call and response, poly-rhythmic pulse, community, and most importantly the crucial role of the master drummer and singer/philosopher, griot.

I knew from this incredible experience it would not be difficult for me to return to my master's thesis board and argue my theory on theological music. I was wrong. Boston University's theology faculty rejected my first thesis. They found my argument for theology based on West African functionality untenable and based on premises that were impossible to argue or prove, which in their minds was the didactic role of music in culture. They further asserted that my findings were not based on traditional theories of music aesthetics. Can you believe that? We fought over it hard at my thesis defense but they finally—after three years—let me graduate. Their approval came only after I switched the focus of my cultural paradigm to European models based on the writings of Nietzsche, Schopenhauer, and the music of a Western European composer.

I am now proving all that I argued was correct and I got the model from traditional West African and Black American music practice. This writing is based on those early models; the active role of musicians in shaping contemporary society comes from West African practices, griots, and European notions of the creative artists. But, "We Are the World," the biggest artist/humanitarian concept to date, raising millions for hungry people didn't come from Nietzsche's idea of a superman. As a Black American musician, I have had to join the fight within the traditional academy to refute exclusionary thinking and understanding—to argue that the rest of the world functions, participates, creates, and celebrates art in very different ways than Bach, Brahms, and Bruckner.

My return to the States was eye opening. At any rate, by day I was pursuing a master's in theology and by night I continued my work as a record producer, while also writing a few song cycles and string quartets.

One teacher, Donal Fox, has become a very close colleague. Donal is a contemporary new music composer who, among other things, experimented with mixing Bach fugal themes and approaches with bebop, free jazz chords, structures, and improvisations based on this mixture. He's winning critical acclaim for his effective fusing and performances. Donal introduced me to more worlds of compositional insights and new music. Even before I entered the master's program and studied composition with Greek avant-garde composer Theodore Antiniou, I was working out structure, analysis, and process problems with Donal.

Another opportunity arose out of my connections with music and the public schools: I was hired to be the music director of the Days in the Arts program with the Boston Symphony, which was housed in Lenox, Massachusetts, at the famous Tanglewood summer festival. Here I heard all kinds of music, taught art and music, wrote new kids' musicals every week, and watched Seiji Ozawa conduct. Along with Stephen Newby, I ran the program from 1982 until 1988. I learned arts administration, along with interdisciplinary and cross-cultural tactics, which fueled my hunger for how to do music in the world. Our kids taught us great lessons. We directed and coached hundreds of young minds and souls during those summers. This was a great time.

I also flirted with record companies in New York, primarily trying to get a record deal from Dr. George Butler, then the head of Jazz A&R at Colum-

Donal Fox and Guthrie Ramsey.

bia Records. And while Wynton and Branford had things all tied up there, George seemed really interested in having me join the camp. He even told industry friends I was going to be signed. Didn't happen. We had set up a showcase, and Delfeayo Marsalis was actually assigned to be my producer. On the day of the showcase at the Hyatt in Cambridge, Dr. Butler didn't show! I was devastated, along with my band, which included Rachel Z on keyboards, Billy Kilson on drums, and Greg Jones on bass. A fight almost broke out between my drummer and the young Marsalis.

After this letdown, I immediately began to reroute my entries into the industry. My company was still doing business, YADI was in session, two records got notable mentions in *Billboard* magazine, and musicians were coming up to my office bringing charts and wanting to write for our artists. One client was Harvard's Divinity School. With the help of my Harvard partners, I negotiated a deal to actually carry their first and only gospel album on the BMagic label. The artist, Garth Fletcher, was a divinity school student who I had actually worked with as an undergraduate at NEC. Garth was an early BeBe Winans with a kind of all encompassing pop/jazz/gospel bent. This experience allowed my small company to see a full album project through every stage: artwork, packaging, and even placing product in local stores.

But trying to get a record deal, trying to keep YADI and BMagic afloat, and trying to be an academic took its toll. Out of frustration and sheer exhaustion, I left Boston. By this time, I had already been accepted into the doctoral program in composition at the University of Michigan in Ann Arbor, but the lure of a recording contract blurred a small and steady compositional voice that would later emerge and be the entry point into a more national artistic identity.

I got the "sign" from the Lord that I was being prepared for something else. My teacher at the time, T. J. Anderson, told me, "We don't need any more 'Wyntons' doing this. What we need are more Black composers. Go get your doctorate and study."

CHAPTER FOUR

Making Music, Finding Meaning
(1989–2003)

Most of the people I began with in the mid-1970s in high school, and the many I name here, are still making music strong and we still keep in touch. The same is true of graduate school friends. From this group we hear about jobs, research projects, and conferences. We advise each other through the difficult terrains of the academy and the music business. This camaraderie underscores the importance of the camp and crew idea.

I entered the doctoral program at the University of Michigan in the fall of 1988. After finishing his graduate degree at U of Massachusetts, Stephen Newby headed out to the University of Michigan as well. Being back on Michigan soil made me feel like a kid who leaves home and returns to old familiar playgrounds. Immediately, I reconnected with family and friends.

In the college town of Ann Arbor, Stephen and I bonded with a new group of contacts which included Chicago pianist and musicologist Guthrie Ramsey, vocalist and musicologist Kyra Guant, singer and pianist Louise Toppin, and so many others. The five of us remain all very much connected in academia and in music. Guthrie is professor of music history at U Penn, Dr. Kyra Guant at Virginia University, and Dr. Louise Toppin is a voice professor at U of East Carolina. Louise actually took over the Boston-based Videmus/Visionary recording and concert/education company in 1997 and asked if I would serve as the executive director of the record company along with composer and conductor Julius Williams.

In 2001 we released our first symphonic record with the Prague Radio Symphony and Washington Symphony. One of the works that was released on

Stephen Newby, me, and Allan Callahan.

that CD project was Stephen Newby's gospel symphony. The important thing about this group at U of M in the graduate programs in music, between 1988 and 1995 or so, is that it was probably the largest and most supported group of Black doctoral students in music, ever. Most of those people graduated and are professors and artists teaching and performing all over the United States. The other thing was that the institution funded us. We were all on incredible fellowships, and we could hold teaching posts as well. If you change the funding structure, place the priority on embracing people's work and nurturing their creativity, you will produce successful results in numbers. Two were responsible for bringing us there; musicologist Dr. Rae Linda and Dr. Willis Patterson. Brother Newby and I met Rae Linda as we cotaught with her sister Carlene Brown, a systematic musicologist at Tanglewood. Rae Linda acted as big sister, keeping us all in line and setting the example for young Black scholars in music. The real foundation layer for Black graduate recruitment and retention at the University of Michigan was Dr. Willis Patterson. A monument should be erected to honor his incredible work and dedication to supporting so many great Black musicians in Ann Arbor. He also is responsible for probably one of the most dynamic classes of Black music scholars and artists across at least two or three generations as he provided leadership as a voice professor, and then dean in the school for thirty plus years.

In terms of Black music, it cannot be done without Black scholars and teachers in the field. Music is a special enough field, but could you imagine the world without Black music leadership? Often I think we would have the industry mislead us into the fantasy that Black music is good on all levels. We are losing great Black training. There aren't enough Black technicians and the development of young performers (musicians) in major cities, which has declined so rapidly over the last three decades that there is bound to be a serious shortage of "serious" Black musicians. This is clearly a result of lacking school programs, the draw of more competitive industries, and the lure of spotlight-popular music traditions which are mostly producing rap and kiddie R & B songs. Forget the classical music scene; it has not grown up out of its racist, exclusionary elitist place, allowing it to be a safe, warm, encouraging environment to support large numbers of young Black artists. But we have to encourage, push, and inspire more young musicians of all interests and stripes to stay on, stay on. This is what we all did and are doing. I hope we continue to pass and keep lighting the torches.

At U of M as a graduate teaching fellow I taught 180 undergraduates in American Religion and the African American Church Experience. This is where I got my chops as a college instructor and it was here that I brought together history, aesthetics, and the socially charged evolution of Black people in the church and in music. Now keep in mind I was a young brother and still am! Perhaps I was in my late twenties. The other class I taught occasionally, after taking it myself, was Harold Cruse's American Culture and Gender course. In Harold Cruse's class I learned a more critical approach to cultural studies and about the powerful African American narrative. Harold Cruse taught like a master teacher and was preparing me to actually carry the torch. He subsequently invited me to assist with teaching his course which I did each year, handling the sections dealing with Black music. His book *The Crisis of the Negro Intellectual* will long be hailed as one of the most important writings of Black American cultural critique.

At the doctoral level I studied composition with Leslie Basset, then William Albright, Bill Bolcom, and a little sharing with American composer Michael Daughtery. This was the coming together of all the worlds I had known as a musician and later as an aspiring scholar and student in the culture of western art music. I had a lot of catching up to do as my master's was not in composition proper. But, I was already writing as much if not more concert music than my colleagues. I had finished my first guitar concerto at

William Bolcom and me.

age nineteen and it was premiered, me as soloist, at the age of twenty-three with the Detroit Metropolitan Orchestra in the venerable Symphony Hall. My second guitar concerto was completed not long after I arrived in Ann Arbor and was again premiered in Detroit.

At this time, 1989 or so, I was also hired at Hartford Memorial Baptist Church in Detroit on the ministerial staff, conducting the chamber orchestra and teaching in their Biblical Studies Institute. I guess coming back to Detroit in the church, doing music in probably one the nation's premier Black churches, plus working on doctoral studies allowed me to see yet another view of what I should be doing with music and culture. Seeing it all played out around and within the culture of Black life in Detroit was an epiphany, revelatory and prophetic for me all at once. I worked under Dr. Charles Adams, the "Harvard Hooper" as he is called and James Abbington, one of the finest church organists and Black choir pedagogists in the country. Our pianist from high school Vernon Fails was and still is at Hartford and the church organist was the music director for Aretha Franklin. I tell this story all the time. Vernon was then writing, arranging, and playing for Anita Baker and the second organist, "Darrel," was the music director for Aretha

Franklin! Music at Hartford Memorial was a most incredible experience. Jimmy Abbington, by the way, was doing doctoral work at U of Michigan in organ studies, and today is one of the leading authorities on Black music performance traditions. The music went from Black traditional Baptist anthems, the traditional hymns, spirituals to Richard Smallwood and the Winans all in one service—performed and sung by incredible musicians and one of the best trained Black church choirs anywhere. A Black music program like that will probably never exist again. It was truly incredible. When they installed their new pipe organ, they flew in a Russian organist to inaugurate it. Yes, pretentious, yes, middle class, and, yes, big Black church tradition. Truly rich and powerful! Jimmy did all the music for the national progressive Baptist conferences and accompanied Pastor Adams all over the world doing Black church music traditions. I required all of my ninety or so students to attend a field trip once a year to Detroit. Hartford's spiritual and musical services changed lives. Since then, as a professor of music, I have always taken my classes to the Black church, the absolute most important carrier of Black music tradition.

During this time I was also playing in Detroit clubs and was actually seen in 1991 or so by a talent scout at a record company. I had no intentions of pursuing, but received a call from Ramon Hervey, then manager of both Vanessa Williams and Andre Crouch. The industry seduces me back again! Ramon encouraged me to come out to Los Angeles. I did and I signed a management contract under which we recorded an album. It was produced by ex-Rufus drummer, producer Andre Fisher, son of famous orchestrator, Claire Fisher. The demo record was followed up with a showcase somewhere in a rehearsal studio in Burbank. Most of the young green light guys in the emerging smooth jazz market were invited. I honestly had not made the jump to smooth jazz and was caught in an awful no-man's zone of stylistic eclecticism of which these new young turks didn't get. And dig this, on bass I had Alphonso Johnson, drums Ndugu Leon Chancelor, and the then music director of Frankie Beverly's Maze, Wayne Lynsey. He was by the way married to old band mate and street performer–partner, the singer Lynne Fiddmont-Lynsey. We actually performed a piece together our first time in ten years. Whenever you see any big name Black singers on the *Jay Leno Tonight Show*, Lynne, nine times out of ten, will be singing lead backup. At any rate, all were L.A. big time music industry veterans. Still, no deal.

The time in L.A. with Ramon was great because at that time Vanessa Williams was huge and Ramon managed the club R&B Live where so many big Black names hung out. My old saxophone player and buddy Najee was sitting in on R&B Live during the time I was in town, so yet another connection.

The Wynans were huge as *In Living Color* was blowing up. Hanging when I was there was Wesley Snipes, Babyface, John Salley, Robert Townsend—you name them, all the Black big names came to R&B Live. This was my first taste of Hollywood. I loved it and it poisoned—or flavored—my palate for the industry. Somewhere in here I met my number one idol, Quincy Jones. During this first meeting, he even said David Baker had mentioned me, but that he couldn't speak with me for at least three years. I met up with Quincy and reminded him of that broken promise at a Smithsonian Jazz Orchestra concert which David invited me to. David did an all Quincy Jones concert in July 2001 at the Lincoln Theater in D.C. But what that initial L.A. trip did was give me a very wide view of music making from all angles: the professional world of being a musician, running a record company, publishing, recording. By this time I could appreciate L.A's industry, classical concert music circles, the academy and the Black church.

While I have many heroes and sheroes, models, mentors, and people I just idolize, Leonard Bernstein is probably one of the examples that shone brightest for me. When I met him I couldn't believe it. I had seen him several times working at Tanglewood, but at U of M he was there to meet five conductors and five composers and I was chosen as well as Stephen Newby. I still have the letter. This was the winter of 1988. After conducting an incredible concert at Hill Auditorium in Ann Arbor, we were invited to a small gathering at the university president's home. There, Lenny was in his regalia, wit, and charm. But this evening he didn't seem to be interested in hanging with that crowd at all. As a matter of fact, he cornered Stephen and me and literally unknown to neither our professors nor the university president and guests, encouraged us to get him out of there.

So, if you can believe this, we called his driver to the side door, Stephen, another New York composer, Todd Levin, me, and Lenny, after politely dismissing himself as tired, hopped into his limousine with us and rushed to a local tavern for drinking. We secretly spread the word to the music students that we were taking Lenny Bernstein downtown to hang! We sat there with him all night listening to his stories and each one of us getting personal advice and instruction. And then, Lenny turned to me and really shared. I know it's the "Black and Jewish thing"; that is, there has and will always be a synergy and connection, a shared history between Black American and Jewish people because of our horrific histories and marginalization. And, there is our deep, spiritual music center. Leonard Bernstein gravitated toward me that night in sincere and honest brotherhood to share. He sensed I believed my own questions, particularly the search for the center of artist-hood and culture, Blackness, vernacular, academy, and reaching a marketplace. He encouraged me to express what he called, "your Blackness. . . . It is what makes you beautiful and different, and somehow as an artist you simply must bring this Blackness out in your music as a composer." Not long after, I remember on a drive to Detroit hearing on the radio that the great composer, the American maestro Leonard Bernstein had died. This was 1990. I cried all day. He meant that much to me for all the many reasons I have already stated. As artists, we must have living examples of individuals who exemplify the principles of artistry, creativity, passion, dedication, drive, and making music that brings people to wholeness. That's what Leonard Bernstein represented to me. I really admired his artistic spirit.

Leonard Bernstein was the second non-Black concert music composer (the other was German composer Hans Henze, whom I met and shared my early work with while I was a much younger composer at Tanglewood) who truly understood the crossroads and the dilemmas of being a Black American and being a composer and wanted to talk about it freely. The problem with too much academic classical music training is that it is anti-Black and even anti-music. It is as if Black people didn't matter, shouldn't matter, and in the traditional music academy there are very few references, links, or sidebars to the rich, deep, and varied traditions of Black music doing and its implications for concert music doing. As a composer I figuratively came to blows and brushed up against these thorns too many times. That conversation with Lenny Bernstein changed my perspective and once again I was as my teacher T. J. had charged, pointed toward a mission in academic and concert music fields, holding up the torch of Black music artistry as a creator, not just as a performer.

Studying composition at U of M, I finished string quartets, song cycles, chamber music, and a lot of jazz charts. I researched the history and writings of Black music pioneers and became committed to charting the lives of Black music thinkers, especially after getting a hold of David Baker's *The Black Composer Speaks* (Scarecrow Press, 1978). Finding that book, I couldn't believe it. A book on Black composers? David Baker immediately became the focus of my attention toward securing links to the long legacy of Black composers, who they were, where they lived in the United States, and what music they were writing.

We had only ever heard of William Grant Still, who was a pioneer, but it was David Baker who became my "Quincy Jones of the academy." I wanted to emulate his academic, jazz, concert music writing, and scholarship. As it turned out, Scarecrow Press later asked me to write the follow-up to David's book, which became the vehicle for introducing me to many composers, the radio interview formats I developed, later the formation of the Undine Smith Moore collection of scores and manuscripts by Black composers and gently pushed me into Black music scholarship in general. I sought him out during an invitation to Indiana University to have one of my pieces performed there in the fall of 1989. After meeting with David, I was determined to be a Black music professor. Until that point, even through my first year or so of doctoral studies at U of M, I wanted to return to the East Coast and see my life running around New York, chasing the broken and short-lived dreams that all too many burned out musicians are forced to accept. Discussions with David Baker and Portia Maultsby convinced me to pursue the life of the academy.

I completed my dissertation, which was my symphony 2 (Dream Realized/ Nightmare Resolved). Symphony No. 2 is a forty-minute work with chorus, speakers, and tenor saxophone that aesthetically looks at the differences and similarities in musical form between the philosophies of Malcolm X and Martin King. Infused among the sections of the symphony are various excerpts from the speeches highlighting what I identified as the central themes of their legacies: spirit, revolution, brotherhood, integration/nationalism, dream, and nightmare. This symphony was chosen the following year of my graduation in 1992 by the Utah and University of Utah Symphonies in a national contest and subsequently premiered with these groups. This was a huge piece that brought together my concert, jazz, and contemporary dissonant languages that were refined from all the doctoral studies of Arnold Schoenberg, serialism, and Coltrane. And as well, simultaneously this symphony put together social and spiritual principles and music, which have provided me with the foundations of my work as a composer. In 1992 I was the first Black man ever to graduate with a doctorate in composition from the University of Michigan. A damn shame! Only two or three more since have completed and Stephen Newby was one of them.

After graduating from U of M, I was actually recruited by David and Portia to Indiana University in 1992. I was hired as an assistant professor in the department of African American studies, was composer in residence with the African American Arts Institute, and later taught in the department of music at the Indianapolis campus. The move to Bloomington, Indiana, was extremely difficult. Going from a graduate student to a professor was like going from diapers to wearing a wrinkled suit in some ways. Nobody really teaches you what to expect. I knew nothing about salary negotiation, arranging to pay for my moves, housing, computer needs—nothing! My father and I packed up an old pickup truck and drove down. I moved into a one-room apartment on the top of a flower shop next to a Burger King. My windows during the summer constantly received the fumes of flamed broiled burgers, fries, and onion rings. I had no clue that this was really just student living and that I should have purchased a house or condo. I wasn't just another graduate student, I was now a thirty-one-year-old professor at one of the most respected universities in the country and teaching students who attended the world's biggest music school. Clueless!

I taught my signature course, the Art Music of Black American Composers, a general Western music history course, and directed the Black Popular Arts Ensemble or then named the IU Soul Revue. Portia Maultsby founded the group and course, in the seventies, making it the first academic and performing course in Black popular music. When I arrived I added to the name, Black Popular Arts Ensemble. I was cursed at for doing this but soul music was no longer in existence and I wanted to give the ensemble and our music a proper designation within the academic setting and so I called it, Black Popular Arts Ensemble. This was radical at the time because the White scholars in the department of music looked at it with scorn, and Black folks thought of it as a holy historical dinosaur not to be messed with. The ensemble, some thirty-five members, toured around Indiana, Illinois, and Michigan, with about twenty performances a year. Unheard of! Again, I was clueless. Most university ensembles do two or three concerts a year and rarely leave the campus. We were on the road! Here I was, a young Black classical music composer, forced to do Black vernacular music—and loving it. My kids only wanted to do current stuff: Tony! Toni! Toné!, Boyz II Men, Whitney Houston, Mariah Carey, Jodeci, SWV (Sisters with Voices), TLC, Ralph Tresvant, Heavy D and the Boyz, and the onslaught of hip-hop culture in the nineties. I revised the performance curriculum and for the six years I directed the ensemble had it doing music from jazz to Motown, seventies revolutionary work to hip-hop and Kirk Franklin. As well, I made my students complete research papers on the music they were performing and attend "other music" concerts. Again I was caught in another cultural revolution or market swooshes first with smooth jazz, then hip-hop culture. Hip-hop is Black music family. But, due to its posture in the industry, the focus around young Black urban poets who use (sample, loop) recorded records that I grew up on, as well as its completely different audience base, in many ways hip-hop is a different artistic orientation. This old school R & B and jazz guitarist from the seventies, aspiring to be a classical concert composer, now teaching eighteen-year-olds how to do Janet Jackson choreography and nineties doo-wop R & B ballads? Wow! But by immersing myself in our vernacular, first languages I grew back into myself as a Black musician, and I must admit it was with the emergence of hip-hop Black music culture that I came back to myself. You have to give as an artist.

To study traditional academic classical music culture too often is the study of non-music giving. As lofty and as rich as that tradition is, it is because of the academy and classical music industry practice, snobbery and pretension, actually an anti-music practice and just sad attempts at European museum music replication. It's not Europe's fault, nor the musicians, just too many pretentious academics and hanger-oners who feel to be involved with European-based music of old is a status and knowledge marker. That's not what the music is for. Being in Black music at that point got me back into why we even do music: to delight, to inspire, to speak, and to move people! I taught at Indiana University from 1992 to 1997.

I taught hundreds of students, engaged with both music and African American studies colleagues, began the Undine Smith Moore Collection and the extensions of The Tradition Concert Music series (both still staples of Black music research at IU), and I wrote a lot of music. I completed symphonies 3–6 during this time, a percussion and tuba concerto, had my sixth symphony commissioned and recorded by the Akron symphony on TelArc, my fifth symphony commissioned by my alma mater U of M, composed large chamber works and my first three operas, and I co-orchestrated with David Baker my first musical, *Eyes* by stellar poet Mari Evans. All this was during the time at IU. I grew because I was inspired by my students, music teachers, and an active academic and musical environment in the African American Arts Institute that fostered excellence and music community among young people. One of the major partners I met here was the incredible classical percussionist Tim Adams, for whom I composed the percussion concerto for the Indianapolis Symphony. Not only have we become great partners, creating a band called Black, touring and recording an album together released in 2004, but we were born both in 1961 and share similar navigation struggles with doing Black music, classical culture, and being concerned about the values in artistry. These kinds of concerns among our generation of artists will surface more and more frequently as we become the power players in American music culture. We must hope anyway! In this great mix I also met my wife Krystal from Detroit and a former music student at Cass Tech. See, full circles.

By 1996 I had been teaching at IU but I was also really active as a concert music composer. So I had been traveling back and forth across the country having premieres, doing residencies, conducting jazz big bands, speaking, and establishing connections with orchestras, foundations, and universities, making friends in multiple circles, never knowing nor recognizing that any boundary existed between the industries of recording, doing colleges, composing concert music, or gigging. My first professional commission (for

With Phillip Brunelle and Bobby McFerrin.

$5,000) was from a recommendation from David Baker in 1992. It was my third symphony called *Job's Song*, commissioned by Phillip Brunelle and the Plymouth Music Series of Minnesota. This would not only be my first of many trips to the Twin Cities, it was the connection to a longtime collaborator in Mr. Brunelle who would subsequently commission a series of works including my seventh symphony and connect me ultimately to that community in some permanent ways.

In 1996 I was nominated for a Guggenheim and Cal Arts Award and received a McKnight Fellowship from the American Composers Forum actually founded in St. Paul. The project I created allowed me to work in residence at the Ramsey School for the Performing Arts in Minneapolis. For the entire school year, every month I drove eight hundred miles (one way) back and forth between Bloomington, Indiana, and Minneapolis, Minnesota. I proposed to ACF that I write a large cantata based on the words of the English classes, using their band, choirs, and orchestra. The final concert included members of the Minnesota Orchestra, St. Paul Chamber Orchestra, and the Plymouth Music Series. For Life Suite, we had more than one hundred kids on stage performing and singing this twenty-minute work. That year culminated with many school visits and lectures in my then future institution, The University of St. Thomas. At the same time, Bobby McFerrin and the St. Paul Chamber Orchestra were there as a part of their CONNECT residence series working in Minneapolis public schools. I actually first met Bobby as a graduate student at U of M. He had come to Ann Arbor to study conducting with Gustav Meyer. Now, some ten years later I meet him as the artistic chair/conductor of the St. Paul Chamber Orchestra. So I had the opportunity to get to know and work with one of the most important artists of the twentieth century, Bobby McFerrin. Bobby and I developed a very close friendship and he has helped to confirm every aspect of what I have been saying about artistry in our world.

We spent many hours over meals and hanging out talking about music, artist's citizenry, and our culture. He is a great model for me. This model was too overwhelming. The Twin Cities was for me at that time a "model" arts community. It was reported then that Minneapolis/St. Paul was second only in arts activity to New York. Consequently I left IU officially in 1997 and headed north and west out of southern Indiana to polar territory! In 1998 I was appointed as the Endowed Chair in Arts and Humanities, Associate Professor of Music at the University of St. Paul in St. Paul, Minnesota. My teaching continued and I developed courses (Theology of American Popular Music, Rhetoric and Music in Popular Culture, Popular Arts Choir, Introduction to American Cultural Studies, Black American Music: A Historical Survey, Creative Construction: Composition Seminar) which were dead center of my research interests and artistry.

Not long after I arrived, with the help of a very energized faculty in humanities studies, I organized an American cultural studies program with some thirty courses examining American cultural experience and was awarded a National Endowment for the Humanities Focus Grant, and later encouraged to apply for near a million dollar support grant. The appointment and living in the very artistic Twin Cities provided me with incredible opportunities to bring all of my work and interests full circle. Minnesota by culture and practice is one of the most important cities for the arts by virtue of its aggressive and sincere advocacy for the arts. No wonder Bobby McFerrin settled there, Libby Larsen, Stephen Paulus, Dominique Argento, author Alexs Pate, many others, and too many composers to name. I settled in and began to get to know the culture. In addition to commissions, including works from the Minnesota Opera, Minnesota Orchestra, University of Minnesota commemorating the building of the Wabash Bridge in St. Paul, my undergraduate alma mater commissioned my eighth symphony. I published articles, and I continued to give lectures on the role of artists in contemporary popular culture.

I thought it was important if I were going to be dealing with culture from these larger vantage points, that I should as well address my own Black

Meeting Coretta Scott King, who attended a Banfield symphony in Atlanta, c. 1998.

community here in the Twin Cities. I had always thought that the Black community had too few hometown critics. I love that scene in *Hollywood Shuffle* where the two principal characters, one played by Robert Townsend, decide to be "real brothers" as movie critics. The Twin Cities paper is *Insight News*. I approached them with the idea of writing a cultural commentary on contemporary music. Many of those pieces are published in this book as they appeared in print.

I organized my BMagic orchestra and began playing at local clubs, the Dakota, the Mall of America, and finally running our own concert series at a local arts theater called Patrick's Cabaret. This was a remarkable thing for us because we were the orchestra in residence and invited younger players and musicians to sit in a real music community jazz orchestra, with radio and foundation support. During this time I was approached by the music producer (Ben Roe) of National Public Radio's *Performance Today* to host a special series of programs which I called *Landscapes in Color: Conversations with Black American Composers*. This was my first national radio broadcast program.

Soon after I was approached by another public radio station, WCAL at St. Olaf College, Northfield, Minnesota, to write and produce an original show where I could explore aspects of my artistry and teaching. I called that program

Essays of Note. The show's philosophy was based on my interpretation of music as boundaryless and having a criteria for excellence, only a continued stream of human expression from multiple places. One of the openings went, "I understand as a concert music composer the world of classical music and its historical place. But as a contemporary artist and educator I'm faced with the daunting task of making music live now and of making it useable and accessible, while still pushing the boundaries of art and expression. Furthermore, I'm interested in breaking down the categorical barriers that separate too much great music. So, in *Essays of Note,* I want to tie Beethoven's rhythms to Prince's rhythms, and Bob Dylan's songwriting to Schubert's as well as Ellington's orchestrations to Ravel's. I want to look at the relevance of hip-hop verse as poetic structure and see Carole King's writing as monumental to the shaping of American musical culture.

Another huge meeting of musical minds for me was hooking up with Morris Hayes. Morris is one of the most gifted and beautiful brothers I know. Morris had served as Prince's music director and was introduced to me through some mutual friends, lawyers we had in common, and specifically, Craig Rice, Prince's former manager. Craig, a huge player in the Twin Cities, still serves as the head of the Minnesota Film Commission. Craig produced the award-winning documentary on Gordon Parks. Morris and I made a musical pact to help each other. His studio is the one our dreams are made of. Probably Prince and anyone in that whole musical camp have been and worked in Morris's studio and have been affected by his technical and musical wizardry. Morris produced my first commercial release as a jazz recording artist, *Striking Balance.* So, Morris helped produce Prince's road sound, then he produced little me. Clearly my connection with him brought my near twenty-plus-year bumpy road in popular music industry to some meaningful resolutions. I am indebted to him for bringing a certain part of my dream to reality and keeping me real.

More on writing music. This idea that there is a drama always to be told in multiple languages came to be tested in what has been my largest work to date, the opera *Luyala.* The work, which was budgeted at $400,000, was commissioned and financed by Duke University, Triangle Opera, and the Lila Wallace Foundation. It was conceived by librettist and fundraiser Penelope Bridgers and was danced by Chuck Davis and the African American Dance Co. The cast included jazz legend Nnenna Freelon, opera tenor Bill Brown, and my dear friend Louise Toppin singing the lead role. Clearly the loving ghosts of my past came to conjure up this work, those being Wagner, Africa, and T. J.'s baptisms in modern music. I had to make all this work, and this opera exposed me to the power and potential of large scale works. Again,

Nnenna Freelon and me.

this was an opportunity that you don't usually get before forty. I was commissioned at thirty-four. It took six years to complete. The opera was premiered at Duke University in April 2000.

This same year my first commissioned piano concerto was performed and recorded by the Grand Rapids Symphony; the solo pianist was Patrice Rushen. Classical pianist Leon Bates also performed it in February 2000 in New York. This was my first New York performance and a *New York Times* critic said great things! "Rigorous organization with harmonization that could be read as typically jazz or typically Bartokian with a combination of gracefulness." As a matter of fact, cultural critic Stanley Crouch met us (Leon Bates, composer/pianist Donal Fox, and me) at the Village Vanguard that night and congratulated me on the premiere. We ended up hanging out all night till four the next morning talking about the role of Black people in the next moves to shape the culture! I learned a lot from Stanley Crouch that night and we have maintained our dialogue since then. The brother is always in pursuit. Even Wynton Marsalis the next day apologized to me for missing the concerto performance. He invited me to attend a rehearsal of his Lincoln Jazz Orchestra, which was preparing for its China tour. Wynton also born 1961 too, so as you can imagine he has been the subject and focus of much of my admiration and envy. I was very appreciative of that soft moment.

Me, Cat Henry, and Stanley Crouch at the New York Premiere of my opera *Gertrude Stein Invents a Jump Early On*, at Symphony Place, 2005.

As an active academic during the first years in St. Paul 1997–2000, I received awards and sat on panels, did conferences (Opera America, American Symphony Orchestra League) and residencies teaching my perspectives on Black music and cultural studies at Morehouse, Atlanta U, and Spelman College, North Carolina Central, University of North Carolina, Duke University, University of Texas, Bowling Green, U of Penn, Carnegie Mellon U, Hamilton and Hunter colleges in New York.

During the summer of 1999 I was invited by Marian Wright Edelman to have a work of mine performed (my *Spiritual Songs* for tenor and cello sung by Bill Brown and cellist Ron Crutcher) to inaugurate the John Hope Franklin Library and Maya Angelou Reading Room on the Alex Haley Farm, owned by the movement in Clinton, Tennessee. Both Maya and Dr. Franklin attended and Hillary Clinton officiated the overall celebration that week. Again, another full circle. I ended up the next year being invited to be the first scholar in residence on the farm. I wrote the major portions of this book while in residence for one week, during which no one else was on the entire farm! Scary, but at complete peace with myself in the hills of Tennessee. I was able to determine that at that point I wanted to pull together some of the seemingly disjointed, yet harmonious portions of my musical struggle to find the right note.

With Maya Angelou.

Henry Louis Gates invited me to be a W. E. B. Du Bois scholar at Harvard during the 2000–2001 school year. During this year I wrote two more operas, one on Gertrude Stein and the other, *Soul Gone Home*, based on a 1936 text by Langston Hughes. For my final required lecture as a fellow, gathered in the crowd were people who knew me in Boston as a freshman from some twenty-plus years earlier. So many times back then I dreamed while walking around the campus, but never dreamed that I would be able to study there, and certainly never dreamed that I would be invited to share my music and research as a scholar. So this event was cathartic for me in many ways because I had become recognized for doing what had been so difficult to make sense of for nearly twenty years and I was doing it within the halls of what is thought to be the citadel of American intelligentsia. The final page of this music academic art chapter was a call from Nobel Prize–winning author Toni Morrison who had heard my work (she was present at the Clinton Farm performance) and received further recommendations from poet Yusef Komunyakaa. I was invited to be the 2002 Atelier artist in residence at Princeton University. Our work was a dramatic music piece with text by Yusef on nineteenth-century Black sculptor Edmonia Lewis. In 2003 and 2004 came the National Loan Museum and National Endowment for the Arts (NEA) commissions for new symphonies in Mobile and Pineville, Alexandria, Louisiana. The Mobile Symphony premiered my *Structures in Sound and Soul* to inaugurate the opening of the Mobile Art Museum. I was in residence in the South for the 2002–2003 year. The NEA commission was to commemorate the one hundredth birthday of Harlem Renaissance writer, archivist, librarian Arna Bontemps. I used his 1924 poem, "Hope," which won him the *Crisis* magazine award that brought him to New York as a young man. Other young Black artists seized this cultural time and created the most important arts and culture movement in history. That I have written my ninth symphony using Bontemps' words as Beethoven used in his ninth symphony *Goethe*, really rang home for me. Ellis Marsalis agreed to be the piano soloist. This symphony with jazz, voices, and Black text and musical styles marks a pulling together of the major thrusts of my work up until the publication of *Black Notes* in 2004.

My final academic test was to deliver parts of the thesis, "The Post Album Age," at the citadel, the birthplace of American popular culture theory, Bowling Green State University in Ohio. On an invitation from Dr. Angela Nelson, chair of the program, and Dr. Ray Browne, the founding father of American Popular Culture Studies, I came there in late February 2004 to present my findings, meet, and discuss this with students, graduate seminars, and faculty, and they gave me my last, "you go, boy." I began this writing in 1999 alone in a secluded cabin on Marian Wright Eldeman's farm in Tennessee, and ended it actually writing in a secluded and quiet university home provided to me by Bowling Green University, with, if you can believe this, two dear ladies (Vi and Mary) who would cook and clean for me each day! This is living large!

With all this I wanted to say that being in the arts is all wide and all fulfilling and that any of us are examples of people who are dedicated, focused and absolutely rewarded first by ways in which our music reaches, inspires, and completes people, and that this activity of music making is what makes us whole too.

We continue to struggle and explore. This is only the beginning of a long journey to stay in the fight, to keep the music right and moving and with meaning and purpose sounding in a sometimes hard of hearing and hard of loving world. I felt it was important to illustrate portions of the walk and my current walking as I wrestle with finding peace in my own sounding spaces as an artist. Probably the biggest stretch for any aspiring and growing artist is how to reach the mark of the high calling of artistry, measuring your own inabilities, failures, and insecurities against that call, and keeping your head in place as you encounter these few leaps and successes. And in 2004 we try to forget, despite what seems like a world crumbling before our eyes, this post-9/11, postalbum age which challenges us to maintain hope with a vision toward fighting and working for a better world. Or at least trying to save the one we are in with our small battles for love and taking care of one another. I am one who still believes art will keep a crazed world sane.

This is only the first chapter in attempting to engage with the ongoing maps of this music culture, charting and paving new roads. Baraka's words (found in the introduction to LeRoy Jones's *Blues People*, 1999) so dearly and clearly come back to instruct the end of this sharing as it did in the beginning: "Writing the book confirmed ideas that had been rolling around in my head for years and that now, given the opportunity, flashed out upon the page with a stunning self exhilaration and certainty. That is, how to measure this world in which we find ourselves, where we are not at all happy, but clearly able to understand and hopefully, one day transform. How to measure my own learning and experience and to set out a system of evaluation, weights and meaning. . . . This is the history . . . this is your history, my history and the history of the Negro people. The Music. The Music, this is our history."

PART II

NOW

CHAPTER FIVE

Hope and New Directions (2004)

As I read my log entries, I became more interested in looking through this window of the past, reliving those experiences. That kind of "in the real moment" representing drove me, and I have included those short snippets of life view (2004–2007) as you (and I) are walking it, not simply writing reflectively after the cool of the storm, but too in the stomach of the pain and hanging out in the win at the races.

January

My year began with a fabulous splash in New York attending the International Association of Jazz Educators (IAJE) conference. I love this conference because everybody in jazz and in the industry comes here to hang out, meet, and catch up. Accompanied by Tony Mendoza, my manager/attorney, I met so many friends, reconnected with contacts, and met some new industry people, including Stefon Harris (artist) and Jason Koransky (*DownBeat* editor). I also had a significant meeting with Terri Pontremoli, executive director of Cleveland Tri-C Jazz Festival (currently Detroit Montreux Jazz festival director), who was considering booking my opera *Soul Gone Home* in 2005. Along with my manager and singer Nnenna Freelon, we met to discuss the potential of a staging of the opera at the festival.

February

I spoke at the University of Maryland's new Fine Arts Center, then spent four days at Bowling Green University, Ohio, on invitation from Angela Nelson, chair of their popular culture department. The department's founder, Dr. Ray Browne, encouraged me to leave University of St. Thomas to seek a bigger post that was more suited to my current research and interests. Several days later, I was informed that I was on the short list (four of us) being considered as a dean at Berklee College of Music!

Stanley Crouch and Cedric Dent of Take 6 at U of St. Thomas, St. Paul, visited and I had a very successful sharing with the two of them. I also had great rehearsals with my BMagic Orchestra.

April 21

Over the last few days, I have been hanging out with Patrice Rushen and Lenny White. They are in town with Buster Williams. It just so happened to be "Patrice Rushen week" in my class, and she called to say she was in town. So that day I invited Morris Hayes, Stokley Williams, Patrice Rushen, and Lenny White to class. It was historic to have all those great legends and musical minds discuss music, culture, and the industry with my students.

Delfeayo Marsalis's visit to St. Paul was so rich. We spoke at great lengths about him producing my next record. He sat in on my regular trio gig at Dixies, and the great avant-garde saxophonist and composer Oliver Lake came down and sat in. I had bassist Anthony Cox aboard and Nathan Norman on drums. We really took it "out there."

While the Berklee appointment did not happen, a dean there reported to me that their provost was already approaching him about pursuing an endowed chair for me at Berklee. Hmmm . . . interesting. I also received a call from Dr. Frederick Tillis, who informed me that there is motion at University of Massachusetts to offer me a "deal."

I made an appointment to see the number one Black music administrator in the country: Toni Montgomery at Northeastern University. I also had a great conversation with Jason Koransky at *DownBeat*, who has promised to help me with my new record, *Striking Balance*. So on many fronts all is moving. At Central High in St. Paul, I taught a remedial English class, using Quincy Jones as a model for excellence, and the kids really responded. I have been having substantive discussions with my new producing team at Minnesota Public Radio, fussing over contracts and the content of a new radio "minute" show. I don't need the hassle, but public radio is a powerful forum and the exposure is so tempting that I hang in there.

Striking Balance CD cover.

May 16

I was commissioned to create a symphony to celebrate the life and work of Harlem Renaissance poet Arna Bontemps with the Alexandria, Louisiana, symphony. The night before, the executive director of the symphony took me out to a local affair at the Arts Collective, to hear the group Men Who Cook. So great. All the artists, along with their wives, have their studios together in this combined work cooperative in the downtown area. Boy, these Southern dainty, Southern wives, so charming!!! Fabulous food and music. During the whole bit, I squeezed off to the corner and played piano. People came over requesting me to play some Southern favorites, none of which I know, but I had marvelous conversations about what Southerners in this part of Louisiana value: certain kinds of defined "Black music." Living "within" Southern White culture, as I have closely observed over the last two years (Mobile, Alexandria, Atlanta) has been interesting. I've never known any real Southern White people before, only those I've seen on TV. Everyone was genuinely nice, and there is a great classic sense of charm, tradition, and elegance that I appreciated.

This morning I read through the Arna Bontemps essays, which reminded me of my missions to document culture and to leave an imprint of my experiences as an artist, as an American, as a Black "human meaning explorer," as Bill. I will never be famous, but I am being counted. The crossroads of my work—music, archiving culture, poetry, teaching, cultural criticism, composing, and playing—seem so fragrantly rich and abundant and clear with meaning. It's making me drunk!

I read Charles James's article on Arna Bontemps, as well as Arna's "Personals," and decided to use the line, "I speak for the tormented souls who struggle through life with unusual and difficult names." Bontemps spent his life discovering, documenting, and disarming human struggles through his writing efforts.

Also on this trip, I decided to use my *Deep Like the Rivers* composition to represent Arna's close connection and exchange with his friend, Langston Hughes. The work is so beautiful, written during the same time I was sketching my symphony, *Hope*. They both grow out of the same creative spirit. It makes perfect since to use "The Negro Speaks of Rivers," as in *Hope*, Arna's piece, because both poems brought the two poets to Harlem in the 1920s. I was also inspired and struck by Arna's line, "In Harlem we were seen in a beautiful light. We were heralds of a dawning day. We were the first born of the dark renaissance."

Our group, the U of Michigan Black artists (Guthrie Ramsey, Louise Toppin, Kyra Gaunt, Timothy Holley, Stephen Newby, Jethro Woodson, Gregg Broughton, Tiffany Jackson, Anita Johnson, Joshua Hood, Rachel Williams, Darryl Taylor, Timothy Jones, Charsie Sawyer, Albert Howard, Ray Wade, and me) were all aspiring Black artists brought to the university to pursue our master's and doctorates in music by our great mentors Willis Patterson, George Shirley, and Rae Linda Brown. We felt called and are now some of the leading artists and scholars in Black music in the field. No other group has made such an inroad. One could speak about Gates, West, and a later group with Michael Eric Dyson, but our generation born in the 1960s is unique in that we gathered at the same drinking pool and were imbued with the idea of promoting classical music made for and by Black artists. We are also the last of the dark renaissance. The generation following us—hip-hop—is most definitely cut from and are about radically different ends.

May 23

I am rich from my experiences in Louisiana. I made more local contacts, including substantive talks with directors of the Alexandria Museum to secure placement and storage for my uncle Zeke's paintings. I also visited the local Zion Hill Baptist Church where the music and fellowship were great! I mentored several local musicians, directed excerpts of the symphony strings, jazz segments with one hundred plus high school students from Pineville and Peabody High. The mayor of Pineville and his lovely wife took me out to dinner where we ate alligator. In short, we set up major community links that will help to pave the way for the *Hope* premiere in the fall.

May 30

I drove to Detroit from Minneapolis, after my gig at the BellaNote. Bella-Note, by the way, is a trendy new restaurant in downtown Minneapolis. I have been contracted to play there for the next six months. My band—just the trio of Stokley Williams (of Mint Condition) on drums, Serge Aquo on bass, and me—is slammin'! All of the "cool" people hang there, and the last night drew many musicians. Great hit. I met a new booking agent, Mark Gurley from Detroit, who I think will move some things along. I have assembled my management, booking, finance, and musical teams. I should be ready to go the next level—at least.

Came home to celebrate with my family. We threw my dad his eightieth birthday party. It was one of the most fun and rewarding times. So many friends and family came out. My best buddies Trent Mitchell and Kenny Scott came, and we played a tribute set for my dad, the first time the three of us had played together in such a capacity for twenty-five years! Great time.

Jamming with Stokley Williams and Serge Aquo.

We spent some time with family today, then Krystal and I drove back to Minnesota on Memorial Day Monday.

June

I flew to New York this month to speak on behalf of the National Loan Museum Network. The following week I flew to Chicago to meet with Jason Koransky and the next day I meet with Toni Montgomery at Northwestern. This is a big and respected music school and I am "shopping around." So it will be a great talk with her. One idea is to bounce in two years to another place and Chicago might be an ideal next move. Toni is the "biggest" Black music dean in the country, and she might be willing to attract strong candidates to her campus. We shall see. In the meantime, I will keep making music, completing my *Hope* symphony, and having a good summer.

My press sent out twelve unedited manuscripts of the new book, *Black Notes*, to Henry Louis Gates, Bernice Johnson Reagon, Stanley Crouch, Michael Eric Dyson, Rae Linda Browne, Gerald Early, Guthrie Ramsey, Ray Browne, and Toni Morrison—the biggest cultural critics and scholars I know. So, here's hoping they will say a kind word about it.

I have also been invited to teach graduate composition at the University of Minnesota next year as a visiting professor of music.

June 10–11

News today is marked by the deaths of Ronald Reagan and music great Ray Charles.

Today I headed into Chicago to meet with *DownBeat* editor, Jason Koransky. He understands what I am attempting to do and I think has decided to help me get a little visibility. Jason feels there is a real story in my work, and I happen to agree, of course. Clearly he will become an advocate and friend. Every known artist, whether they are twenty or forty, needed a little visible push like this that can make a big difference. So *DownBeat* will do a feature story on my work in October, about the same time my symphony *Hope* premieres, the record *Striking Balance* is released, and the book breaks out. I have waited sooooo long for this kind of recognition.

July 30

I was in New Orleans, principally to see Delfeayo Marsalis, then off to hear and see Ellis Marsalis. On Sunday I head out to Bloomington, Indiana, to work for three days on my *Gertrude Stein* opera and *Hope* symphony with my copyist, Peter Kienle. We are in the last leg of summer, but it has been rich and rewarding. I consider this trip to New Orleans an investment in my general progression to the next steps. I had projected that by the age of forty-five I wanted to find my place as a jazz guitarist within the system, and already I'm two years ahead of the game.

Two days ago, I spoke with Branford, and my discussion with Delfeayo will focus primarily on the next potential project, and you must meet a producer face-to-face. I think the Wes Montgomery identity—a serious Black jazz guitarist—has really moved me lately. I have been studying concert/film DVDs of him and other guitarists, as I anticipate the CD release of my "guitar essay" *Striking Balance*. In the meantime, I have been appearing around town and gearing up for my debut on the road in Detroit in early September.

My new book, *Black Notes: Essays of a Musician Writing in a Post-Album Age*, arrived in page proof form. I have five days to turn it around to make publication in September. I go next week to D.C. to meet with Scarecrow Press to discuss the cover design, publicity for the book, and my appointment as contributing editor in cultural studies. *Black Notes* is all I dreamed about and worked on it to be more. It is my musical memoir, a cultural commentary, and history and philosophy of Black music. A comprehensive book of its kind, it covers fifteen years of my essays as a musician, and ends with me reporting on popular music from the Black Entertainment Television (BET) awards program in Los Angeles. My appointment at Scarecrow may signify my role in a more elevated post as a Black cultural theorist. Perhaps Ms. Morrison or Skip Gates will be able to help get me into such circles, but, when I think about it, I ain't doing so bad without 'em. At forty-three, there isn't a territory of my dreams I have not attempted or brushed with significantly, and I must admit, it's pretty cool. I am not famous or rich, but I am sailing pretty high. Yesterday I was interviewed by a local writer, Robin James, whom I have supported and mentored in some ways. She was hired by *DownBeat* magazine to do the November feature story on me! Slated for November, this feature story could be *the* national break, the springboard I have been waiting for in jazz circles. With the release of *Striking Balance*, my book *Black Notes*, the *Hope* symphony, and the long-awaited *Gertrude Stein* opera, I couldn't ask for a sweeter mature launching. These projects should *finally* bring me some visibility. This has been a very, very slow-cooking brew, but with all the flavor and richness.

It's 1:30 a.m., and I just returned from Snug Harbor club in New Orleans. Ellis Marsalis and his driver gave me a ride home. Incredible performance, with Jason Marsalis on drums. Got a chance to hook up and hang a little

With the cast of *Gertrude Stein Invents a Jump Early On.*

with him afterward. Five Marsalises is too much gift in the world!! Ellis was very gracious, and we talked very extensively about the book, which he feels I should not have to make any apologies in, as our music and culture is transcendent. He invited me out to his place tomorrow.

Delfeayo and I spent the evening together listening to various Bill B guitar performances, discussing the recording project, and talking about the next direction. Great sharing!

August 5

I was at my usual stopping place in Northwest D.C., the River Inn. I always get a top floor facing 24th Street. The main objective is to finish proofing *Black Notes* and see my publisher in Lanham, Maryland, on Friday. I'm very excited about this most-needed book written by a musician about Black music. Henry Louis Gates, Stanley Crouch, Ray Browne, and Ellis Marsalis all signed on with powerful testimonies. So, my goal over the weekend is to stay locked up in my favorite hole here and closely read these pages.

After leaving New Orleans, I spent time editing and composing in Bloomington. I also had dinner with my main mentor David Baker, saw the great opera diva Camilla Williams, and worked on both the *Gertrude Stein* opera and my *Hope* symphony—in short, completing what I think will be my last

Kissing the opera legend and original musical diva, Camilla Williams, in Bloomington, Indiana (c. 1995).

concert/symphonic works for a while. I am really geared up to focus my attention on my jazz guitar identity now. So I am here finishing this book, my "memoir" at forty-three. W. E. B. Du Bois wrote ones at fifty, seventy, and ninety. Stravinsky, Ellington, and Copland completed theirs at various creative bridges too, so maybe it's not too early for me.

Upon arriving to my room at the River Inn, I found an express package from Peter Kienle with the completed *Gertrude Stein* opera and a CD version of the *Hope* symphony. All three of these projects, at the close of the summer of 2004, with *Striking Balance*, represent a plateau of sorts and clearly mark an ending and beginning point. I have little time to waste chasing dreams and begging for acceptance and with this "maturity" comes a feeling that in some ways I have finally arrived and deserve to be allowed to resonate in my proper "seat."

October 10

I am sitting at an old bed-and-breakfast in Vicksburg, Mississippi, at 8 a.m. on Sunday morning. Built in 1840, an old Victorian mansion, complete with huge pillars, porches overlooking gardens surrounded by willow trees. Pure

Southern comforts. Krystal and I arrived from Memphis, via St. Paul, and we flew into Alexandria, Louisiana. We were picked up, then brought into Alexandria, then another set of friends who had driven down from Vicksburg met us and then drove us back here to Vicksburg. I have been invited to this historic Southern community to speak on the new book and music, my "Hope" song will be sung and I'll sign books and CDs. I mean my idea about it being better to be "almost famous" is in gear. People are so nice and so very helpful as they perceive you have something to share and are "on your way to being." So gracious! But the real deal is my weeklong stay in Alexandria for the premiere of my *Hope* symphony. More later. Returning to the even deeper, richer South is comforting; despite our turbulent and troubled history, there is something quite really American about the South, some real history that my destiny is ultimately tied to. On the long highways we passed over the Red River, Black River, Mississippi River, and cotton fields. I had never seen real live cotton fields before. My mind could picture hundreds of Black people lining those fields and roads—it was deep.

At 2 p.m., I gave a presentation in the historic Vicksburg Constitution Hall (where *O Brother, Where Art Thou?* was filmed). In the back were photos of bands from pre–Civil War time, as well as photos of the musicians who appeared in the Coen brothers' film. The talk was sponsored by local music teachers. Unfortunately the entire coast had been hit by four major hurricanes this year, and we were in the middle of a mild one blowing in. A lot of rain diminished the crowd, and those from Vicksburg don't come out in the rain, I'm told. But there was still a good-sized crowd of families, music teachers, and community leaders. I spoke about music culture and afterwards signed CDs. My host sang the "Hope" song from my new symphony. Very thrilling.

October 18

Krystal and I arrived in Alexandria, Louisiana, on the eleventh and have been here for a week. It was a great drive from Vicksburg. We drove across bridges that run across the highway in Mississippi, including a beautiful forty plus miles of forest reserves. Just gorgeous.

It has been both a great week and a long stay in Alexandria. The premiere of my *Hope* symphony went very well. The big thing for me was bringing together the various ideas of Arna Bontemps, and celebrating and documenting the life of the community. The piece had a number of singable, memorable tunes that stick. The orchestra performed very well, and the piano soloist, although fearful of not playing to his best, managed to pull it off.

The youthful college choirs found some of the dissonances challenging, and it showed! But, all in all, the energy and spirit were there, and the audiences were so moved, they stood on their feet. I can't think of a better reason to feel this was a successful time.

The time here with Krystal and hanging out with my mentor T. J. Anderson and his wife Lois, made this an especially valued time. T. J., of course, schooled me on all kinds of things. We ate together, taught a class of young musicians and composers, and spoke on a panel discussion. Arna Alexander Bontemps Jr. was there, along with scholar Charles James and Ifa Bayeza, sister of Ntozake Shange, author of *For Colored Girls Who Have Considered Suicide When the Rainbow Is Enuf*. Not only did we participate in panels, we hung out on the porch of the historic Bentley Hotel drinking wine and discussing hip-hop and the need of another "Black arts collective," that is, a new Harlem Renaissance, until two in the morning! Great hanging with these cultural historians.

Yesterday, my cousins Omar, Dwight, and Myra arrived from Detroit and Mobile, Alabama, after attending my uncle Zeke's opening there, then attending the opening of the Alexandria Museum of Arts exhibition of African American culture. I was able to meet Stella and Harry, the Black couple—experts and collectors with a gallery in New Orleans—who put the exhibition together. Another great meeting! So attending arts openings, the premiere of my ninth symphony, sitting out after the concert selling books (five copies!) and selling out of CDs, holding public radio and TV interviews, connecting with college and high school groups, hanging out with friends drinking wine, eating great Louisiana cuisine, and being with my mentor—what more could you ask for?

This has been a great and rich time, but I'm really tired. In the past few years, I realize I have been overloading. I have decided to basically drop out of the whole "hustling" scene—radio shows and gigs, etc.—so that I can step back and consider what creative ventures I need to pursue. That means I have to literally drop out. If I don't do anything for the next two years and really study, I could focus. In the meantime, I am going to complete the Free Jam record with Delfeayo and the Tim and Bill AB2 project—both ending this period—with releases of the discs in 2005. These recordings represent both an ending and a look forward. While *Striking Balance* fizzles out due to the lack of label support, I will consider some new music ideas. Though *Striking* represented a mixed bag of ideas and commercial explorations, there are some wonderful productions on that record. But to achieve any kind of market penetration, you need promotional dollars to compete. That I do not have. Although *Striking Balance* is not a big seller, the people who have heard it really, really love it. I will continue to sell them wherever I go, but that will be sustained only for so long. But here again, even after costing more than $60,000, it has achieved the goal we set years ago.

After finishing these recordings, the release of my new book, and the end of the teaching semester, I will head into the holiday season with a realistic eye on focusing and trimming back. Before that, however, I have another scheduled trip and performance, CD performance with my younger mentee, the talented saxophonist Michael Burton, in Jackson, Mississippi, and a performance in New Orleans with young trumpet great Maurice Brown. We have scheduled a few more regular gigs with my trio in town, and I'll probably do a BMagic Orchestra hit in January. I also have to focus on the spring semester as I prepare for my stint as a visiting composition teacher at the University of Minnesota. I'll have all graduate students, and this post will really benefit me as I step out to look for a new job. I really want to study and practice my guitar as I look for the next station to dock. But I have decided to pull out of the whole "race" so that I can emerge again in a few years a bit more seasoned and studied.

I am really disappointed with the public radio culture. I find these producers to all be shortsighted with no idea about the longer, larger view of culture. Even the news end of public radio is starting to be driven by sound bites. Neither of the major carriers I am working with seem to want to cover the ideas of culture I want to develop, and I'm being directed by clueless young White producers who were born in the 1980s, so I end up reporting about issues I have already discussed, not exploring new ideas and people, which sucks. And my book, as preachy as it is, highlights my general suspicion of the current "industry" with its continued attack upon strong Black culture and its limited coverage of sustaining ideas and images of Black people.

Ralph Ellison's *Invisible Man* and Spike Lee's film *Bamboozled* have really reinforced how a Black thinker gets treated in this culture. Other than shackled to the institution of the classroom, we are not really visible, nor do our radical critiques keep in check the deafening barrage of negativity hurled at people of color. Again, a significant Black thinking voice is unheard. So, I have desperately been trying to find a space for research and focus for my thinking and refinement of my new artistic studies. Only by dropping out, taking a sabbatical, a study fellowship abroad, or another artistic endowed chair can save me from the industry rat race. Having finished this last symphony and the Stein opera and seen the release of my book, I should chill for a long minute.

Of course, I will focus on the new appointment as a Scarecrow contributing editor, sinking my chops into that. As the appointment will bring me into D.C. every month, I will also travel more often to other parts of the East Coast to solidify contacts (Gates at Harvard, Morrison and West at Princeton, Bobby McFerrin and Michael Eric Dyson at University of Pennsylvania). My hope is to land a new post within the next two years, and by that time, emerge a bit more seasoned as an artist. The other goal is to enlist the help of a high profile agent who will help me get in with an established label for my new works. I imagine this will take a few years to put in place, but ultimately expect to land a new post by the age of forty-five. Krystal and I both are looking forward to new plateaus.

October 20

Ode to Bill Brown. Today we all received the incredibly horrible news that singer Bill Brown passed, dropping dead of a heart attack after his regular morning run. I had just spoken with him, sending him music of mine that he was to perform next month! This man was, by far, a major musical friend, advocate, and mentor to me—as well as to many others. I felt this death hard. He was the person I called first for everything, and there was nothing I didn't consult him about, from marriage to money, from people management to making music matter. His voice was unforgettable and unmatched. There was no sound like it, and the energy and focus he put into being a music maker is unparalleled—"No question," as he would always say. Everyone knows this extraordinary personality who would not only light up a room when he entered it, but the floor would shake and heads would turn, because he went through life making it louder, fuller, and more dramatic, but also more humane. As for us composers, no single musician championed, performed, advocated, or fought for us more than he. He was our music soldier. I will never forget this man, and every day I will feel the hole that his passing has left in my life. And I will continue to honor him by believing in the sanity and sanctity of the music as he did.

October 27

I'm still greatly hurting from the death of my friend and mentor Bill Brown, whose great magnificent voice I am listening to right now, as I sit here crying like a baby. This kind of loss can make no sense. Thank God for music recordings of artists, because even after losing them we can access a small portion of joy knowing their work goes on. We can piece our souls together with them, even when they are no longer breathing. Their notes still pierce our souls and make us appreciate the great gift God gave us to touch people's lives. As I continue to reexamine my next directions, I take Bill's example to heart, so that I can honor him and the work of one hundred others before him. I must commit to getting out there my most impactful music—the best, serious stuff—and through my efforts with the press and my teaching preaches the word of Black art and culture as the important pulse of our time. While part of me feels the need to retreat to a quiet place, this is soooo hard, because I thrive on multiple energies. It's so difficult to say "no" until I have shaken off this addiction, to allow myself space and time to find the correct notes. If I stand still enough, maybe Bill Brown will advise. If I find some quiet, I might hear him say clearly, "Go brother man, go brother, go brother man."

November 2

Finding Out Mark Ledford Died

Election Day. I voted at 7 a.m. in my precinct in St. Paul. I was the second person in line to vote. I arrived at the polls at 6 a.m., and when I came out there were hundreds of people outside, wrapped around the corners for blocks, standing in the rain! This is an important day. For the first time in my life I am a registered voter in the state and community I live in—a tax paying, home-owning citizen with a driver's license and car registration in the same state. I've lived the life of a rambling, noncommitted, unsettled, roaming musician. But now, at the age of forty-three, I have "become" an American. I voted in an election that is seeing the most crucial issues of my life, and as a conscious voter, I know what I believe and I know who I trust in.

Today too, this follows the tragedy of the loss of my dear friend Mark Ledford. Just as we are getting through the death of Bill Brown, we must endure this second shock. Two dear friends, great artists, mentors of mine, and Mark, my brother, was only forty-four. Unbelievable!!

November 3

The day of the election, Macalester College kids were protesting on my side of town. One of their placards read, "Fuck Southern Retards!" While it is about time that this generation voiced its political and social consciousness, one has to feel concerned about a sentiment that is divisive and mean-spirited. But bad-spirited politics have divided our nation into some very problematic camps, even as the usual divisions are represented: republican and democratic; conservative and liberal; warmongers and peacemakers; rich and poor; White and Black, gay activists and religious zealots. Maybe it boils down to those wanting a change and those resolved to complacency. Either way, it's never been this bad before, unless I have lived thus far with my eyes shut, ears blocked, and heart empty of feeling and being totally disconnected from reality. But the reality is that we live in a frighteningly divisive and disconnected society, one of conflicted consciousness.

November 4

Here in Minnesota, I have grown immensely as a guitar player. Stokley Williams, Serge Aquo, and I have grown incredibly as a team, an ensemble. Last night we played our regular Wednesday evening gig at Rossi's Blue Room. Between sets I skirted over to Nicollet Avenue to hang out at the Dakota, and it occurred to me that Minneapolis has its own kind of "scene." So like Boston as a teenager, in my forties I am in something of a "player zone," revisiting the foundational path that I have strayed from as a composer and academic.

At 6 a.m., while most of the guys are asleep, I am here checking cultural studies midterms. Engaging in these multiple duties is pretty amazing, actually, because I know of so few colleagues who are doing this, conducting in so many broad strokes. So this continues to be a very special time. My label submitted *Striking Balance* for a Grammy nomination in the Best Jazz Instrumental category, and the album made the cut to the remaining forty. This affirmation is quite meaningful and affirms my growth as a guitarist, as an artist.

On stage last night my heart was ripped with thoughts about good friend Mark Ledford, my brother who we lost. What an incredible musician, voice!! Like so many—*too* many—jazz artists, Mark may have destroyed himself with substance abuse and selfishness brought on by the demons of public artistry and a lifestyle that can come with it. We have to be so watchful, so conscious not only of our gifts, but of our vulnerability as well. Music can make you selfish and self-centered. I am forced to reexamine my own consumptions, my own selfishness, and to be more considerate of others.

November 7

This weekend Tim Adams flew in and we completed the mixing/recording of the AB2 project. After nearly two years of planning, it's finally coming out on Albany/Videmus recordings.

On Saturday, I took twenty-five students along with my colleague, Elise Marubbio, to the Mille Lacs Indian Reservation, in upstate Minnesota.

Wow, what an experience! I had never been on an Indian reservation before. To know there are sovereign nations here within our country, and which were set up centuries ago, is beautiful in many ways.

November 13

Mark Ledford's Funeral

"If you find your head in a lion's mouth, don't kick him. Rub his paws and he might let ya go." Mark Ledford's mom spoke these words to me, sharing her wisdom as she retold some nice things about our dear departed brother.

I came home here to bury one of my dearest friends and mentors, and words cannot bring forth the meaning of the loss we witnessed today. Almost two weeks since his death, Mark doesn't even look like himself! We are still all shocked, very sad, and miss him much. It was extremely difficult to see Ajare, his daughter, and Mark Jr. part with their dad.

Though Mark was only a year my senior, in many ways he mentored me and my crew. At today's funeral, Jeff Stanton, Trent Mitchell, Kenny Scott, and I stood as brothers to "represent" and speak as Black musicians who had been in each other's development for twenty-five years. And while the "readers" at his funeral service did not make enough of his supreme gifts as an internationally known artist, we had to share this, to speak of his energy and lively spirit.

When we all went into this thing, we never thought that we were going to lose one of us so soon, so suddenly. Being an artist can sometimes create a feeling of eternal, indestructible youth. Some days we feel like children, who never stop dreaming, and who find a way to live those dreams. As musicians, our hearts are filled many times with an indescribable joy when our audience seems like it's made up of kids from another playground blocks away who have come to listen. We seemingly never tire of sharing, of showing, of making music. And we all feel like play pals. And Mark, while mature in some ways, was the biggest kid of us all.

That we would face death in our prime seems so surreal. So we four forty-year-olds, almost elders now, stood there talking about Mark and our lives as teenagers. It all seems so distant, when we ran through the streets of Boston, chasing dreams of being famous, of being liked. And Mark, our brother, did it. The Pat Metheny Group is one of the most successful jazz ensembles in the history of recording. Mark got to play with Metheny, to record with him, see the world many times over as an artist, heard in so many venues. I think Mark was very happy that his brothers spoke on his behalf.

I thought of our Thanksgiving dinners together, and even of two with Bill Brown! With Mark's "going home" service behind us, K and I will fly to Jacksonville, Florida, for Bill's memorial service. Celebrating the lives of musician friends who have died ain't fun.

Those deaths will continue to resonate with me, especially as I look in the mirror and ask myself, yet again, "What will you do now?" And these days, the harder question to answer is "How can you do *less*?" because it feels like I have an endless list of things that are always bubbling, ideas that are constantly brewing, and it's difficult to turn away from them. I'm not sure what or how to cut. And sometimes I feel that things are crumbling, when my self-critical mind takes charge and I give myself little credit, I'm unable to savor the moments that matter, because I'm always moving. And there are other struggles—with health, with the seemingly endless mounting of paperwork. Sometimes, so many wonderful blessings can bring heavy responsibilities, numerous disappointments. People don't always deliver what they promise, but I'm always expected to produce more than is ever given to me. But I never let these disappointments and setbacks slow down the creative process.

It would be impossible to name all the melodies in my head, these testaments of living hours, weeks, and months in solitude. Soon, I will need to figure out what to do with all this music. At these crossroads, a new Berklee opportunity comes nipping at me again. What if I am meant to return east, to connect with those roots, to build a new dynamic Black music program?

November 15

Jacksonville, Florida

Mark's funeral and then two days later, I find myself paying respects to another passed friend, Bill Brown. I have never been to Jacksonville and as I came through the airport, I realized that Bill must have passed through here hundreds of times. I felt as if I was walking in his paces, his steps. Bill traveled the country, the universe, and he passed through this airport to make his connections as an artist who represented, who reached out to touch the world again and again. And so I come here, to Jacksonville, not to meet him but to remember how he went through this world. Not at all cool to be participating in death salutes to your friends, but many have come— Louise Toppin, T. J. and Lois Anderson, Dwight Andrews, Vivian Taylor, and Alvin Singleton—to celebrate this man, his life, and his dedication to artistry.

A memorial concert for Bill was held at North Florida University, and it was just beautiful. Louise Toppin, as always, sang like a dove. Big brother

cember 16, 2004 • Volume 21, No. 22 $3.50

LACK
SSUES
N HIGHER
DUCATION®

w.blackissues.com

20
Years
1984-2004

With All
Strings
Attached

NIVERSITY OF
T. THOMAS PROFESSOR
ND COMPOSER
ILLIAM C. BANFIELD
EAVES TOGETHER
ORLD OF MUSIC

LEADing students to careers in
business, Pg. 28

■ Black Coaches Association grades
minority hiring, Pg. 8

■ Alternative to Greek-letter
organizations, Pg. 32

Black Issues in Higher Education cover story.

Dwight Andrews and others gave fitting talks and there were marvelous musical tributes as well. The moment that touched me most was when the sixty-voice choir was asked by its director, "How many of you are Bill Brown students?" Thirty or so kids raised their hands! To see his life here, on his working soil, wow.

A group of us (T. J. and Lois, Vivian Taylor, Dr. Horace Boyer, and me) were escorted up to his office, which remained untouched since his death. The room was filled with framed posters of his performances and pictures—of all of us, of every Black composer, of world famous conductors. Bill's books, notes, music, travel items, and CDs rested on the walls, on shelves, and all over the floor! Just like him, completely "full up." Marvelous sight!

I came away inspired by Bill's life in another profound way, by his role as a giver to young musicians. I can't help but feel called to continue to search for a place where I can contribute and shape young musicians. This is the truest mark of our contribution and our sharing; because those young artists go on to reach others, they will carry on the traditions. So I have to find a teaching home where I can mentor, like Bill did.

December 16

Today I made the cover of *Black Issues in Higher Education*, and it will go far to "represent." Already, *Black Notes* is making connections all over the country. My press developed a very aggressive promotion and outreach for this book. My publisher, Ed Kurdyla, has finally finished my appointment to Scarecrow as contributing editor. So the work continues.

Two thousand five will be an interesting year. . . .

CHAPTER SIX

Slowly Contemplating Boston (2005)

February 2

Bobby McFerrin, the walking note, was in town last night. K and I went to see and hear him. He was fabulous, of course.

Today I completed my second full week of teaching at the University of Minnesota, and I'm loving it too much. Actually, I began at St. Thomas this week and love my kids this semester. But teaching at U of M, my goodness, it has changed me. My seasoning as a composer/teacher has caught up with my work, so now I can speak as someone who "knows." It's a little bit frightening to teach a graduate seminar, because it doesn't seem too long ago that Stephen Newby and I were at the University of Michigan. Now I'm the composition professor at a major Big Ten school. I never thought I had the stuff, but apparently my work over the years has prepared me. I truly love it.

I am preparing to go to New York for my opera *Soul Gone Home* which will be performed at Avery Fisher Hall and Merkin Hall. Also, Lenny White invited me to play with him and Victor Bailey at The Jazz Standard to celebrate Mark Ledford's life. So, for the first time I am going to New York as an artist. And then I go back in June for my opera *Gertrude Stein Invents a Jump Early On*, which is playing off Broadway.

February 6

Over the last few years, I have been trying to unite three interdisciplinary divisions—American cultural studies, peace and justice studies, and women's studies—since they share similar views of the world and academy. It is taking root finally this year—in a way I think will unite some of our discussion and activities, mainly, the engagement of faculty discussions. We have created an initiative called "Troubling the Waters: Interdisciplinary Forum in Society, Culture and Humanities."

As chair of Jazz American Popular World (JAPW) music studies, I have been encouraging the fragmented adjuncts in music to be more visible. We organized an all ensemble meet, which last year brought together the jazz band, African drum ensemble, jazz ensembles, voice and guitar ensembles—some one hundred students. I encouraged them to attend each other's concerts, come together for an annual Christmas concert, and stage an area recruitment tour. Last year for the first time these areas were introduced at the opening music majors meeting, giving music majors an opportunity to see and hear about the other ensembles.

This year I introduced a measure that would, I think, radically change options for music students to participate more fully in these ensembles: The students should be allowed to participate for at least one semester outside of their required standard ensemble. I had the same battle at Indiana University, but Dean Charles Webb allowed a provision in which these students could participate in my ensemble. This similar idea at Minnesota can diversify the department, without all of the curriculum hubbub.

I have also asked our American cultural studies faculty to be involved more in the community outreach initiatives I began around town and at other campuses—namely our Mille Lacs Indian Reservation trip with the American Indian studies program at Augsburg College, the Weisman/Walker Arts trip, and the Central High humanities residency, where I bring more than one hundred students to study on our campus. All of this is teaching me how to be a better administrator, but more importantly it is expanding the curriculum and educational programming. This area is so important because people don't spend enough time thinking about outreach and resource sharing, except when it saves money. Collaborative education and interdisciplinary exchanges are truly enriching.

I am preparing three papers: one for the Popular Culture Conference in San Diego; another for the William Dawson Symposium in Atlanta; and one for Black Issues in Higher Education Conference in D.C. My presentations include multimedia, interactive demonstrations of music and video.

I am still in discussion with Scarecrow Press about my possible appointment as a series or consulting editor.

Preparing for my trip to New York next week, which besides a gig to honor Mark Ledford, I will see Andre Guess and perhaps Wynton Marsalis at their new Lincoln Jazz Center Auditorium—"The House That Wynton Built." I will also see Fran Richards and Cia Toscanini (Arturo's granddaughter) at American Society of Composers, Authors and Publishers (ASCAP).

I returned home for a solo guitar performance with five other local guitarists at Hamline University's Sundin Hall. The following week there is a Barnes and Noble book signing in St. Paul.

I had a great meeting with Sarah Lutman at Minnesota Public Radio, our nation's biggest public radio station. We are working on creating a ten-year space for me in public radio. At this point the seasonal commentaries and short-lived shows are a waste to pursue. We are working on a model that allows for growth, while reaching an important commercial, cultural niche. I think this move, even if it takes a few years to develop, will ultimately pay off.

I am not chasing that old dream of being a famous young musician. Those days are clearly gone. But the pursuit of ideas, the evolution of my artistry, and the cultivation of friendships within the industry is sooooo gratifying. In days past I have spoken to old friends Regina Carter, Carla Cook, and of course, Kenny, Trent, and Jeff, all old Detroit musician partners. This kind of sustained sharing is quite satisfying right now.

February 12

This morning I got up at 5 a.m. to decide what clothes I was going to wear in New York. While the *Piano Concerto No. 1 No Mirrors in My Nana's House* performed at Hunter College was my first New York premiere (2001), and the reading of *Gertrude* was another first, my entry to the city this time comes with a full performance of *Soul Gone Home* in two major concert halls. That's new.

February 17

New York. For the first time in my mature, professional life I arrive for my music, from performing to the acceptance of *Soul Gone Home*. I'm meeting all the right folks this time, so many of the pieces are coming together. I stayed close to midtown, Merkin Hall, and Lincoln Center.

On day one I met with Andre Guess, the Lincoln Center's Jazz's executive director, Wynton's main boy, to sell him on *Soul Gone Home*. After a great talk, Andre walked me over to Wynton's new "house": the main concert hall, studios, full jazz club, and a second smaller theater overlooking Central Park. Ridiculous!! No Black artist in jazz history has been given so much power or sold himself to the "machine" to deliver such a slick, well-oiled product. I admit that the educational series, concerts, restaurants, gift shops, and retro-style concerts diminish the firm commitment to the "art" that jazz hardliners would demand. I mean the shops at Columbia Circle have huge pictures of Wynton wearing his Modavo watch. What can you say about this? Wynton is *doing* it!

March 4

Atlanta. At Emory University with a fabulous gathering of the best Black concert music musicians, composers, and writers in the world for a symposium celebration of William Dawson. I gave a wonderful presentation and am enjoying the exchanges, especially among us composer/performers: Donal Fox, Anthony Davis, Geri Allen, Oliver Lake, T. J. Anderson, George Walker, Alvin Singleton, Tania León, Rae Linda Brown, Louise Toppin, and Dwight Andrews, our host and coordinator. The symposium has been nothing short of fantastic: seeing all the artists and friends, hearing and participating in all this music and culture. Last night was the finale concert with the

With Dwight Andrews.

Tuskegee Choir and other local choirs, including an incredible performance by Clark Atlanta University. Our brother Andrews really pulled an incredible thing together.

Although not centralized in a city, we are witnessing a Harlem Renaissance of this generation. This is a "moment," and we are moved toward excellence. But a few of us are going beyond the symposium with books, radio, teaching, and such. We are moving traditions along.

I need to spend some time writing more vocal music for choirs. William Dawson left an incredible legacy of music with those arrangements and compositions for voices. Let's face it: The regularity of orchestral, chamber performances is slim.

Speaking of Dawson, I spent the morning at the Emory library where there was a Dawson collections exhibit: letters, scores, records, books, and a photo history of his life. Here again is another example of a map for my life. In this collection of artifacts, I can read Dawson's path, philosophy, and evolution, his challenges and accomplishments. He was totally dedicated to his life as a musician, teaching and preserving the traditions of Black artistry. This is a model for me.

March 17

I got the call yesterday from Berklee College of Music: They fly me out on Monday, I present on Tuesday, I interview, and then they send me back home. So this is it. I have already made appointments with folks at MIT to discuss a potential production of my chamber opera *Edmonia* and will perhaps see big brother Henry Louis Gates at Harvard. Berklee is the gleam in my eye, drawing me since last year's visit. I'm well prepared and adequately equipped, but will they want me or some other guy? There are all kinds of nice bubbles in my stomach and wild thoughts floating in my head: What would I be able to do? What new connections are there to be made? What young musicians could I share with? Where would we live?

We completed the semester after returning from Boston. Next week, K and I fly out to San Diego. We are both presenting papers at the American Culture and Popular Culture conference. As soon as I read my paper, I'm out the door and to the beach for seafood!!

Yesterday the *New York Times* mentioned *Gertrude Stein Invents a Jump Early On*, my opera with Karren Alenier! And *Striking Balance* has finally been released nationally, internationally. I got a record promoter who has the record playing all over the country, a first for me.

With Krystal.

March 21

Well this is it! I am heading to Boston to interview again, this time for the post of professor of Africana studies. I feel pretty confident that I will be able to deliver. It's pretty exciting to be given this opportunity to possibly change or refine my direction. My dean, Connery, actually encouraged me to take a two-year leave of absence. This relieved my guilt of going through this far because St. Thomas has been so supportive. I do want to be loyal but I also feel a calling and need for my work and now is the time to reconnect with my East Coast roots. I'll meet Lori Gross at MIT to discuss *Edmonia*, go see Gates, and see friends at Harvard tonight. Tuesday I interview all day.

April 19

7:15 p.m. I waited here at home. I was told yesterday that the Berklee search committee would meet today, Eastern time from 4 to 6 p.m. to make their final decision. It is past the hour and no word yet. I had K take out a bottle of wine and two glasses, but if it was a deal, I would have heard by now. I know this feeling, one I've endured for the third time, and it doesn't feel nice. I'm reminded of W. E. B. Du Bois waiting on a call in Ghana to hear if his Africana project was going to be funded. So, I wait in a sweat, stomach tied all up, because this position would launch me, I believe, into the next phase. The prospect of creating a Black music program in a powerful music institution excites me, and I have placed a lot of my hopes into this Berklee post.

I have prayed for this one as hard as the last job hope. Still, I wait. I guess this is what the blues is about.

April 21

Yesterday morning, I received the call from Berklee. They offered me the position of professor of Africana studies, music, and society! I am still trying to catch my breath, so excited about what God has blessed us with!!!

I had a great discussion with Berklee president, Roger Brown, who is on the same visionary page. So much of the things I have been working to include in my pedagogy, my philosophy of music and culture, are very much what he has been thinking. At this point the possibilities at Berklee seem endless. Being at this great music school, among all those talented young people, is mind boggling. Think about how much I will learn and absorb, how many great conversations and challenges I'll have from and with musicians. In my mind this will be the last music school stop.

May 7

Washington, D.C. I arrived yesterday to work with the two presses, Scarecrow and *Black Issues in Higher Education*. Took the train to the Scarecrow Press office in Lanham, Maryland, to meet with my publisher Edward Kurdyla and speak with the two other consulting editors on staff. In short I began a new leg of my professional career as a book editor. I am officially on staff, on salary, with a responsibility to create six new books a year and oversee African American cultural studies publications. This is pretty unbelievable. In our discussion, we considered the new face of Scarecrow Press music, of which I am now directly involved. That in itself was a major mind-blowing experience.

June 10

I then go to New York for a first time full run of one of my theater works. A real big deal. Topped on this is the move to Boston, a whole lot to consider.

And now, Michael Jackson. As we wait for the jurors' verdict, we cannot help but think, "How sad." Michael means a lot in the cultural equation: history, artistry, hero, our maturation. Beyond the cult status and paparazzi considerations, some of us grew up with Michael Jackson. I am sickened by the insensitive treatment of this Black man, an internationally loved artist and symbol. I am sickened more, though, of possible improper treatment of young innocent victims.

First, Michael is a musical enigma, a major music and cultural force, an impeccable artist of genius accomplishments. The sound he had as a youngster—the sound of an old man singing the R & B blues yet through a preadolescent and adolescent body—is of note. His artistry as a singer, vocal innovator, and tradition interpreter is unprecedented. White cultural media will run to Elvis or Sinatra, as they consider anything White newsworthy, but critically viewed, Michael is one of the finest singers American culture has ever produced. His transformation of down-home Black style into international pop still maintained its Black cultural sound, yet pushed the envelope of aesthetics, technology, movement, and visual narrative. Michael is an arts wonder. So it saddens us to see a great, meaningful person fall like this. It hurts because there are so few sacred Black icons in the popular marketplace, and the media are only too eager to sharpen the negative spotlight on them.

When White public figures make mistakes, their behavior is often treated as just another minor antic. When Black people do stupid things (Mike Tyson, O. J., R. J. Kelly, Kobe Bryant), their conduct becomes a lightning rod for racists who project such behavior on all Blacks.

And now, it's Michael's turn.

One cannot judge Michael based on hearsay evidence and a media angling for advertising dollars. But the charges he faces, along with the knowledge that he paid other accusers off, smells of something problematic. I don't know of any grown man who has "boy sleepovers" and claims it's just friendly mentoring. There is a problem here. Regardless of guilt that may or may not be proved, if Michael Jackson is criminally charged, this problem is serious.

Michael Jackson is human, and we ask God to heal him. We also thank God for what Michael has given us. His fall marks a major tragedy for Black artistry, and we will miss this great artistic force.

⌢

The Move East: Space, Serenity, Peace of Mind and Creativity, and an Essay about Arriving Home

August 30

Brookline, Massachusetts. So, I was sitting in the Village Fish, a wonderful quaint seafood restaurant near my new home. Brookline Village has restaurants (Greek, Thai, Japanese, Chinese, American, Irish, Italian, and French), Starbucks, local grinders, Dunkin' Donuts, Jewish bakeries, markets, shops, wine stores, and cleaners, in circles that wander like most streets here, cow pastures simply paved over. I can imagine old world, or present Europe for that matter.

Boston still combines urban East vitality with old world sensibilities, and I'm now delightfully retrapped in this environment. I first arrived in Boston many years ago, and I return now twenty-five years later. The days as an eighteen-year-old are still burned into my being and yet there is something fresh about this old space. You have to find a creative space to be, to be "in." That "in" is so important to the creative voices in your head. But this kind of selfish, self-absorbed space comes at a high cost. Sacrifice, loneliness, being misunderstood and misread, perhaps. But such is the cost of getting divine time, which is highly valued by artists.

I sat there drinking a spicy Merlot, a bit buzzed actually, waiting on my fish, eating bread and butter, and thinking I had died an early death and was stationed in heaven's waiting room. This move, as desired as it might have been, was a sacrifice: I left a well-earned tenured post, endowed chair, and a successful program that I helped build, along with a lovely and rich Twin Cities supportive arts and education community. I left behind a beautiful home and great friends to meet new challenges, both financial and emotional. Yet still I can feel some reassurance, as I anticipate my meal, that God has delivered a great answer to many prayers. And my wife, who is expected to join soon, successfully moves in her own well-deserved and fought for stations, hundreds of miles way. Missing her warmth, I wish for us both to be fulfilled. But I start our journey as a scout of sorts. As far as I can see, through thick brushes ahead, we will settle our camp here. This is a kind of peace that comes in later years: a peace of mind, of place.

K and I have no children, at least as yet; my only children are the "babies" I created. Boston is a creative place, a space where great minds have passed through, and you can feel this kind of accommodation in the air. And yes, it is a hard place too, with race and ethnic relations always strained. The divide between the "rich haves" and the "poor ain't got nothings" is as sharp a line as the train track. From community to community that line has existed and separated folks throughout our rich, soiled social history.

I had a cousin, Nelle, who was like my mother here. She watched over me, gave me a home to stay in, and was a great mentor. After I had moved away, I would often call "Aunt" Nelle, playfully harass her by threatening to move back into home. Days before I arrived, I called to alert her of my return, but Nelle had died and been buried days before my call. Crushed, fighting back more tears, I refused to be "taken out" by another death this year. A few months prior, I had two very close friends die, two friends die from heart attacks and only a couple of weeks apart. Both were great musicians and singers, both mentors. The year before, another mentor, my uncle Zeke—a great artist—had passed away, and three months beyond that, his daughter, and three months beyond that his wife, then her mother—back-to-back—boom, boom, boom.

After a gig this past spring, I rushed to the hospital with heart palpitations. What the hell was going on? Months of doctor's appointments followed: internists, cardiologist, gastroenterologist, doctors of all sorts. I quit all gigs, dropped out of performing commitments, and in the process made some enemies. The opposites of serenity and peace are stress and distress. I felt cracks, creeks, and sore muscles, and that ain't sonorous. So, at forty-four, I have learned a few lessons about tritones.

In *Black Notes* I included a poem, "Wearing Afros in Late 199?" that I had written while I was a resident composer in Utah. Looking at snow-covered mountains after visiting the Mormon Tabernacle, I was feeling a bit out of place. That was more than a decade ago. While I try to grow my "fro" again—literally—I realize there are several places where my hair just doesn't stand as alive, and there are spots of graying. I can't eat what I used to, and my knees and feet ache many days at a time. My hands are pained at the nerves from thirty years of piano and guitar, from banging at the computer. My insides feel just as young, but my body is different. Besides peace of mind, I wonder how to allow my body to be well, too. I am an old man, I guess, but this realization opens up creative spaces that I could not have imagined five years ago.

September 1

As we watched the devastation done by hurricane Katrina, there is feeling of disbelief. The events of 9/11 were over the top, sent us into global warfare, chasing after al-Qaeda and terrorists to noneffect, as Iraq and Afghanistan have ballooned into more madness. Now our shores have been hit in places that have little resources. New Orleans, one of the world's greatest cities, is nearly destroyed. Sodom and Gomorrah come to mind, although it almost seems insensitive to say such. The very depressing part is that the majority of folks in New Orleans are Black people—caught in the chaos with no way out. Stranded. How could this happen in modern America? The richest country in the world and still people are reduced to living as if in a third-world nation. It will be months before the city is dried out and some order is restored. I can't help but recall the time I spent there this past year—walking through the French Quarter, meeting with Papa Marsalis, roaming the streets, savoring café au lait and fried dough cakes at Café du Monde—

thinking "What a grand place, New Orleans." All the great civilizations fall, great city by great city, and one has to wonder: Will it come back? What will it take to rebound? We pray.

I left my father in Detroit, after the recuperation from his surgery. Today I learned that some cancer remains. I can't go into depression, but thinking about my dad, thinking about New Orleans, feeling my loneliness got to me. Still early in my journey here in Boston, but all days don't feel glorious. I am in a new place, and as much as I talk about coming home here, it was quite an uprooting.

November 13

I am headed to Philadelphia to visit Bobby McFerrin and family, staying with them in their park. On Monday I head into New York to see Lenny White and I will stay with him in Newark, New Jersey, then on Tuesday head into Princeton to meet with Cornel West and Toni Morrison. This is my first Eastern Seaboard train tour out of Boston. I had longed to move east and be able to travel up and down the coast and see these mentors.

Life is challenging in Boston. Some days I ask, "Why did I leave the peace of mind and comfortable embrace of Minnesota?" Nobody bothered me. I was free to roam. The culture was not complicated. Here in Boston, nothing is easy. The Berklee environment is contentious among all kinds of factions. Some days I leave exhausted. But, every day I go into work exhilarated, and most here are moved by that same energy, especially these wonderfully excited music students who dream about being the next great star. This is the same dreaming most of the professors felt, and to be able to shape that dream into reality is what we are all about. So, while I could name about three or four downsides, when I really consider what drives me and why I wanted to come east, I could easily list thirty-five-plus reasons for joy.

I can't even begin to fill in what has been happening since I arrived. K comes every month and I go to Minneapolis every month so we see each other two or three times a month. It's not wonderful, but we are managing this. For our eighth wedding anniversary we went to Martha's Vineyard. This is God's country, for sure, one of the loveliest places I have ever seen. We really enjoyed and luxuriated, taking a room at the Harbor Inn looking out over the ocean.

Here in Boston, living in a luxury condo complex in the hills, the Pill Hill area of Brookline, has been quite a nice thing. My living area is completely set up to study and I immerse myself in music for the year. Most evenings I may walk around JP Pond, a few blocks away, have meals in Brookline Village at the Village Fish or other restaurants. Evenings I study films and read.

I am writing a new book and part of the visit with Cornel West is to see if he would consider cowriting it with me. In it I interview a number of famous musicians and ask them, "Why does Black music matter?" With the continued barrage of attacks against Black humanity, we find that if the music dies, we die. So I am engaging in a discussion that I hope readers will take up again, to take the music back, as it were.

I finished a voice and piano piece, "It's All Good My Brother" for Louise Toppin. The work is in homage to Bill Brown, who always said, "It's all good my brother." The work will be performed at Carnegie Hall, on my forty-fifth birthday.

I am also orchestrating this for chamber orchestra. I have been involved in teaching all kinds of classes, presentations, and meetings at Berklee as I prepare to launch my work here as a teacher and administrator.

Many days I am anxious about how I will fit in here. The academic structure and culture at Berklee is completely different from any teaching environment I have been in. So I don't feel safe yet. But, slowly, I'll get over it.

I went over to a concert at Jordan Hall, which I remember walking across the stage in 1983. I was invited by a former teacher of sorts, Ran Blake. My challenge is to find my niche here, grab onto it, and make it work. As I write this new book and work through my research models, I have again landed on the work and writings of W. E. B. Du Bois and his efforts to not only understand the conditions of Black folks but to change them by researching, documenting, and advocating Black culture. I would like music to be my great contribution, but there are so many more talented and important voices. While committed advocacy at this level is rare among my generation of artists and scholars, I *live* in this passion.

I took over as the chair of the Black music culture area of the American Association of Culture and Popular Culture Association. Some forty scholars, my cochair, Angela Nelson, and I are coordinating. I am very proud of that.. And *DownBeat* has hired me to write a regular column on culture. With a wide range of topics I can review, this will give me another international platform to share some ideas. I think this will be fun.

Meanwhile, I am playing, practicing. And I have a weekly sparring coach to work through some sight reading and analysis issues.

So, I am trying to reinvent myself on several different stages.

November 15

Princeton University. To meet the prophet of your era, to be affirmed in his eyes is a most meaningful encounter. I arrived here shortly after 1 p.m. My meeting was at 2 p.m. I sat waiting briefly in his office, one of the most spectacular, in terms of books. Each one, with a cover of the author, is placed by the hundreds cover to cover, facing outward, for visual effect. The feeling is that all these great eyes and minds are upon you—from Beethoven, Monk, and Coltrane to Baldwin, Mahler, and Morrison. Thinkers by the hundreds all looking at you.

And then he enters, with all humility, in characteristic Cornel attire: black suit, scarf around the neck, Afro high, and that marvelously wide, wise smile.

We talked about music, market forces, thugs in office, and things in the streets. And he read through my things—my CDs, my books, articles by me, articles about me—with great admiration and interest, calling my work, "Unprecedented among us." A very honorable and lofty claim, and because it was from him, I dare not deny it. Cornel is my most profound writing influence.

In recent times I can't remember a meeting as exhilarating, so meaningful to me as this—not since 1988 when he encouraged me to seek out Jon M. Spencer. Not only have I met the prophet, but what's really cool is that the prophet listened to what I had to say, liked what I had to say. Here is the most brilliant brain one can encounter and to feel his deep concern and willingness to learn from others is something to behold and experience. I have known Cornel over the years, but this moment is different. While my journey is in no way complete, this plateau is worthy of mention, a professional moment that we were able to meet.

Cornel invited me to dinner, then to accompany him to his class in Black intellectual development. After announcing to the class my presence, he asked me to speak on the students' discussion. They were brilliant, they did not need my comments, but I did share.

Afterward, I joined Cornel for drinks. I feel very well treated by the gods of destiny.

November 25

I arrived from New Jersey after visiting Cornel West, Bobby McFerrin, and Lenny White. A quite successful trip all around. Staying with Bobby and Debbie McFerrin at their home in Philadelphia allowed me some close time with Bobby that I had not been able to experience since they left Minneapolis. Lenny and I bonded as musicians and friends, as we hung the entire next day in his studio, playing and listening to music (I brought my guitar along). Then in my visit with Cornel, we walked across the Princeton campus talking of old friends, the intellectual life, and the value of music. At that meeting he not only agreed with great enthusiasm to come to Boston and inaugurate my new

Africana studies program at Berklee, but to coauthor my latest book, *Black Music Matters*. In this book I trace the development of an aesthetic that led to the study of Black music, then discuss with Black artists about why music matters. Cornel enthusiastically agreed to interview some of the artists, as well as to edit the book. If it comes to pass, it will be phenomenal.

As I land in Boston, I am off to see my biggest hero, Detroit guitarist Earl Klugh. I left the Thanksgiving holiday early—to my wife's great disdain—hoping to connect to this great artist and teacher of mine.

CHAPTER SEVEN

Life Lived East (2006)

Jazz culture for me represents how I was brought up in this culture. I was taught by older musicians. I came up in the [Black] church, where there is a family, a community, a lifestyle and there is a sensibility, right things to do. Things that are wrong, invisible rules, and things you observe, a decorum. You don't run up over somebody's solo. When someone asks you to sing in church, you might expect payment, and your answer is always, "Yes," you stepped up to the plate. All these things existed in a larger community. It was not a thing where the music is over here and culture was over here. These emerge from the culture, it shaped, fed the culture and reflected back to us who we were through the performance of it.

—Nnenna Freelon

February 9

Much has happened. How do I even begin to fill in the empty spaces, pages, with this writing? Acceleration defines my life. Arriving in Boston everything got accelerated. I just returned from New York where I had a great time with my wife and friends, authors Alexs and Soo Jin Pate. We roamed the streets of the Village, ate, shopped, and went to the awards concert for IAJE. I met my buddy, Billy Childs, who was there for the Chamber Music America conference. Billy won two Grammys last night for his chamber jazz music. Unbelievable!!

With Alexs Pate.

When I returned, I gave a Berklee Teachers on Teaching (BTOT) lecture/ workshop at Berklee on my work and vision of Africana studies. The most attended, I was told. Everybody showed up to hear the "new kid" on the Berklee block. It was a great beginning here.

Then I was asked to interview Ornette Coleman onstage for the awarding of his honorary doctorate. That made the newspapers! It is very difficult to get Ornette to commit to tangible answers, as all his reflections were those of a great spiritual teacher, which of course, he is. So I had to relax and go with it. We think we had a nice exchange in front of my colleagues, a couple hundred Berklee faculty. I survived and most of my colleagues came up to me and were gracious about the exchange.

The following weekend, I flew out to L.A. for the purpose of hooking up with Stanley Clarke and Lenny White. Both were attending the National Association of Music Merchants (NAMM) Conference, so we decided to meet there. As a member of the Black History Month Committee, I suggested we bring the dynamic duo to Berklee to discuss their work, then to join myself and faculty in an evening concert. While at NAMM, I saw Morris Hayes, my old buddy, now entrapped again in the seductive web of Prince as his music director. Morris and Prince tore up *Saturday Night Live* this past weekend. I also saw my old college friend, Lynne Fiddmont, and drove to Altadena to pick up dear friend Patrice Rushen. We had breakfast and were able to really connect and share, catch up.

At NAMM, I also got to meet my old idol, Al Di Meola, who happened to hear me playing as I was testing out new gear. As a matter of fact, the mighty trio—Clarke, White, and Di Meola—all came over to the booth where I was playing, unknown to me. Can you imagine, looking up and there are three of my biggest musical influences actually listening to me as I wailed on the Japanese guitar distortion unit?

I returned to Boston, two weeks before classes were to begin. I have thirty-five students in what is the first official new class of Africana studies, the Sociology of Black Music in American Culture. Great students! Can't believe I am teaching all music students for the first time in my career. They are young, gifted musicians, and it completely amazes me that I don't have to re-explain aesthetics to them.

But shortly after New York, I began to experience a significant headache that lasted weeks, and sister, wife, and niece made me go to the doctor. MRI results came up negative. We concluded my pace and stress caused a severe reaction. I had to go on blood pressure pills. It was scary there for a minute. After K flew here to take care of me, my headache began to dissipate for the first time in three weeks, and today, I am painless. Amazing love. I took deep breaths, figured out how the stress was affecting me, and readjusted. I will pace myself. But the environment at Berklee is abuzz 24/7. With all the job expectations placed on me, people pulling at me, and all eyes and ears on me, it had taken a toll.

I was invited to speak about my music before some thirty young composers. Then, my "Lyric for Violin and Piano" premiered in the David Friend Recital Hall this past Monday night. Both of these events allowed me to make great connections with my composition colleagues.

So I head home this weekend to see Krystal and friends in Minneapolis.

The concert, "Black Music, The Dippin' Pool: Bill Banfield and Friends with special guests Stanley Clarke and Lenny White" will test my limits as a leader and as a player. These guys are at the top of their game as colleagues and major artists. I have to come up a few notches more to at least be a respectable player. It never occurred to me that any of this was an extraordinary acceleration or anything. I just landed and started doing my work. But after the February concert, I will really be able to slow down. I just have to get through it. But truly, if I get these guys up on that stage and we play well and make good of this, and I play respectfully, I will have truly accomplished something.

Another unforeseen turn was a major lead story on the front page on the *Boston Globe*, citing me (with my picture) about hip-hop culture and my courses. Along with an effort for the Hip Hop Alliance, Berklee College, and *Essence* magazine, I was keynote speaker. This all turned into a big media event and before I knew it, I was on the front page billed as "Professor who advises hip-hop." There have been all kinds of other people in this loop, but I just got put out there, and so, well, things don't come as expected sometimes. Although I am not a big fan, nor advocate of mainstream hip-hop, I have been quoted as someone who has hope for the genre to grow. Also, my column, "Essays of Note with Bill Banfield" appeared in *DownBeat*. This is my first, nationally—actually, internationally—syndicated column.

Another wonderful surprise was the super glowing review of my book, *Black Notes*, in the February issue of *Jazz Times* magazine. The writer of the very glowing review called the book a "balanced cultural treatment." More blessings from heaven.

April 1

I celebrated my forty-fifth birthday in New York City with wife and many friends. Louise Toppin threw a concert bash and commissioned a bunch of composers (T. J. Anderson, Olly Wilson, Donal Fox, Hale Smith, Adolphus Hailstork, Dwight Andrews, and Alvin Singleton), who attended, along with cultural critic Stanley Crouch. The concert was held last Friday, March 24— my birthday—at Carnegie Hall, the first time my music was ever performed there. Louise premiered works written for her to honor the life and artistry of our dear friend and mentor, Bill Brown. Afterwards, about twenty-five of us went to an Italian restaurant. All Black contemporary classical composers, singers, musicologists—and again Stanley Crouch—attended and came for the hang. History!

April 22

I'm here in the mountains at Hamilton College in upstate New York. I drove down yesterday, a lovely four-hour drive. My friend, Mike Woods— "Docc-tah" as he calls himself—invited me here to premiere my work for jazz orchestra, "It's All Good My Brother," the Bill Brown work I enlarged. Rehearsal went pretty well yesterday. It feels nice to conduct again.

It is really lovely here, very serene on this little but impressive campus tucked in a hill and nicely appointed with stone buildings, landscapes, blossom trees, creeks—completely picturesque. I have been watching Henry Louis Gates's documentaries of Black folks. Very inspiring. I wrote him a long letter which I will put in the mail this week. Reflecting on the importance of his work, I noticed how much of my directions mirror his. My work of late is finding its own way, and in doing so, I am finding my long-awaited

Michael Woods.

peace of mind. Perhaps at forty-five I have finally caught up and am having sanity within myself? Took long enough!! I spoke to a class of composers today. With ease I shared, like a master, about the meaning, process, and the life of "composering" as I call it, and it all flows, makes sense. I think my life will become easier.

May 11

Today I completed my 1,626th class as a professor, and led my sixty-third section through a fourteen-week journey—my first year of teaching at Berklee. As I turned to the last late student, a fine young singer named Carmen, I said to my class, "This lady is my 1,740th student." I calculated these stats before addressing them, thinking that I have started, again, a small though contentious, revolution. Some of my superiors are coming down against me, alas. But as I was reading the coda from page 300 of *Black Notes*—speaking about the love and caring of artists, and how I'd rather be giving this speech to a room of future agents of culture who are musicians than to a classroom of lawyers or politicians—I saw the gleams in their eyes. They were, for a minute anyway, believing. And believing can spark a moment of opportunity in a young person's mind, one that could be the inventor of a new order or a new song. At the end of class, one student announced, "I have been here four years and nobody has spoken about being a musician like this." So, it is true that if even twenty hate, but one is loved, the world can be a better place.

June 18

Today, I take a train to New York to attend Toni Morrison's retirement party. Yes, I guess I have reached some elite artist circles. Who knows? Maybe I'll get to meet Halle Berry or Oprah Winfrey!? At 6 p.m., I meet with Paul Bongiorno, manager of Sweet Honey in the Rock. Sweet Honey is the featured act, and those in attendance will include Bill Clinton, Nikki Giovanni, and many others. I guess that Stanley Crouch and Amiri Baraka will be there too. It's being hosted at Wynton Marsalis's "house"—the Rose Theatre, Jazz at Lincoln Center. Perhaps he will be there too. I'll hang with Lenny White at Birdland, then head back to Boston in the morning.

June 22

On Tuesday I headed over to Harvard Square to meet and have lunch with old school chum and colleague, Ingrid Monson, at Grafton's. Ingrid holds the Quincy Jones Chair of African American Music at Harvard, now chair of the music department, and is a member of Skip Gates all-star team. Ingrid and I were in school together at NEC, and it is so funny and wonderful for us laughing about how we never dreamed we would be in these places, able to push buttons. We are making plans for a collaboration between Harvard and Berklee. Ingrid also oversees the Fromm Festival composer commissions. I definitely will submit.

July 26

Yesterday and Monday I was in Norfolk, Virginia, the Tidewater area. My first time. I addressed the National Association of Negro Musicians (NANM). To speak to 150 seasoned Black music educators was a major milestone in my career. I emphasized the importance of valuing hip-hop and young people's music and cultural spaces to reach them. Giving a paper or talk is quite different in terms of the performance energy needed for a clinic. It's almost like being at a political rally and navigating the different factions, allowing all to speak. This was quite new for me in some ways. Awadagin Pratt, the Black classical pianist who has drawn so much attention by playing Beethoven with dreads and dressing casually, was the evening's featured artist. He was a beautiful soul, and we really connected. I will send him music and stay up with him.

I returned to Boston, came straight home, then headed out again to a rehearsal with a new colleague here, drummer Kenwood Dennard. He is playing with me this week, on my first Boston gig. Kenwood is a great musician I tried to meet in New York twenty-five years ago when he had already made a name for himself. Now we seem to bond like brothers. Dave Fiuczynski and Thaddeus Hogarth, a couple of great guitarists, have also become close friends. It has been really gratifying for me to come out of my Midwest academic cloud and be accepted by these professional musicians.

On Friday I moderate a talk on a new film about the "death" of Black Rock Coalition. Filmmaker Raymond Gayle will be there and he and I will discuss his film. Then K and I drive to Martha's Vineyard for a Berklee event.

Krystal was appointed the director of the City Music Program of Berklee, a signature staple education-annex of the college. Just so happened that the post opened, she applied, and she got the job! This ties us both to Berklee and has been a significant blessing.

November 13

I spent the weekend mixing the new record, *Spring Forward*, at Master Mix Studios in Minneapolis. I booked the studio for two days, just me and a young engineer, Colin McArdell. This was my first time having a studio lockout like that, I think. Both Stokley Williams and Serge Aquo from my band came down to hear. We got incredible results: ten tunes mixed in two days. Really quite amazing. This is actually three records brought together, three years of recording (summers of 2004, 2005, and 2006), and at least three different music directions. A major company would never allow this, so I will

Spring Forward recording session.

release and finance it myself. It really is my best guitar-composer-band leader concept record. The artistry of this work—the direction and function—is clear to me. I realize that *Striking Balance* was very unclear, and because of this, it didn't communicate as well as I would have liked. It is difficult for people (industry executives, DJs, promoters) to see to the heart of something without that heart put out on display. So, this is a major win and accomplishment, at least from within my own little life.

K was also in Minneapolis finishing up projects with Philip Brunelle. Late at night we were able to do our three couple dinners with John and Serena Wright, and Soo Jin and Alexs Pate. We have these great dinners at restaurants—all writers, artists, and professors talking about our students, teaching, writing, politics, philosophy, and Black folks.

November 20

Heading home yesterday, our plane made an emergency landing in Chicago. I arrived in Newark at 6:30 p.m. and decided it would be best to go directly into Princeton. I'll visit Cornel's class, perhaps have dinner, discuss his visit to Berklee, and, maybe get him to commit to the book I'm suggesting we write together. We shall see.

I think being in these circles makes me take up Richard Wright, Langston Hughes, Ralph Ellison, and others whose missions were to pose the questions, document the culture, and focus education on the refinement of the Black voice in art. As Black people, we have an "art force" that is wide, one with impact and purpose. It is our legacy. I am proud to be invited to our march forward. I found a note in Amiri Baraka's book, *Black Music*, that I had written to myself in 1988, where I vowed to pose questions regarding the definition of Black artistry. By 2004, I had written two books with exactly that charge, not to mention the radio shows and news columns I produced. This thinking came out of my work with my mentor Harold Cruse. About that same time I began idolizing Cornel West, and now, almost twenty years later, I find myself at Princeton getting advice from him, as a junior colleague of sorts.

December 9

I flew to Philadelphia this morning to interview Bobby McFerrin for *DownBeat* magazine. This is my first major story with them, and I wanted to start with my good friend. Bobby has been on sabbatical for seventeen months. Bobby met me at the train station and drove me back to the wooded area around his home in Chestnut Hill. Our talks today were the kind that can only emerge from Bobby after a lot of years of trust—ten years actually. Usually shy and modest and not drawn into talks that revolve around him, Bobby spoke more openly about his artistry. He considered what artistic responsibility means for our generation, particularly how he has reshaped his thinking about what he wants to do now. His father, Robert McFerrin Sr., who died less than a year ago, factored largely into his thinking. Bobby considered what this signals him as the one McFerrin who is left singing, and what this may mean for three who follow: Maddy, Jevon, and Taylor. We listened to his father's 1957 recording—scratches and all—of spirituals. As we listened, Bobby yelled out with excitement, "That's my dad, one of the greatest baritones ever." I had never seen him so pointedly proud.

This week, Marcus Miller, one of the great musicians of my generation, was at Berklee and spoke to my class. Marcus and I really connected. The week of Thanksgiving, young composer/performer Stefon Harris was in town, and we had him over to the house—another opportunity to connect with a great voice in my time.

I'm playing my guitar, composing again, and the teaching is going great. I'm reminded again that our move east was the right thing.

CHAPTER EIGHT

The New Essays (2006–2008)

Don't call it Black music. Many people have a perspective on this. I had a teacher who did and he called it "White music." And that would make me cringe because that would mean I couldn't play it. I grew up endorsing it [a culturalist labeling], but now I don't. So I would teach it as American music. The greatest people who created it were a great people. It was Black people. So why isn't it that that's the achievement of America?

—Wynton Marsalis

Days with Ornette Coleman
(*Published for* Berklee Faculty Development Journal, *2006*)

Friday, January 13, 2006

Ornette Coleman stands out, with even a casual cursory glance of the history of American music traditions, as a giant. If not just the man, or his music, it is the radical shake-up of a "sacred" jazz tradition that sparks a deeper read. A legend, myth, artistic hero, and person with a deeper way of approaching the music are what you pick up about Ornette Coleman. And so, I was asked by my school to interview this great figure and these comments are about that journey to meet, greet, and be seated with him to conduct a public interview on stage. This is an essay about that experience and what that exploration into the personhood of a musical legend was like.

There were many days spent in preparation doing readings, listening, and trying to imagine what the exchange was going to be. The myths as much as the music created anxiety, and at the same time an excitement about how rich and how meaningful the time could be for myself and my colleagues who shared in this. And what we could all walk away with if we had a chance to "walk a little closer with" . . . ? During the weeks leading up to the visit, everyone remarked how difficult this might be. "No one gets to talk to Ornette," "He doesn't give interviews," "He doesn't talk to the press," "He won't talk about those days, that gig, those comments made about him." So, besides the normal anxieties associated with interviewing someone famous, added on were all the "professional cautions" of how not to scare him away. Added to this was the additional heat of interviewing this great artist in front of colleagues from Berklee College of Music, many of whom are older, had been around, knew Ornette, had written about him and "knew" the book. For me as well, this had to, above all else, be an educational moment where all listening would gain from this exchange. But how was I going to negotiate these various waters of expectation and angst meeting the man and collegial raised eyebrows?

For this interview, live, I simply decided to create an exchange by which a conversation about the values of what we do as artists, what we hope for as educators, and the meaning of that as applicable to a new generation of learning musicians would emerge. I felt if I could create that kind of a sharing that many of my anxieties would fade, and we could have a talk with Ornette. I had interviewed, met, and had talks with Leonard Bernstein, live NPR radio interview features with Russell Simmons and Yusef Lateef, and my first book was a compilation of forty interviews with such artists as Dr. Billy Taylor, Bobby McFerrin, Ysaye Barnwell, T. J. Anderson, and Herbie Hancock. But, this time was different, because it was Ornette.

Well, a talk with Ornette blossomed into a walk down a path toward not only a deeper appreciation of his music, but a chance to "window into" new and well-formed beliefs he has about being in the culture, many lessons hard earned and graciously shared. In addition to a musician with tough convictions and an armament of sound seared with convictions, he is such a gentle spirit. Here is a musician who was ostracized by many who saw him as a threat to their way of life. Threatened by colleagues, admired and maligned by critics, loved and misunderstood by a jazz record buying public, his work embodied all the sides of the mythical misunderstood artist.

During those weeks of preparations, after exploring Ornette Coleman's music and experimentation, I came to appreciate his emergence as one of the most important breakthrough moves in the history of music. Ornette saw as foundation, a primary focus, the expression and meaning of the melodic line, free rhythmic associations, the improvised invention after the statement of line, the communal-artistic engagement of the ensemble to sustain creative environment, and the absence of stacked harmonic dominance but heterophony as primacy. This was a great break back into Black music culture, during a high art time within bebop's development which moved in somewhat opposite aesthetic tracks. Ornette's move was back to communal expression, invention, roots of the African call, and free rhythmic complexity and the idea of master drummer-griot-ensemble music making. So, I thought I should go down and meet the man. This turned out to be a very helpful step through these explorations. Associate dean Karen Zorn at the college arranged for me to get in touch with Ornette's manager. When I called, he answered and said, "Oh great, here is Ornette right here." To my complete delight was this gracious, warm, and eager to share, Ornette Coleman. I was headed to the 2006 IAJE Conference in New York, and during the visit there I planned to sit and do a pre-chat with Ornette. He gave me his address and we set up a time that I was to come up and visit with him.

So I'm leaving Jazz at Lincoln center, at about 60th and Columbia, having to walk downtown, eight avenues toward the thirties where Ornette lives. I was actually having a meeting at Jazz at Lincoln Center prior to our interview. Phil Schapp, in-house historian, stops in to exchange in a friendly debate about the origins and movement of ragtime. As I am enjoying our exchanges I realize I am ten minutes late for my meeting with Ornette Coleman! Schaap exclaims, "Oh my goodness you're going to speak with 'God' I'm coming too. . . . When you get there, please tell 'God' I said hello." That began my journey this day to see Ornette Coleman. When I arrived at his home, I entered in the traditional New York apartment, stepping off the elevator directly into his living room. Opening the elevator door was Ornette Coleman, just as humane, warm, and lovely as the Ornette sound we have come to know. Such a gracious and giving soul, so warm, courteous, and open. The apartment was huge, custom designed, and appointed with paintings, sculptures, art tastefully placed with modern furniture, nothing like the stories of the earlier loft days. His home was straight out of a New York designers' magazine, adding yet another layer to this already elevated mystique. We sat and chatted about things related to music and culture in America. "If you had your say of how music culture today should be, how it is made, created, performed, disseminated, educated, and reported on, how should it be done?" His first response to me, "I would take away all the rules that restrict ideas and love." I inquired further, "Are you happy, concerned, surprised, encouraged, or disguised with the way artistry is handled in the marketplace today?" "I have been all of those at one time or another. I'm concerned now with what they [young musicians] should be doing, which is trying to achieve bringing love and spirituality into their music. Except for music and religion, all else is method. I'm concerned also with the quality of their 'sound.' All information comes from the same places and those are human places, and so much of what we do has to do with human needs." Those ideas really stuck with me, that we live in a market-based culture where there remains a restriction of creative ideas, innovation from artists, or that all is channeled through only commercial and profit-based ends, instead of a focus based on human expression and value.

So, the bridge had been made. Now, how were we going to take this "conversation on the road," landing it on stage? What we tried to do was implant that exchange directly to Berklee. It worked, except our myth hero goes even deeper into the realm of unexpected responses. I did what I could do to harness this great figure's wisdom into a traditional set of "walk away with a pocket full of wisdom" from Ornette on teaching, but the master wouldn't be held down to any easy definitions in a response. His characterizations of our human responses, this culture's lack of sensitivity, and our need to eradicate hate from all our exchanges, was the kind of experience left on our minds that we don't usually expect to get from a "musical giant." This was the day of the deeper read of an Ornette exchange. I think many of us took away more about what the human experience should be about than just the musical experience. We took away not just the meaning of what we were doing, but an expectation in what we should be hoping to understand about the human condition in a challenged society. It was perhaps not the note some would have expected but that exchange provided us with some resolutions we needed to hear. This was again, much more about that experience, the personhood of Ornette Coleman, reflecting after four decades of artistry and figuring out what the real meaning of musical exchanges are about, and what for us was an exploration into the personhood of a musical legend still living onward.

Connecting Jazz to Contemporary Culture:
How Are We Making Jazz Culturally Relevant?
(DownBeat *magazine, April 2006*)

Musicians came up with bebop to challenge the narrow minded museum-like character of jazz. . . . The reality is that the different styles young people invent are an attempt to mark their own particular environments with the style they are accustomed to . . . and style is an attempt to put your stamp on your existence . . . we should not resist the edifying character of hip-hop Culture as a tool of aesthetic, economic and social expression for young people.

—Michael Eric Dyson

Jazz criticism has always been involved in the edgy debates of culture, Americanisms, ethnicity, experimentation, exploitation, marketing, and original voice. As a musician, I'm interested in how artists connect, collaborate, conflict, and communicate culture. We often forget that music is a by-product of our lives. Equally, it's important to make the linkages and bridges between popular cultural phenomena, industry mythologies, artistic practices, and practical questions of where we are headed, who's teaching the next generation, and what that generation is saying about itself.

This being said, how are we making jazz relevant to our contemporary cultural experience? When hearing musicians speak about the '60s, they talk about taking the music to another place using the influences of electricity and popular music. A cultural transition synonymous with that leap of the '60s jazz community is how today's traditional jazz community is dealing with the heavy flood of mainstream sounds of hip-hop music culture—the beat, poetry, lyrics, and rhyming over music, the use of prerecorded sounds (samples, loops), turntables, and the always present image of the rapper.

In the '60s, *Time* placed Thelonious Monk on its cover. This past September it was rapper Kanye West on the magazine's cover. While many have already made that leap into "hip-hop-ville," many younger musicians (jazz or just in general?) are in a new reckoning space somewhere in between hating the marketplace and wanting to expand with it for fear of missing the entry point or not hearing where their generation is today.

Many are simply culturally ambivalent about the "whole hip-hop culture thing," and it may be because we associate these new musical trends with urban black and youth culture. But jazz and most mainstream American popular music has always been cooked up in emerging new brews from within the Black community. And as well as some of the most edgy critiques of American culture, hip-hop carries that voice as well. So, how does hip-hop fit into jazz's historical/cultural frame?

It's important to separate rap and hip-hop style, commerciality, rude lyrics, and profanity—market-driven entertainment images—from the musical stylistic and rhythmic aspects of the music. This presents a great challenge. There may be a greater challenge though in hearing or being open to discovering what may be the next relevant place for jazz, what's musically, stylistically relevant, what matters for the development of the music. Many times we may miss the boat. So these questions are at the heart of the future of this music really.

American music has always been a cross-section of different musical impulses colliding, borrowing, and inspiring. Thomas Dorsey (the Father of Gospel Music) pepping up church music with blues changes and feels from his days being the musical director with Ma Rainey, the fusion of bebop into mainstream big band culture in the 1940s, or rock and soul in the hard-bop era of the late '50s are all examples. There has always been a rub between the market demands of popular culture and the tastes of artistry. "Caravan," "Manteca," and "Cubana Bop" were cross-cultural stylistic examples of blends that have made lasting marks on the culture of jazz without diminishing its musical values and artistic codes. In many ways, hip-hop's musical frame has already been successfully integrated into jazz culture.

There is a variety of respected contemporary musicians—including Pat Metheny, Branford Marsalis, Erykah Badu, John Scofield, Don Byron, Jill Scott, Soulive, Roy Hargrove, and Terence Blanchard—who have leaned successfully in this direction. Jazz has made the next organic pairing it seems, its next inner-cultural revolution, a kind of a "be-hop." Yet, few jazz educators, aficionados are speaking to the obvious or taking the leap in this direction. Hip-hop culture and contemporary musical impulses probably cause upset stomachs for traditional jazz educators. In each musical generation, the reemergence of the grass roots comes, and each time the more "rough and silly" conventions of the common cultural vernacular are ignored and dismissed by the establishment.

With radical accents, new phrase construction, new aesthetic conventions, and the emergence of a new generation of creators, establishing their own unique voices, Dizzy Gillespie and Charlie Parker were harshly criticized for their radical shake-up of performance conventions. Hip-hop music culture is becoming a foundation for a great deal of contemporary music. Is hip-hop music culture providing as style direction, a viable road map for where contemporary jazz music culture is, and is heading? I think the music is "racially and pop market stigmatized" and therefore easy to dismiss as irrelevant. But be careful. A closer look reveals a twenty-five-year music culture development of note and some major rhythmic, melodic, even harmonic shifts, which are impacting today's jazz conventions. So the edgy debates of culture and how artists are connecting, are communicating culture, is where we are headed in this discussion.

iPodology: What Are We Being Asked to Plug Into?

Set your music in motion
iPod put music in your pocket, now it puts it on the screen.
15,000 songs, 150 hours of video . . . gives you the ultimate music experience.
Sight and sound in thinner design.
Music to your eyes.
Which iPod are you?

—Ad lines from iPod

Do you sometimes get the feeling that our world is being run by something that is running it, out of control? Yes, I raise questions about, "iPoditus." I'm all for technological access, but today's sensory overload and excess bothers me, mainly because our cups runneth over and we may be desensitized by it all. I'm interested in music culture. I appreciate, use, and understand the importance of technology. I know inevitably products are marketed, manufactured, and sold to a waiting public. I am a big fan of popular culture and I know in this area young identity rules! However, it's time for a reality check. Today we teeter on the edge of auto-culture. Everything is automatically assumed that it's "all good." The mechanized construction of a view of music as a prepackaged, convenience sound module that is made to order is iPodology. The process allows us to adjust the order, that is, to custom make, style, fit, and flavor the music.

Music professor Matt Glaser opened a teaching session at Berklee College of Music with a strange order of music for his audience to consider. This sequence came up automatically on his iPod. While he pondered the uncanny ordering of this diverse music selection for observation, I began to think about what it means to be doing music under digitized automation. Your iPod may set your music into motion—along with Clear Channel, Fox, CNN, Hollywood hype, *People* magazine, and Pro Tools software—but we may as well be shutting down our minds and allowing our realities to be preprogrammed by a cultural apparatus gone mad. How much, how fast, how frequent do the changes have to come before we slow down and think—and take care of what we mean by "doing" music?

But still it's not technology and the "toyism" we swim in that bothers me as much as the mentality of the menacing marketing monster that controls, constricts, and consumes culture today. To be "in" we have to give up and give in. I'm sure as hell not going to jump off the cliff before I ask why and where am I going to land if I take this leap. Remember: It's more than just downloading, transforming, and exchanging data; it's music made and played before it's stored in those hard drives.

So, my record company asks me to do a podcast interview—a three-minute commercial where potential buyers hear me talk about my music and listen to a sample. Then a purchaser can download the slice for 99 cents. Why not? I'm "Papa Bill's Music Pizza." How do you want me to slice up and serve it to you? Without album cover notes? Without tune connections or album themes? Without the experience of hearing my unique invitation of musicians playing together? My artistic voice and artistic choices are dislocated, reconnected, and swimming in a new thread of meanings preselected by iPod casting—slice and sound bites of entertainment. Is the music made better because it comes in a more accessible form to a larger ready-to-order market? Should I care? It should mean more buyers, more options for purchase, more meanings, more usages, and more methods of payment, right?

I gave one of my CDs as a gift to a waitress whose restaurant often I go to. Several weeks later, I asked her if she liked the music. To my horror she said, "Oh I can't listen to the CD 'cause my iPod is broken." She has no other way to play music than by downloading? No CD stereo player, no CD in a car, no home stereo system? All her music experience comes through her downloaded iPod: iPodology.

A larger chunk of popular music seems to dominate in mainstream culture today, and I think this is great in many ways. But the way music is used to fill up the space around your head so that nobody can get to you? That bothers me.

Music as an iPodology is so commodified, so packaged for high power market value, that I wonder if it is still music in the end. Music is a shared expression and experience. But are people now hearing music in different ways because of such market-technology representations? Are there new ways to emote? Are there new ways of hearing? Do people feel only in the preprogrammed inner ear? What is today's musical identity and ownership? These are the questions I ponder in my iPodology.

⁓

Hop Ain't Hip without the Music (or What Happened with the Music in Popular Culture Markets?)

January 2007

We want to talk about the richest tradition in the history of modernity, and that has to do with musical tradition(s), from people of African descent who were able to transcend and transfigure their moans and groans into an art form . . . Black Music Matters . . . bringing together those voices that actually connect political engagement and social reflection with music, music, music. I want to disabuse you of the notion that music is simply a form of stimulation and titillation. It's not about superficial entertainment. We have to peer back into the spirituals and listen to those nonliterate peasant folks who had to struggle against laws that didn't allow them to read or write, listen to that art! . . . We want to remind the younger generation, that they were not singing for some search for a cheap American dream. They were not looking for some narrow conception of success. No, they were looking for a greatness and a magnanimity and an integrity of self-respect, self-regard that allowed them to love themselves but to do it in such a way that did not require putting others down. Spiritual maturity, moral wisdom, connecting all folks on the human scale. Any time you talk about the Black music tradition, be it Louis Armstrong, Sarah Vaughan, John Coltrane, or Alice Coltrane, we mean beyond superficial classifications.

—Cornel West, from a speech delivered at Berklee College of Music

I am seeing some problems in the industry related to creating great music: our megacultural values transfer, and the projection of images that help us to sustain who we are have been problematically screwed with. Another critical question apart from what the music means and carries and who are the current artists is, What is the music in today's "music"? What happened to Black and popular music? Black mainstream commercial music (blues, jazz, gospel, R & B, reggae, urban contemporary, African pop, Caribbean) used to be music made and performed by musicians. It is sad to say that the generations coming up as consumers in the public marketplace today were never brought up on a culture that is centered in music made by musicians for the purpose of being music. Post-1990, things changed drastically, and we are living in what I termed the Post-Album Age. To really define what Black music is and when its codes of definition were initially set, you have to look closely at the music history, the culture, and the artistry. For many musicians who grew up in the public school system in decades past, these codes and standards for music excellence were set by trained, serious, and dedicated teachers. So today, facing and participating in and with the "beast"—the mainstream popular music industry—we have a culture that exists on prescriptions of mediocrity and a fast sell for a buck. How much money is made can never truly be a defining element that qualifies what is good in art. So dedication, focus, commitment, and integrity are the kinds of mind-sets that have to be strongly cultivated, and that is what artistry and creativity are set upon.

We have to ask: What do people hear when they are responding to what they like and value musically? In today's marketplace, what defines what people like in music? A good beat, a catchy hook, and a video. Much of our popular music is market sold—a salty, fatty, or sugar-filled substance—and is manufactured crap for a dollar. And while most conscientious consumers recognize this, they can do nothing to change what the market is doing except choosing not to buy. In 2007 that began to happen, and the market took note. If the radio-listening public hear enough bad music, they become stupefied, then pacified, and then become addicted to impulses they are fed as the "sound" they want or love and need. But this really is just like any other drug—an insufficient fix for what music could be and should be about. What you really want to hear is the artist's soul. That's what really affects listeners: the sound, construction and form, the execution, mastery, and craft of music. An artist's ability to move my insides with creative expression is what inspires me, not dazzling titillation.

But these values are lost in today's mainstream popular culture.

Although we definitely have a music-buying public in this current generation who are hungry for the "feel of music," they have been sold dance beats, popular icons, and an empty music culture. When did we get to the point where we allowed market forces to promote Master T., Biggie Doggie, Snoopy Poppy, Poddy P.Q., and such clowning to define the culture for young people? How did we pimp the system so that real, young aspiring musicians, singers, poets, and artists would have fewer places to market their art? How did we come to a place where our values of expression have been so diminished?

～

Wrestling with a Black Aesthetic in Contemporary Living

Today's prevailing early millennium commercial, public Black and mainstream popular aesthetic seems to be a prescription delivered not by artists but by Hollywood culture for cash and commerce. At present most of the music is based and defined on popular market forces and not artistic expression. No art approach that is based solely on commercialism can serve nor survive. Art is imagined to serve. Second, the current Black popular aesthetic, especially in Black music, is almost completely defined by an "urban monocategorical" niche which undermines an aesthetic based on excellence, achievement, self-expression, communal collective or about being about the betterment, the preservation and presentation of Black people. Sadly in these times we find ourselves falling into positions where posturing in poisoned, pained, and problematic pathologies are normalcy. We live today in a world, a larger culture now where predatory greed is considered a high sign of a modern cultural success formula.

Any art that attempts to be reflective of this social conflict and class conflict, indifference could begin to be representative of a code that helps people see through all this. An empowering arts belief that examines today's sense of frustration about the lack of success, access to the power keys, control of images, prescriptions for access to power, and that too critically examines the poisoned marketplace, needs to be maintained. Art addresses and dispels counterhuman impulses. I have always spoken of younger artists being in critical, clear dialogue with those artists old enough and in place to know how to and what values, images, and strategies can be projected aesthetically as a part of the contemporary voice for healing, critiquing, and mobilizing new progressive ideas for change. I believe this dialogue and artistic flowering can come from today's next collective artistic expressions. Now is our time to execute, sing, dance, and write a path.

Now it becomes necessary to talk pointedly among artists about a more well-defined, purposeful aesthetic that draws deeply from the past, forcible from the present, and actively projecting a future. Keeping it real, being "ghetto," "gangsta," "big pimpin'," and only a contemporary urban identity have become substitutes for a more formal and sustaining concern for taste, tone, expression, and meaning, which must be the center of the departure of artistic expression.

One has to wonder then, what happened to art that cultivates and represents the young mind and culture? All the resourcefulness, the conviction of moral, cultural, spiritual uplift, the power to name inequities, the strength to face them and dismantle and to create a powerful art perspective that took these as "existence tasks" as I call them, and made these the objective for focused art, living commentary, and beautiful expression that moved people seems to have disappeared!? What happened to . . . what happened to Black music? What happened, happened, happened to mainstream popular music?

⌒

The Aesthetics of Sales in the Contemporary Marketplace Post-2007

It is important to mention artists who have emerged contemporarily such as Jill Scott, Musiq Soulchild, John Legend, Kim Burell, Erykah Badu, India.Arie, Christian Scott, Mary Mary, Macy Gray, Stefon Harris, Alicia Keys, Omarion, Mary J. Blige, Jennifer Hudson, Kelly Price, Lalah Hathaway, Fantasia. These current great young musicians, artists, singers are now firmly in place, and that's a great sign. But these examples are evidence that the gene pool for Black popular music artistry and talent did not dry up and go away. There is talent out there, there is just a need for demanding that the marketplace support creative artistry. New music and musicians must be allowed to flower to create the new path settings in arts culture. Again, the examples are plentiful and all around us.

There is simultaneously though a greater amount of bad noise not made by well-intentioned young music creators. Check the artist and repertoire directors who sign bad acts. Much has been said about the "White executives" who have shamelessly turned the music industry into dollar and trash image commodities at the expense of Black, American, and global music and culture, and at the expense of millions of young people of all kinds. There should be culture tribunals where these industry heads are tried for the death of Black music culture. Music must be made and cultivated in culture by musicians. Period.

Check the Record on Sales

Consumers did tire of negative cultural expressions in 2007 and in subsequent years. You can't keep selling negativity in the marketplace as a viable sustaining aesthetic commodity because it will fold in onto itself when you simply create a "better buy." Then everybody says, "Oh, this music was bad, it couldn't sell." A moment of clarity about this hit when it was reported in the summer of 2007 that, "The public has made a choice, hip-hop sales are suffering due to marketing strategies, lack of creativity as public tires of gangsta images.... With declining sales and rising concerns about its quality, gangster images, hip-hop is in crisis ... it risks being irrelevant. Due to drops in sales, once a driving creative commercial force in American culture, hip-hop sales are down 33%, twice the national decline in other music" (*USA Today*, June 15, 2007).

In 2007 there was a reported 20 percent decline in CD sells nationwide among large record companies. Some speculated that the decline was due to shifts in what everyday people now do, where they spend their leisure time, and the inevitable change of tastes in consumers. The "on-demand" idea of freedom for consumers is seductive. Many musicians rejected the "money greedy positioned" mega companies and began to take their work to independent record companies and distributors. That trend blew up with the power of Internet marketing. There were CD compilations, better TV, better home entertainment technology, satellite radio, and competitively priced DVDs. Why spend $20 or spend $60 for a concert when you can have the artist front row in the comfort of your own home? That's what nearly twenty years of MTV has given us, and that is good and bad for music. This has come to mean more things, more channels competing for our attention, Internet sales, downloads and sharing, YouTube, MySpace, online TV shows, the fall of big outlet carriers like Tower Records, and companies spending less money and development time on new artists.

While marketing strategies now emphasized singles and more downloads, it was the American-buying public and largely among White suburban buyers that tired of gangster images, attitudes, explicit lyrics, and tales of consumption. And they made a qualitative decision that had quantitative and economic results: the aesthetics of the marketplace. Rapper KRS-One set it straight: "The music is garbage. What has happened over the past few years is that we have traded art for money, simple and plain, and the public is not stupid."

For the first time in many years, in 2007, rap music was not among the nation's ten best selling songs. Rapper Nas released his album *Hip Hop Is Dead* with lyrics proclaiming, "Everybody sound the same, commercialize the game. . . . They forget where it started, so we gather here for the dearly departed." But again: Why pay $17 for massproduced copycat material when you can purchase exactly the piece for 99 cents? The digital revolution has changed the game almost completely. So the only hope for the genre is for this generation of truly creative people to reinvent the form and infuse it with music, lyrics, and a creative force that lifts, not degrades, people.

～

The Closing Argument on Hip-Hop

The hip-hop and mainstream popular recording industry has not taken responsibility for the immeasurable damages done in popular culture to the soul and imagery of Black music culture, due to its emphasis of building cash and commodity and the abandonment of cultural core values: music and the health of Black people. Despite this, one can't help but love the fact that this is a Black-invented powerful form. Secondly, its roots as pointed out in the section on hip-hop's potential theological, social protest, and popular spiritual roots, give it lift enough to be recoded. Like the blues which is Black song and Black sound, Black form, Black worldview, Black social commentary, and a Black truth, hip-hop is a form of Black creative expression.

Given the pervasiveness of the form and its centrality to the identity of twenty-first-century contemporary aesthetic conception and its family connection to traditional Black music forms, the beauty of hip-hop and young Black expression is boundless, fluid, creative energy, innovative gifting, and ideas. If we could harness all that beautiful energy and channel that into a productive direction, we could energize and transform an entire society.

What must we do to be saved?

1. Our industry must move back to where music making is again at the center and neither secondary nor serving market constructed description.
2. This generation has to be exposed to melody and music with a real story that may illuminate soiled, challenged conditions, but also inspire people to rise above and change the conditions that affect our living. For musicians, music is more than just music; it's a way of being in the world. Blues great David "Honeyboy" Edwards said, "That's what the blues is: It's a leading thing, something in your mind that's keeping you going."
3. Enlarge the cultural playing field to include educators in music, art, business, cultural criticism, and spiritual leadership. Infuse and include more Black artistry in the mix, such as poetry, dance, visual arts, and literature—more icons, approaches, a broader collection of creative values.
4. Pull the plug on the power and influence of negative, damaging imagery, music, and cultural product. Decrease, diffuse, suffocate such by

calling for its irrelevancy as it relates to the sustenance of productive Black life and representation.

5. Educate young people to the power of history, new language and expressive modes, values, and aspirations of excellence.

6. Extend these definitions, expressions, and applications to the American and international community at large, so that people are too affected, moved, and reflectively defined by such ideas, outlooks, and expressions. Black arts—*all* arts—must always be for the betterment of people and uplift the society we live and participate in.

All over the world, young people are engaging ideas creatively to "speak" and sustain lives with this forum. A global read and extension to our "hoods" abroad extends the potential here. Our best return in this endeavor is to refine a pedagogy of sustained artistic action that has musical and poetic potential for growing and nurturing artistic ideas and creativity.

Without Fear of Shame: The Eighty-Year-Old Debate

> We younger Negro artists who create now intend to express our individual dark-skinned selves without fear or shame.
>
> —Langston Hughes, "The Negro Artist
> and the Racial Mountain" (1926)

> Sweet relief . . . here ordinary Negroes . . . played the Blues, ate watermelon, barbeque, and fish sandwiches, shot pool, told tall tales, looked at the dome of the Capital and laughed out loud. . . . I tried to write poems like the songs they sang. . . . You kept on living and you kept on going. Their songs had the pulse beat of the people who keep on going.
>
> —Langston Hughes, *The Big Sea* (1940)

Through his artistic efforts the Negro is smashing an immemorial stereotype faster than he has ever done through any method he has

been able to use. He is impressing upon the national mind the conviction that he is an active and important force in American life . . . he
is a contributor to the nation's common store, he is helping to form
American civilization.

—James Weldon Johnson, *Black Manhattan* (1933)

The "low-down folks" (Langston Hughes) who "hold their own in the face
of American standardization" still brew a cultural soup of nourishment for
Americans that sets the standard for tastes in popular culture. Amazing. I
came across these polar opinions, viewpoints and they raised in me the question, do we still even find the questions being asked? I stand now somewhere
in the middle of two existing value streams, like in Langston and James
Weldon Johnson's day, between divided groups on the one hand and my own
disdain of problematic projections of hoods, pimply and thuggish youngsters,
rump shakers, white T-shirts, gold chains and teeth, the devil dog, cars and
materialism as values; yet as a musician, I am intrigued with the riveting
grooves and the energy of Black youth and hip-hop culture. My age group,
young forties, places me in an uncomfortable grind, a generational split with
allegiances to both sides (baby boomers and hip-hop). I sit on a shaky fence
of values that wishes for better days and ways for Black people. I have fear
and shame when I see, in every city I go in, Black youth seemingly unaffected
by the rise in their confrontational attitude, heroic status of criminal identity, demeanors of noncivility, and their seeming disrespect for the simple
traditional social rules like, smiling or saying "Excuse me." No, it's not just
Black youth, nor youth; these ills are reflected in every cultural expression
from George W. Bush's grand imperialist strategies masked as protecting
and providing American democracy, to the confrontational, "You're fired,"
and crime and reality TV. And the low-down folks still play their low-down
music as a commentary corollary to it all.

The eighty-year-old debate: How do Black people rise above their social
and cultural circumstance in America as cultural creators? Do they reflect
and refine an art that uplifts, believes in the American dream, or carry their
common street view, their existential street truths, and rhapsodies (read
"rap-sody") on the American-soured nightmare? And where will these tales
take us ultimately? I am finding both are an important and vital journey, and
both trips are real. Unfortunately the megaculture divided the camps and
controls the amount of stories we all get to hear. I don't believe the Internet

or digital means has enough programming power to make the difference and provide all the balance—yet.

Despite the power we have to punch the button SEND, the megaculture provides the bigger portion of our cultural programming. And what sells for them, don't seal our fates in living in Pleasantville. As my teacher and our great social critic Harold Cruse reminds us in *The Crisis of the Negro Intellectual*, "since the 17th century the historical/cultural prerogatives, expanded continuously in each generation of Whites, created a well entrenched social position characterized by a dominant economic, political power structure and a strong cohesive group solidarity" (pages 8–9). In other words, the high-up folks still set the patterns for how the cultural machinery will operate. The operators find more profit in an off balance of views to inform the general public fairly about the ways of the low-down folks, and in one way and direction. Many of the same debates still rage among folks about the current generational, class, technological, education, and economic divides among Blacks in contemporary America. Do you want P. Diddy, Master P, India.Arie, Wynton Marsalis, Beyoncé, or Dr. Dre to tell the tall tale, sing the ballads, tune the instruments, or dance the dance? My own read is that the majority of common Black people of this generation breathe on the versions, visions, and values of the lowdown from BET, VH1, MTV, TRL, *Vibe* magazine, and "we down wid it." I struggle with this but I am fearful and shameful of the results of some of our predominating expressions. What will it take for Black people to keep a check and balance on what we create as the substance of our cultural plates? And who is asking the questions from the younger side, like Langston did? Are we speaking across generational divides, caring what each side does or thinks? Is there a healthy dialogue to determine what the questions are and what the consequences will be if we don't come to an answer?

In my mind the debate is still strong. Young people's vision, impulses, and reads—no matter how vulgar, apolitical, or nontraditional—are always important to allow to flower from their experience view; and Black arts provide the best solutions for creating a strong foundation for cultural sustenance, but must inspire and instruct people in maintaining and forging a value system that ensures excellence and uplifts. The creativity has not stopped, the debate has not abated, but the balance has been offset. James Weldon's hope that we are, "smashing an immemorial stereotype impressing upon the national mind the conviction that he [Black artistry] is active . . . helping to form American civilization" is today a distant echo of time we want much to recapture.

⌒

American Idle?

A recent *USA Today* op piece drew attention to the plusses of the current TV show, *American Idol*. A friend and I recently had some disagreements over a pleasant passion of ours: popular music culture. At the center of this debate is the question of an out-molded critique, that we have lost a certain "musical values set" in the popular culture marketplace. I claimed that we should maintain a serious concern, critique, and caution about the chaos of this palpable and perceptible decline of music in our times. The criteria for what constitutes worthy commercial artistry has fallen to an all-time low. I see *American Idol* as a commercial boxed lunch, and though it may be help-ful in cultivating a new generation of would-be commercial artists, much of what is being replicated over and over lacks original, innovative, and inspir-ing artistry. I blame the industry. My friend finds such a position untenable and calls it another generation's expression of old fogyism that has been heard since the emergence of popular culture. Throughout history, he asserts, there were similar complaints about the emergence of the new music from minstrelsy to ragtime to blues, to jazz to R & B, to Elvis and to rock and roll, and all these "haters" have ached from the same sounds, movements, and popular market idols in popular culture. I must admit being aware of these cultural upsurges, my friend makes a great stab at the validity of my current cries for the culture's well-being.

The *USA Today* piece makes a convincing argument for the plusses of *American Idol*: thirty-two million homes watch, which compares to the popular *Ed Sullivan Show* in the 1950s; it launches careers; it cuts across the American gender, social, racial, generational divide; it features a democratic nature of participation since anyone under a certain age can try out; winners are ultimately chosen by the viewing audience; it binds the nation around a single focus; and it encapsulates the American dream of instant celebrity.

Okay. That sounds really fantastic, I guess. So my question is: All of this is at what cost and for what? In terms of costs, they are making bundles of money and it is entertainment; this is nothing new or shocking. But what are we looking to, to be an idol? Is this artistry at all innovated or original? The quality of the talent is amateur, in most cases. At best this is a hi-tech, big budget talent contest. It creates and feeds into a push button, pick-what-you-like-this-week mentality. There is a serious talent racial imbalance among those "call-in" TV voters who support contestants they like the most; leaving the number of ethnic representations in talent does not reflect, to me, the real numbers, of young Black, Latino, and Asian American talent. These multiculturals could never really break through fairly except in the cases of exceptional talent. In most cases, all it takes is a cute and adorable White kid and forget skin tone equality in these popular TV-based Hollywood-flavored contests. In terms of stylistic diversity within this racial question, those adorable White contestants can diversify and be hip-hop, R & B, jazz, country, soul, whatever; all is acceptable. The American cultural contests get tricky these ways when the King of Jazz is named Paul Whiteman, Benny Goodman gets titled the King of Swing, Elvis is the King of Rock and Roll and now, the Soul Patrol is being policed by whom? So, whose American dreams are really being served here? What is and who is "pretty and popular" is still scripted by the same Hollywood recipes. And lastly, what is most distressing for me is the same fame saturation of the fifteen-minute "Warhol wipe away." In this game they discard each new winner, after the record contracts and fame, providing little, it seems, of a real sustainable presence for these young artists to blossom and grow. *American Idol* in title alone begs for a cultural critique and reeks of hegemonic suspicion, layered with the fact that the show's lead character carries a "smart" British accent.

The racial question, as tiring and inflammatory or evoking indifference as it can be, is not only essential; it is inextricably elemental in American cultural discourses. To not run anything American through the racial, social, class, gender wringer would be to leave nails in the roads, cramps in the legs, and thorns in the side of this country's identity. As a writer taking the leap into this, you get to speak from these angles, sometimes poetically asking the irritating questions, projecting hope, causing conflict in thought in a kind of covered, protected role that means you stab at the establishment rib a bit. At the center of the American popular mythology are the narratives of race intrigue, social and class prescription, the values of the world of the powerful and the common person, and how this gets represented. Many times the designated carriers symbolic of these ideas are the famed idols, the projected and constructed heroes of the common folk (Miss America, Superman, Shaft). A lot is at stake here with playing the game, *American Idol.*

After lamenting my friend's deflating of the relevance of such a noble critique, I continue to be open, patient, and possibly hear my sourness as an indication that I am growing older and less hip. But while I am holding my breath and peering through my hands covering my glare into the idle box, my musical ear waits longingly for that surge of new and promising talent the network executives promise is worth being, our *American Idol.*

~

Using Your Creative Voices:
An Essay on Race and Artistic Action

Dear reader, close your eyes and imagine a young professor. His name is Miles Brown. Imagine yourself being engaged in what he is trying to get you to envision yourself as. Imagine you are a young singer, or poet, or guitar player, and he is speaking to you!

I want to speak to the artistry as a place to aim from. You have to be proactive with the reach of excellence, and yes, you have to be proactive orientated with hatred and evil. I'd rather not just call it racism, because racism as an idea gets too much attention, starts to sound like a cliché, and is really not worth all the hype. I call it stupidity. Gain for yourselves personal worth dignity, move toward excellence, and put yourselves at the buttons of power, and racism will be seriously undermined. There are really two aspects to racism to be concerned about: first, the debilitating bite and sting, hurt, humiliation, insult to your intelligence and the affront to your humanity; and second, your nonaccess to power. Two things will seriously dismantle racism: it's lessened by your excellence and then putting yourselves in position to have access to power by being "there at the button." The biggest reason why there is racism at your institution is largely because you are not there teaching, administrating, and making decisions that affect change. That's what is meant by power, not having the means to execute decisions that affect people and meaning. Though I believe, in my experience, at the end of the day, racism will not matter if you can't play your axe and you are failing in your school studies. I have rarely known a 4.0 student who was having severe problems with racism. Excellence is the best weapon against this kind of stupidity from people or from an institution. And by creating solid patterns for success, this wave creates an impenetrable mind-set that ensures motion and looking forward; history is full of examples of this. We applaud all of you for being involved in this forward action.

Having lived through the 1960s, 1970s, 1980s, 1990s, and into the twenty-first century, I can say each period of musical activity in our culture helped connect people across the lines of racial/social/cultural divide. Soul music of the 1960s, social protest of the 1970s, universal groove of the 1980s, urban choices of the 1990s, and now, I struggle with the ghetto fabulous imperative, "thou must be this to be Black." People in most of these eras were concerned and connected to some shared ideas of our common citizenry:

education, housing, political representation, jobs. My concern is that the power of contemporary popular culture BET/MTV worldview, these prescriptions for cultural identities, are limited and doing a disservice to our recent slipping racial divide. Why? Because the definitions of what's beautiful and Black, virtuous and excellent, prideful and progressive are limited, and even our criteria for what defines Black is limited.

So there are, in many ways, fewer options, fewer substantive debates of choice, fewer positive projections that make it easier for people to settle into "stupidity-isms," and be comfortable and high-minded in their complacency.

I share with students that through real conscious activism, creative activity, musicians, poets, artists, must produce an art environment that challenges and suffocates this stagnating media assault. This way, you produce an identity, a contemporary cultural identity that uplifts, empowers, helps to level the field, raise the expectations of cultural production, projection with an array of believed-in values that make it less possible for racism to suffocate, because it isn't being fueled.

What fuels racism, is it the fantasy of White superiority? When you know your history, you excel in excellence, you know your craft, you are "bout it, bout it" you then create music, images, creative activity that lifts you above the snarls of the fantasy of White superiority and racism. To evoke a Malcolm X affirmation, ". . . once you change your thought pattern, you change your attitude. Once you change your attitude, it changes your behavioral patterns, and then you go into some action." For the artists, diversify your fields, and not only create it, but think it, refine it, produce it, manufacture it, market it, teach and administrate it and you will successfully change this condition for yourself and thousands of young people who will come after you. That's how you first deal head-on with racism. That's how you come to your White, Asian, Hispanic, Muslim brother and sister and bring something to the table about a shared humanity of greatness.

Your issues of being Black are not more important, although it may be more pressing than other problems in the universe of issues. Because really, today's reality is that we are less divided by Black and White and are more diluted, derailed by the inhumane mind-set of greed and power hunger that is exhibited more brazenly and bold than ever. Katrina's example was that poor Black people suffered the most, but what was underneath this hatred was a blindness that was fueled by greed and disregard for their humanity.

Today, you have to come together on what are common strategies. But to Black young people who are artists, you have to come to the table from places of power. You get this power from an identity of knowledge of culturally, historically, spiritually grounded self, and all that comes by and through the gift of your art.

A Culture of Conflict and Confrontation

Our enemies are innovative and resourceful, and so are we. They never stop thinking about new ways to harm our country and our people, and neither do we.

—G. W. Bush (2004)

Not a single army in the world will be able to dismantle our resistance.

—Hassan Nasrallah Hezbollah (September 22, 2006)

We live in a culture of confrontation and conflict. That sprit among us is palpable like the taste you can imagine after walking through an area with the sickening smell of a dead animal. It's all around us, we drag it with us, carry it everywhere. We live under a regime that masks its hegemony and imperialistic arrogance in the name of a false gift of liberty shared abroad. But the people don't want the gift, would rather return it, and have what they had before sad Santa came with the false idealistic toy. Our children have fewer and fewer substantial, impactful, visible, meaningful, sustainable iconic symbols, heroes, movements, or healthy shared values. Such an idea could seriously disrupt these current larger corrupted codes in our society.

Our music, movies, magazines, popular cultural projections, TV shows, videos, campaign ads reflect this high level of confrontation as a cultural reality and style of rhetoric. Confrontation, competition, class division, and incivility are as common as the daily news and reflective of humans disconnected and in chaos. Kings, presidents, princes, politicians, and preachers all over the globe are seen as corrupt, untrustworthy, and immoral, and their advances are marked and measured by greed and an insatiable quest for power. From rap to the gates at Bush's White House everybody wants to be a pimp, a hustler, a thug, and a playa. So what options do we have? We have to create and insist and depend upon our communities of friendships, teach-ins, cultural-social soirees, partnerships, grass roots political movements, faith gatherings, art and music creation that is committed and based on our collected humanity. This can and will dislodge the thickly layered corruption and disarm "the devil." We have to illuminate the dark spaces where corrupted frameworks, people, and institutions mechanize, menacing maniacal minding. We can confuse and diffuse the megacultural poisons. And we simply must, or we will be poisoned and choke.

Many of us are holding out and hoping in what may be perceived as naive, a mythologized utopia, but as John Lennon sang, "You may think I'm a dreamer, but I'm not the only one."

⌒

A Letter to My Students

Studying more closely the life, music, and artistry of Bob Marley was very meaningful for me. These journeys through the history of music, ideas, and artists' lives, as you know, are not a casual walk in a day for me. Music for me is life or encourages meaningful life. Remember Jim Morrison's, "Music is your special friend, until the end."

I was struck by a special I saw on a flight to Minneapolis this weekend. It was a special on life and culture in modern Ghana. At every occasion as this reporter journalist (who, by the way, was completely uncultured and insensitive to the meanings of the roots of the cultural history and people he was reporting about) made his way to communities both urban and rural, dignitaries to commoners performed music that used to carry the values of the event and the beliefs and customs of the people. It hit me hard that it is so easy to be deprogrammed away from this. I have studied and performed in West Africa, and as a Black artist you can't know what that meant to connect so deeply and primarily to root. As we viewed Marley, it caught my mind and soul again as to the importance of the work of the griot, the healers, the prophet, a spiritual advisor, the musician.

And notice, it is the simple poetry and song that the common community grasps forcibly, its ideas, values. The best examples of this come from a balance of simple repetitious, but not long poetry. It's funny how powerful and simple ideas repeated in the depth of style, performance, and sincerity hit and impact deeply. And you see this in grass roots, roots music like country, blues, spirituals, folk, and gospel.

It occurred to me that my beliefs, passion on this have been baked in a pot buried deep within a stove that cooked and simmered continuously in the generation of my youth of musicians in the seventies. As we move within our study of this very musical time, I hope it will inspire you. Seems like these artists had a chance to see and say that their music counted for their beliefs, focused on what they wanted to say, and the industry for various reasons, not all lofty, gave a product imbued with creative excellence. Our work still to this point is only in the best sense of the word, view, a broad survey of significant artists and tracking this work, ideas related to social critique, construction. We consider the best of these to be the inner convictions that the voice of the artist is inextricably bound and related to a "spiritual consciousness."

In the cases of John Lennon and Bob Marley, these men were assassination targets during a time when great leaders were targeted. Bob Marley became the first national hero of his people, then an international symbol for what it means to demand peace, peoplehood. John Lennon magnetized a generation with his music and ideas.

It occurred to me that these days the talent is far more diversified, far more technically informed, and the information about the work of popular culture, technology, the world around us we have literally a grasp on in some significant ways at our fingertips. This is incredibly compelling.

I sometimes tear when I listen to all the music of this valued period, and realize we will probably never have a generation who will be able to deeply be moved by the meaning, the feeling of a music made by their own generations of musicians, and that work be supported by a system that at least markets that expression as music. I am finding our music, I may be wrong, marketed for many things beyond the appreciation of what music sounds out and feels to express and to mean. No, I don't preach, I inquire, is there something I am missing? But, my tear is dried when I think of your possibilities; in many ways you have a pass beyond what we had, although I encourage you to tighten your belts, lace up your highest boots, and be ready for "them."

It is a matter of meaning, commitment, and values too. If you don't take time to think about the joy, the gift, seriousness, inspiration, and the causes and effects of your works as artists, why even bother? Do your artistry for joy that it brings you and do care for the way it connects to the world around you.

Always my best,
Dr. B

Out of the Woods with Bobby McFerrin

(DownBeat *magazine, April 2007*)

My dad was the greatest baritone that ever lived and everything I have done musically is directly influenced by him.

Have I gotten quiet enough inside to really hear the music now?

—Bobby McFerrin

∽

Bobby McFerrin is now "out of the woods." The very idea that one was in the woods, perhaps lost, perhaps searching, had gained sight, provides quite a powerful image in the mind. In this way, crossing over, coming out of the valley, making it to the other side, are all symbolic of journeys. Bobby McFerrin's musical life is more than symbolic in this way, and for us it has always been one marked by multiple directions ending up in many musical places. No other artist of our generation, with the exception of Prince or Madonna, has been able to redirect, redefine, recast their direction based solely on artistic choices so directly. A picture of Bobby McFerrin coming out of the woods as well points to some realities. He lives, literally in the woods, in a wooded area near Chestnut Hill in Philadelphia, where his custom built home stands beautifully surrounded by nature. After living in Minneapolis and serving as creative chair of the St. Paul Chamber Orchestra from 1994 to 2001, Bobby and family headed east to settle in a different environment. And one can only imagine that somewhere in the haze of making music in this clouded industry, it inspired him to take some time to rest, reflect, refine, and re-find his directions. So he moves east to the woods in 2001, begins a blistering itinerary of performances, clinics, conducting, and touring. He exhausts himself, faces a near tragic health challenge, and not long after decides to stay home, contemplate, revisit, and recharge. Now Bobby McFerrin in 2007–2008 emerges, fully rested and ready, artistically imbued with what the time had instructed him to do next. Bobby McFerrin, out of the woods. What is Bobby coming out of the woods with and for, what is he going to do now? Bobby has been on sabbatical for seventeen months and on this day, in December 2006, as we walked around the woods that surround his home, with two dogs, Harley and Mo (for Mozart), conversations revolved around everything from the meaning of his time off, what was achieved, what is coming up, his new APT formula and what all this means: all new engagements must be artistic, profitable, and timely. Our talks on this day were only the kind that can emerge from Bobby after a lot of years of trust, ten years of friendship actually, where we fussed about the openness or not, of the Christian narrative as it relates to other faith experiences.

He owns more Bibles than a library is allowed to hold. And in this Bible room is where his studio, piano, rare recordings, and his reading chair rests.

But Bobby moves comfortably to discuss what music and faith means, what artistic responsibility means for this generation of artists, and how his music making is now imbued with renewed insights into what the value of time teaches, how time, or the power of time, has reshaped his thinking. His father, who died less than a month ago, factored largely into what his voice means, and what this signals for now one McFerrin that is left singing and performing and what this may mean for three now who follow: Maddy, Jevon, and Taylor. The walks around the several acres of woods that surround his home segued into sitting and listening to Robert McFerrin Sr.'s 1957 recording of spirituals on Riverside records. To sit there and hear Bobby yell out with excitement, "That's my dad, one of the greatest baritones ever," I have never seen him so pointedly proud, usually shy and modest and not drawn into talks that revolve around him. So this coming out of the woods is literally and symbolically leaping out of the woods with a new sense of direction, in time and fine tuned. And boy what a leaping out: European, American tours with his staple voice band Voicestra; a new recording: a choral CD with a hand-picked choir representing many stylistic disciplines, with original music by Bobby and Roger Treece (arranger, producer) which has been in the works for five years. We've been told, "It will challenge and completely change the way people will think of choral music. . . ." We listened to this. Wow!!!

Festivals, guest conducting orchestras, clinics, and more festivals, conducting at La Scala in Milan; conducting a unique program with Bobby improvisations, conducting the Munich Radio Orchestra, Seattle Symphony, Baltimore Symphony, in Ellensburg, Washington; more performances in Budapest, Paris, London; workshops with Voicestra in Switzerland, Germany; doing the Schleswig-Holstein festival (northernmost state in Germany); performing and recording with the NDR Symphony, two NDR Big Band new music CDs; and being honored at Carnegie Hall in a series of concerts in 2008 with special guests Alison Krause, Yo-Yo Ma, and Chick Corea, of course! And the year ends with him settling down to write and record. So after the walks, the listening, the hang, we broke out the food and wine and I then asked him, What did you set out to do, personally with this break, to do artistically? Did those two goals come together in any significant way in your music, projects, and perspectives? What was the process like, what did you do each day, week? What was, is the artistic process like in preparing new music, rehearsals conducting, rehearsing a group; and of course everybody's ultimate McFerrin question, what is next?

I did this to find my center again, to get quiet inside, to be still, to be in one place. To sleep in my own bed, raid my own refrigerator, be with my family, snuggle with wife, hug my daughter, walk the dogs, sit on my front porch swing, read my Bible and pray, get up early when it's dark, look at the stars, take deep, deep breaths . . . Now that's living, and I was very successful in doing all those things. I thought at the beginning it was going to be a writing sabbatical. It turned out that I did very little, in terms of writing. I would start and work for weeks at a time maintaining a certain writing schedule. But I never found what I was supposed to be doing. I kept looking for creative entrances, into myself, but nothing happened. What would happen if I started with words, or acoustic guitar, writing at different times of the day? I did a lot of experimentation. I was almost too relaxed to write. I did not have enough passion. My passion was to sit still and to think. I didn't have the engine, the heat to write. I had this open-ended seventeen-month period to do absolutely nothing. I found great pleasure in just sitting in a chair with my Bible on my lap. This was my great, great privilege and pleasure to sit and think. It turns out that that was what the sabbatical was all about, examining myself and what I had been doing. How did I want to come out of this time? What did I want to do or say? I watched myself on DVD, a couple of performances. So what did I find out? I didn't care for what I was doing. I thought, "You big show off, that's not what you want to do."

Then I watched a film of me during the summer of 2004 where [with Voicestra]. I literally looked like there was no moisture in my body, every pore in me was dry. I looked dry, as if everything had been drained out of me. Looking at my face, bags under my eyes, yes, it was evident that I was very tired, and looking forward to my sabbatical. But the most interesting thing about that was, that as soon as I started singing with them my life force came back. I realized again I should probably devote myself to something that has this kind of spirit. I wasn't sure exactly what this was until my father died. My dad was the greatest baritone that ever lived and everything I have done musically is directly influenced by him. The night he died I played his album of spirituals, the only one he recorded, called *Deep River*, which he did in June 1957. And I realized that that is what I wanted to write. I wanted to write spirituals.

We live in a society that is so fast. We want fast solutions to our problems. We need to know immediately what we are supposed to do. What I am saying is, it took me a year and a half to figure out creatively after stopping, where I wanted to start again. I am so glad that I took this long, and that I had this time.

It takes a long time, and we become so impatient with our choices. We may do things that may be fun, challenging, but are we nourished by them?

Voicestra gives me a lot of nourishment. I need certain conditions, for solo concerts to work. In small, enclosed dark places, with a single light. Every once and a while I would think to myself, what are spirituals? I believe they are those kinds of songs that talk about God in very simple ways.

My father grew up with Hall Johnson, who taught him how to sing the spirituals. Hall got it from his parents, he got it on the front porch. This is what these spirituals are about, this is why we sing them, and this is the way to sing them and they sound like this.

So my father with his classical sounding voice, got to learn spirituals with all the dirt, the bones, blood, the sweat; all that was thrown in there. It wasn't just open your mouth and sing. You could feel my father singing about his passion, his beliefs, about God all without preaching, just singing. There is a verse in the Bible about speaking to one another in song. I thought, maybe, maybe, this is what my next musical journey is about, writing spirituals. The new album, could be the next step, untitled at this point, is all voices, choral and is culled from past Voicestra, improv concerts. Voicestra is a twelve-person ensemble, and all the concerts are completely improvised on the spot start to finish. It takes a tremendous amount of trust. Some of these singers I've known for twenty-five years and they trust the process. The stage is a platform for adventure. They are walking into a musical stream, standing in the waters. We start, then the singers grab onto an idea, we open our mouths and trust that God will fill it with music.

I decided that what I am going to do is to start thinking about words, verses, and poems. The music is one thing but the music has got to be resting on thoughts, words experiences. I write poems, or I may start singing full blown songs. I have got to come up with something to say and let the music be born from the words.

I am not on a mission. But, I do want to write an album and talk about God. I want to talk about how my life has been influenced by my faith. I want to honor my father's memory through spirituals.

I am out of the woods. I just want to have fun now. I'm trying to limit some things. When I go back out, I don't want to spend all my energy, and have none left to be a person. I am a person first, a father, husband, man, a Christian before I'm an entertainer. You can wear yourself out; I was so tired of entertaining. You never want to get to the place, walking out on a stage where you look out at the audience and not recognize yourself or them. I had gotten to a place where I said, "Is this what I want, do I want to really be doing this?" But now, I'm eager to get back to work. I want to be able to see how being quiet will affect my conducting. I'm going to conduct smaller, am going to move less on the podium. Have I gotten quiet enough inside to really hear the music now?

You know what's wonderful about living in the woods? When it rains, you can see the rain, when it's windy you can hear the wind, you can hear the snow fall. I have had the wonderful blessing to sit and drink all that in. To have all the nature move in, and now I am anxious and eager as everybody else to see what will come out.

～

There's Something New There, but You Have to Find It

David "Honeyboy" Edwards
(DownBeat magazine, May 2008)

Playing the blues with David "Honeyboy" Edwards is like sitting down with a repository of the history of spirituals, country blues, shuffles, jump blues, R & B, and rock. He's not a musical library, but rather, he's an artist with a distinctive sound and distinctive story. And there was a generational values transfer.

Last August, in his hotel room in Boston before a performance at the Boston Blues Festival, Edwards, ninety-two, took out his guitar. I took my guitar out too, to trade some licks with the legendary bluesman.

He called out a jam blues in E, he sang, and we were home in it. The blues is a national musicians' native language, the mother tongue, and this felt like being at a meal with my uncle, hearing stories, and learning musical ropes. True to tradition, this talk was story, note, song exchange, and listening.

That same session a month later was extended to the Berklee College of Music, where David "Honeyboy" Edwards played, spoke, and shared his story with a few hundred mouths-dropped-and-awed students. They had never heard a ninety-year-old, true born Delta bluesman talk and play.

In many ways, this musical exchange felt like the story of jazz, blues, and other American roots music—from its origins, passages, and journeys—and how styles got, as Edwards claims, "cooked around." Perhaps this was what it felt like for Edwards when he sat down to play with Robert Johnson.

"I played with Robert Johnson in 1937," he said. "He, Son House, and Willie Brown used to go to little towns and sit and play in the streets for nickels and dimes."

David "Honeyboy" Edwards and me.

Edwards also had plenty of experience playing in the street for change. He now plays blues festivals around the world, but he has seen the blues tradition evolve around him. Born in Shaw, Mississippi, in 1915, he started playing before the phonograph came into common usage in American homes. Almost the only music Black people in the South heard was "homemade" singing and playing on guitar, piano, banjo, violin, and mandolin. In 1929, at fourteen years old, Edwards began to take his home-learned musical lessons on the road.

"At the time I began playing I was raised in the country and my father was a sharecropper in the Mississippi Delta," he said "My father played violin and guitar. When I tried to play, he'd listen to me. My father could read music; he had education from New Orleans. I played in one key so long he said, 'Boy, don't you have another key to play in?'"

Through this prodding from his father, Edwards began to develop his playing, becoming more advanced on the guitar. "I started switching around, playing in other keys, playing with other musicians and it began to come to me naturally," he said. "Naturally, I wanted to play music. At that time people had families, or a man would leave a woman, then somebody starts playing the blues, and you start thinking, 'When did she leave me?' But the music would keep the mind moving around.'

"There were so many guitar players," he continued. "But many of them played the same thing. But I could play many tunes. I used different tunes and chords, because I had learned a little from here and there."

In 1931, Edwards caught a freight train with bluesman John Henry and headed to Memphis. In 1932, he hit the road with Big Joe Williams. He played for $2 a night, and when home he paid $6 a week for room and board, which included two meals a day. Music for this early generation of traveling musicians meant more than just music. Music was a way out, a view of the world, a chance to see other places and a meal.

How did he react to the emergence of jazz?

"I knew about jazz because I used to play with a sax player out of college, and he would teach me what he was playing," he said. "We used to play things like 'Stardust,' 'Blue Moon,' 'Out in the Cold,' and 'Sophisticated Lady.' I played chords behind him, and read that music. The White people wanted to hear this thing, always had money, and always had the jobs when Black folks didn't have any," he said. "So we played for them, serenading them at night. Looking out of the windows and they would throw quarters out of the window."

Today, Edwards gets a lot more respect for his art than having quarters tossed at him from windows. In 2002 he received the National Heritage Fellowship. Last year, he released *The Last of the Great Mississippi Delta Bluesman: Live in Dallas* (Blue Shoe Project) with Henry James Townsend, Joe Willie "Pinetop" Perkins, and Robert Lockwood Jr. The album won the Grammy for Best Traditional Blues Album in 2008.

The awards are a proper recognition for Edwards, but they do not make him rest on his laurels. Rather, he continually searches for new paths in the music and does so by firmly knowing the music's history. "There's always something new there, but you have to find it," he said. "In the blues you hear the rapping, then your mind falls back on what's happening in your life; it's really something. Every time I played I felt like that. You have to play the blues in different styles: slow blues, a boogie-woogie shuffle, take it up tempo and make it rock and roll. The same stuff my mama and daddy did."

Our culture works quickly to forget its past for the gratification of the new find. But every generation of musicians must look back toward which streams of the past they find floating up toward them.

"I tell younger musicians, to stick with it, hold on to your music," he said. "It will turn out to something one day. There's something new there, but you have to find it. When you find your own style, you can always use somebody else's sound, but always make your own, then you've got a different style."

CHAPTER NINE

Representing Culture (2008)

We are the beat generation. We are concerned with the feel that keeps
you moving. We don't build from the harmonies and the melodies, we
build from the beats up and float the melodies and harmony second, because that's what the people are tapped into. But I study all that music,
I know that music and I flip it. I give you all that tradition, but use it to
bring them in a new way.

—Charles Wilson

July

Dear One (A note written to friends, but then didn't send . . .)

After the recent deaths of my brother (January) and mother (June), I need
to slow down but not to a dead crawl. I need to reason and feel through what
this moment means. My writing—*Cultural Codes*, *Black Music Matters*, my
essays, and a novel—along with my teaching, reflect what I am seeing and
responding to creatively. They are not music—as my friends would like—
but they are musical and they are creative expressions. I have to be satisfied
that these are okay, that it's okay to not write music. I have been writing,
but no major concert works.

Over the last two years, I have been playing, performing, and leading the
band a whole lot. I have been studying, practicing, and taking weekly coaching on guitar and improvisation techniques.

I have been teaching, an extraordinary amount, and I have certainly been thinking about music, culture, and history.

I have been exercising and taking care of my health, regularly.

I have been teaching Sunday school and enjoying great spiritual growth, mentorship, and community at my church. I work at the greatest music school in the world. I have been building, building, and fighting for the building of Black music culture programming at my institution, Berklee. I have had great success and some disappointments. I have made many friends and some vocal enemies, too.

Then my brother and, worse, my mother die within six months of each other.

So now I need to stop, slow down, and in another way, grow.

I need to drop out of sight and hear the air for a minute, a hard thing for me to do. But I need to make some internal peace of things. I just need a moment to search from the inner core about how all this matters and what it means, and that's a good thing.

In the next few months, I need to listen deeply to music. I need to read deeply and reflectively. I need to walk, to think, to pray. I need to compose again, richly and focused. And I must teach and give to these younger people who inspire me tremendously. But no more fighting, no more championing

My brother Bruce, my nephew Doug (Duvaughn's son), me, my father, and my brother Duvaughn.

the good fights. I need to stop pushing and selling things for a while. I need to settle a bit, chill out to a well-seasoned simmer, then cool and be deeply and richly flavored for the next lasting good.

August 19

I just spent a week in L.A. with a mixed bag of things to do, most of them connected to my work at Berklee and with *DownBeat*.

If there is one area of mystery that still looms—large and bright, simultaneously—for me it is popular music publishing. This golden carrot is the key to not only gaining access to popular music, but getting cash as well. As non-artistic as that sounds, publishing and cash flow are the only ways to survive and make inroads in popular music because "if it ain't selling, it don't mean a thing." Unfortunately, too many of the things that don't mean a thing sell.

This time in L.A. was different. Usually I have to chase some*thing* or some*one* down, but this time people were receiving *me*. That's different. The first night I met with my old buddy Billy Childs, hung at his home, and then went out to some fancy dinner place in Pasadena. I interviewed Billy on issues we had long talked about, but this time we focused on the current jazz industry. He is so brilliant and has earned a reputation as a singular thinker in music, both in the jazz field and as a composer.

The next day at Warner/Chappell Music on Santa Monica Boulevard, I spoke with Bob Fead, my friend there who has been sharing with me some publishing myths, secrets, and ways in. Bob was generous with his time, listening to me and to my music. This reminded me of early days in the eighties, sitting in the New York offices of Dr. George Butler. George, who died this year—God rest his soul—would pontificate, plan, and then execute jazz concerts like a king planning his own triumphant parties. He was probably one of the last great Black music producers, a rare musician in power from that generation.

Bob outlined the industry for me in terms of what pays, how it pays, distribution, royalties, licensing, and product placement. We made some plans for what I hope will be a publishing deal with Warner/Chappell Music for my *Songbook*, a publishing/production of contemporary songs sung by friends and produced by industry insiders. We shall see. Another meeting was with my cousin, Charles Wilson, who is now on tour with some new young lady, Rihanna, who is hot. Charles met me at the house of my buddy, Morris Hayes, who was playing with Prince again. I am planning on having Charles and Morris help me produce new pieces. They both listened to my plans and schooled me on the reality of what the market can bear. I quoted them in my

DownBeat article, since it's important to hear about popular music success as a living rule. You can't beat nor join the monster dancing if you don't know where the party is. For me this is on-the-job training which I take right back to my kids.

I then visited George Duke at his home studio. Seeing George is like visiting the master, but the master with arms and heart outstretched, because he is so warm and inviting, unassuming, and *real*. All musicians record and stop in to be with George in Hollywood.

I was especially excited to visit A Place Called Home, which is an afterschool program developed in South Central L.A. (I had never driven through or been to South Central. It looks just like the movies.) This is a fabulous program begun in a safe learning zone, complete with a barbed-wire fence, cement compound, metal detectors, and guards. Inside they have created an incredible alternative arts and achievement school for kids in the South Central neighborhood. The staff is so dedicated. As they gave me a tour of the facilities, we talked about what they needed. I was hooked.

Another day I headed to Beverly Hills to meet with Lee Ritenour at his studio. We played a bit on his guitars and talked about the industry. To be there with him was like sitting with your memories, yet alive and your dreams speaking to you in real time. I interviewed Lee about the history of commercial jazz, since Lee is one of the founders of what is problematically called smooth jazz.

I also met with Rae Linda Brown, now vice president of Undergraduate Education at Loyola Marymount University. Rae Linda and I met on Hermosa Beach and we had dinner while the "other" ocean roared behind us. Rae Linda is one of my mentors—along with Henry Louis Gates, Charles Davis (the great teacher at Yale), composing great Anthony Davis (son of Charles), and Dwight Andrews. The idea of mentorship is essential and yet it is being lost, as selfish motivations have replaced our priority to extend and share, and the important links are often broken.

One of the teachers at A Place Called Home had recently relocated to the Leimert Park area (where some of my novel takes place) and he showed me around. He introduced me to a few shop owners, and people who had grown up there in the 1950s, 1960s, and 1970s. I could feel the same vibe coursing though the street, the park, the historic cafes, stores, merchants, and music theaters.

Driving around, meeting with friends, speaking with industry thinkers, and immersing myself in those communities inspired me. I find these connections relevant, important, and the necessary ingredients for art and culture to represent all we do, think, share, and create. These thinkers and artists need to share their connections, mentor the generations that follow—those generations for whom most knowledge has been sold in condensed, freeze-dried containers with the essential nutrients sucked out. The generations that follow us are in need of something real, something vibrating with life, to inspire them.

Our work is really cut out for us, cut deep into us.

August 28

Today, the *New York Times* headline reads, "Heralding New Course, Democrats Nominate Obama." This nomination makes him the first Black candidate of a major party for president. So many millions around the globe read, watch, and hear the news, feeling a movement sweep our world. In a jubilant frenzy we all called one another, text messaging, back and forth. I haven't experienced anything in my life as monumental, in a history-making moment of greatness like this since the King event, which I was too young to remember. The convention last night was held in Colorado's football stadium, the largest political event in American history. Added to this was the fact that on the same night forty-five years before, King delivered his "I have a dream" speech. So we were able to witness a phenomenon that also connected us to the past. King dreamed, and we heard the wake-up call from a two-hundred-year-long American sleep. Barack Obama becomes the embodiment of another dream in which American power is represented in the form of people who are not White and not privileged. I watched the tears streaming from the eyes of so many people on television. With water-filled eyes, dry throat, and pounding heart, I listened to the poetic, powerful, and finely placed cadence of his speech. He was truly better than brilliant! The pageantry, the staging of this convention event was the best that has ever been produced. This movement occurs at a horrific time, under the modern slick-dressed tyranny of the Bush presidency that has torn the world apart. But here was Barack Obama, born in my proud year of 1961, who held the world waiting, holding their breath for his words, as he said, "Enough. We will wait no more. Now is our time, your time for change."

This was a monumental moment and is marking my own development toward clarity and maturity. For anyone reflecting, Obama's committed, focused, and passionate charges of integrity and care make it clear that we must demand a new, revolutionary spin on all we do. Taking his example, all it requires is a few strong voices out there, and people can see a better way out of the mired mess we swim through in today's culture. I am moved to a new inner level of confidence, because all that is percolating within me tells me that this is right, this is how, and this is now.

September 5

"I hear worse than that on the basketball court." We now have a Black president nominee. This was a comment I heard Barack say to the press when questioned about the rebukes and cuts vice presidential nominee Sarah Palin made about Obama and the movement. It occurred to me that here is a man who speaks of the forums where truth, integrity, ability, and working for the common good of the team happens: on the basketball court. I knew then we would have our first Black president!

September 13

We are in the midst of what has to be some of the worst storms—Gustav, Hanna, and Ike—and hurricane season in American history. Now you have to ask yourself, "What the hell is going on out here?" Katrina, tsunami were wake-up calls enough, but to have the coasts pounded by God's natural wrath—no pushing red buttons or invading coast with tanks—this is some real, uh, deeper shit.

What we saw brewing was political trickery. They stole, rigged, and cheated two elections in a row: Bush from Gore, then Bush from Kerry. They led us into a war, imperialized Iraq, started messes with everybody in the world almost, began to pick at Old World war scabs with Russia, North Korea, China, and Iran, bankrupted the nation and the trust of the world, and sent thousands of young men and women into harm's way. Much of this was fueled by the greed of men in power who were more interested in their corporate investments and maintaining their ridiculously opulent lifestyles. Then to camouflage their corruption, they created a scam with colored security alert codes and empty propaganda about the daily lurking threat of "evil terrorists." If you spoke up, if you questioned them, they called you "unpatriotic" because it was "un-American" to speak out.

They rigged the financial markets to hike up mortgage prices, which then exploded. Gas prices rose, banks folded, and government bailout plans were hatched, while we all sat around asking, "What happened? What is happening?" I'm neither an economist nor a historian, but my eyes are open, and something's going on. This ain't right! Besides "our money" evaporating— along with truth and integrity—so is public trust in the government, now at the lowest in our nation's history. And guess who's come back to dinner? Racism. Along with incivility, incompetence, and rampant ignorance, as many have abandoned decency, morality, and sometimes just everyday common sense. In the midst of this cultural storm, there are train wrecks, every-day business fraud, and airlines charging for pillows and peanuts.

Then along came a moment, perhaps a minute when we were looking for change, and there were agents in place. More people in the history of our voting consciousness, with feet and conviction, swelled to the polls to nominate Barack Obama for president—a visionary and a smart man. Revolutionary!

But just as it looked like Democrats were going to take back the presidency and possibly restore a bit of hope and change in the national psyche, along comes Sarah Palin. Typical political trickery to distract the nation by propping up in the midst of very possible change, a cardboard figure, a woman from nowhere who had done nothing. The thoughtless Republicans threw her in to create a media frenzy, and too many Americans fell for it. It's *American Idol* all over again! As a nation of hero seekers, we worship nothing as much as the instant celebrity, and the Republican Party produced one in a photogenic spokesperson with no real credentials. In the past, our political leaders represented *something*, and we believed in them. We believed in their merit, and they gave us hope. These days we are a people who are bereft of such worthwhile beliefs—from sides left and right. If the Republicans steal another election with their trickery, I will lose hope. If John McCain and Sarah Palin are ushered into the White House, it will be yet one more symbol of this country's spiraling social and moral decline.

Too soon after the cynical appointment of Palin, corporate greed reared its head again. The news came September 15, 16, and 17: Lehman Brothers, Bear Sterns, Fannie Mae, Freddie Mac, Merrill Lynch, then AIG all failed. Major banks Washington Mutual and Wachovia defaulted, crashed, and needed government intervention—buyouts and bailouts to the tune of $700 billion. On September 29, the stock market lost 777 points, the lowest dip in history, accounting for $1 trillion in losses. This was the worst American business rupture the world had seen since 1929 (see *New York Times*, editorial section September 2007). Economic anxiety lain again at the feet of risky investments, spearheaded by overpaid, under-regulated executives. The buy-outs were hoped to restore the interdependent financial system that held up Western society. But at what costs to Americans? At what security of living as we have known it? Nobody is answering these questions. Even the bailout plans Congress wrangled over for days was speculative, and still is.

After living under the cloak of lies, failed policies, and false financial window dressing, the painful and real fallout of this are the job losses and home foreclosures. American workers faced a loss of pay, reduced benefits, and ultimately, their jobs, while evil executives profited with no shame. Their unregulated selling allowed incomes to balloon, while the boys in Washington, under the cloak of free market expansion, failed to temper this or ask real questions, allowing such activities to go undetected and unpunished. The Kenneth Lay Enron nightmare apparently faded from memory, because it was actually the prelude to a long, living nightmare of a crippled American economy.

For me, documenting the times, teaching the younger generations, representing culture, has been the be-all. In some ways I have fallen into complacency, and I wonder if it represents a time of healing or just plain being tired.

I feel more compelled to write what I am thinking, talk about what that means and listening to what, particularly, young people have to say. My writing—and just that—excites me more than everything else. Documenting what goes on right now seems as creative as picking up my guitar. And, as a matter of fact, I'm doing that more than I have in years past, and much of those reflections seem to be coming through the axe. I'm anxious to see what effect this will have on the writing of music.

I wrote a couple of long essays over the last two months. The published one, "Don't Use the J Word," came out of discussions with artists about where jazz culture is today. But more important to me was the idea of jazz in the context of the larger megaculture. I still don't know what part of that article will finally be published by my editor at *DownBeat*, Jason Koransky. But it has led me to deeper places about the representations of culture by artists, not advertisers.

I also wrote about Bernice McFadden, an author whose work I had recently discovered, and whose book helped me shape the final chapters of my novel. Very appreciative of this author, I got up the nerve to e-mail my homage piece to her. She responded yesterday sooo sweetly, saying, "How did you know it was my birthday week? This is so lovely, such a gift."

I found in her writing the maps to some real connection techniques you need to tell a story. I love her book *The Warmest December*. She writes from her experiences growing up in the 1970s and maturing into the 1980s and 1990s, as she and I are of the same post–civil rights generation, what the book says is the "right generation." What I found so compelling in this work was a moment of brilliant clarity on the role of Black music to connect and relate our experiences. This little segment was vividly and poignantly scripted. And for that, we must represent and document.

Look, it's very simple: We must transform these last days so that maybe they *won't* be the last days. We don't need a prophet as much as we need to be operating under the belief that these are prophetic times, for people to feel a calling, to find meaning again. I feel so confirmed on these points, that that is what drives me to be more grounded, to move more deliberately, and to think more deeply about what we believe that matters. And though it is difficult, I am totally convinced that art must heal and prepare and sustain. Approaching fifty, I don't mind as much that I am getting older. I appreciate that are there are now more things to *absorb* than there are things to *do*. That's the difference at this stage. I am in a moment of reflection, allowing myself to absorb, to regain my senses.

Homage to Mentors: Harold Cruse, Cornel West, Amiri Baraka, Bernice Johnson Reagon, Henry Louis Gates Jr., Toni Morrison

There have been several defining conversations and sharing experiences that have given me salvation, sustenance, and clarity. And I share these as I realize how important the reach and the transfer of values from generation to generation is. I was extremely fortunate to be a student, sometimes literally, with six great thinkers: Harold Cruse, Bernice Johnson Reagon, Henry Louis Gates Jr., Toni Morrison, Cornel West, and Amiri Baraka. They give me clarity.

At the beginning of my career as professor, I assisted Harold Cruse in his classes on gender, society, and American culture. I taught under him from 1988 to 1992, while preparing for my doctorate at the University of Michigan. I learned from Professor Cruse that the most powerful force shaping our lives is culture. Our identity is one complex satellite orbiting and feeding back to the base we call culture. For hours, we would all sit listening to him at various cafés in Ann Arbor as he spoke about communism, jazz, and James Baldwin. I learned the way the old masters would teach young apprentices by talking about experiences in context. That's the way I learned to be a teacher. And he said to me, "You have to attempt to explain its [Black music] implications."

Cornel West, for many of us in our studies, was that "big mind" out there who knows all, hears all, and speaks for all. His writing lit the fire in me and made me value—more than anything else—how words and ideas should inspire. For a period of nearly twenty years we spoke: He encouraged and I leaned in, listened, and learned. In our sharing, big brother Cornel made it clear to me that by examining artistic excellence, it would be my challenge to explicate the deeper dimensions of it as more than documentary exotic market forced appeals, but a meaningful philosophical probe into the questions music raises.

With Alexs Pate, John Wright, Cornel West, and Allan Callahan.

He would state, "Artists ask the courageous question: 'What does it mean to be human?' Artists wrestle with the cultivation of what it could be to be alive. So, what kind of human being are you trying to be as you are being an artist, and coming up with a sophisticated form: music?" I read his books, I watched him in classes, I attended the lectures, we dined, and I engaged him on these matters. And so our conversations about Coltrane and Ornette Coleman would translate into connections about how and why Black music matters—and that would become our compelling theme to ponder.

As a W. E. B. Du Bois Scholar at Harvard in 2000–2001, I was very anxious to catch Mr. Gates at his office for whatever I could get from him—on the rare occasions when I could have a sit-down conversation. I attended his seminars on African American topics, and I learned greatly from watching his teaching. My best lesson in teaching—how to work a class and work the material—I learned from working under Mr. Gates during that year at Harvard. He allowed students to present their ideas, questioned, then passed those questions onto the next students, suggesting all at once different ways to interpret Amiri Baraka's *Dutchman*, intensely pouncing on each question, each student, but with great care, finesse, and love for the engagement. I never have forgotten those teaching sessions.

Henry Louis Gates and me.

Toni Morrison commissioned an opera from me in 2002 and invited me to be a visiting Atelier Arts professor at Princeton University. The librettist, by the way, was Yusef Komunyakaa. Our dinner time was very special, and as I was being "schooled," my sweaty hand gripped the fork directed to my mouth. I listened intensely, holding on to her words as tightly as the fork in my hand. At times, I worried about what detractors said of my work, and at other times I believed it merited acknowledgment. I became too concerned about perceptions among my peers, so I asked, "Ms. Morrison, what should I do? What will people think if I do this, do that?" She responded quickly, curtly, and directly: "Bill, what difference does it make what they call it or what anyone thinks? The only thing that matters is what you do with the opportunity that has been given you."

Over the years Dr. Bernice Johnson Reagon told me directly, "I wanted to live being clear and articulate as an artist about what I thought about the world, my people, and the society we are living in and helping to shape. If we are a socially conscious people, and if a point of view, a system of principles and values are going to affect the space we live in, it will be most effective if we 'put it out there.' We can't talk about living in a time when we're losing ground and losing young people. You lose ground when you don't hold it." The idea that music prepares you for your battles is profound.

And lastly, another mentor, the poet Amiri Baraka. As I sat in his living room listening to music, as I interviewed him (2007), as we performed onstage together, as we dined while reflecting on Sun Ra—or Ornette, Coltrane, or Miles—as we cotaught my classes, he pointed to me and said, "It's your turn." Baraka, in those teaching moments, was helpful too in pointing out what the poet does. He asked, "What's the poet's gig, man?" Pointing a finger on his brow, he answered, "To light up the head." He mused on: "Time, place, condition, and context, these are the operating windows of artistic expression. You got to know that. For whom do you create? Can you create another golden age? Truth and beauty are the only things artists should be concerned with."

Each generation needs shoulders to lean on, advice and wise counsel to move with, and opportunities and encouragement for the building of the next generation. These six—Harold Cruse, Toni Morrison, Bernice Johnson Reagon, Henry Louis Gates, Cornel West, and Amiri Baraka—are beacons for a generation of artists and scholars who may never achieve fame and fortune, but will be richly enlightened nonetheless. So many of us are given hope and inspiration because of their works, presence, and brilliance as examples to emulate.

Modern Media Music Culture Madness:
Themes, Threads, Criticism

We cannot predict the shape or direction of things to come. But we can interact with each other in a manner that can influence the way people respond to the coming chapters in our human history. I write this at a time when there is tremendous mistrust in our nation. But I also believe that education and artistry will be the transformative mode of exchange that holds us in place, helps us weather the storms ahead. It will be the next generation that comes gifted with voices others must hear. The future of the music rests upon artists whose outlooks are balanced, who recast the codes. I do think there are enough new artists connected to the best of the older music, who embrace our music and art traditions while at the same time can create something new as well.

Artists such Lauryn Hill, Jill Scott, Outkast, Erykah Badu, India.Arie, Kirk Franklin, Kanye West, John Legend, and others released the most innovative, fresh sounds since the beginning of the new century. They were market smart but not artist dumb. In their first projects, they all drew upon multiple levels of Black artistry. They were global, they had something compelling to say, and their voices are original. Their works were not produced on an industry conveyer belt. They sang in conventional forms but in nonconventional record formats. These products made me feel like a musician.

Other artists of note who have emerged since 2000 include Kim Burrell, Usher, Christian Scott, Mary Mary, Stefon Harris, Alicia Keys, KEM, Jennifer Hudson, Kelly Price, Lalah Hathaway, Fantasia, Janelle Monáe, Raul Midón, and Esperanza Spalding. These artists give us hope that the codes are being handled by musicians of all stripes in popular culture. They are evidence that the gene pool for Black music artistry and talent did not dry up and go away.

In its September 2007 issue, *Vibe* magazine—a premiere popular culture magazine founded by industry leader Quincy Jones—noted, "Rap's problems loom larger than some foul language and a few loud talking heads . . . the vitality of this culture we all know and love has been called into question. So is hip-hop truly dead?" This aesthetic in Black popular music has fallen and is burning. The soiled commerciality of the form is indefensible. Take, for example, the advertisements in this same issue, which feature—you guessed it—hip-hop artists, but mention nothing about music: Beyoncé and Solange Knowles (clothes); Russell Simmons (clothing line, Argyleculture); Kimora Lee Simmons (baby phat clothes); Nelly (Apple Bottom clothes line); Queen Latifah (Cover Girl makeup line).

That issue also references Sean "Diddy" Combs's reality program, *Making the Band* (an MTV-produced music show which takes some potentially talented young people and "false fuels" them into thinking they can do "music" and get famous). How is he supposed to "make" a group when he knows zero about music? And the problem here is that a young, White ignorant executive probably got to "green-light" this. That's who determines how our music gets to be made. This is a sad commentary on modern pop music culture, and we can only hope that it will not continue to set the codes for culture and the arts so pervasively and unchecked.

In an exercise called "The artist meet and greet, make or baked by the culture," I had my students explore industry practices and cultural influences on race, identity, class politics, power, commerciality, sexuality, gender construction, musical artistry, image representation, and spirituality as they relate to the work of contemporary musicians. Using primary articles and media sources, including magazines such as *Billboard, DownBeat, Vanity Fair, Ebony, Vibe, Source, Black Enterprise, People, New York Times Magazine,* and *Newsweek,* they examined cover stories, interviews, ads, and photo layouts to address the following questions: What is this about? To whom does this speak? Who does this represent? What does it suggest about the relationship between music making at present, its connection to contemporary life and culture, and its historical trajectory? How does this shape contemporary living and society? Artistry? Does the tail (media, public tastes) wag the artists? Are the artists puppets of the industry, and if so, how do you suggest we change this, challenge this?

Most if not all participants found that:

1. Music doesn't stand alone anymore, but as an industry commodity.
2. It is no longer good enough to be *just* a musician. You have to sell something for somebody. Not one article could be found that didn't sell something, whether it was the artist, soap, cosmetics, or an industry-shaped lifestyle.
3. There were consistently a higher number of entertainers representing product lines than their own artistry.
4. Hard-core rappers were sold as "artists and musicians" over everyday practicing musicians.
5. The industry identity was largely a commercial construction that projects a weakened authority and artistic credibility. The recording/sales media industry was seen solely responsible for driving this.

Writing about Black music, I sometimes feel I have been too heavy-handed and long-winded. And during rewrites, some of my comments struck me as a little high-minded, pretentious even. Who am I to suggest what or how music today needs to be written?! But even when I have doubts and lose my courage, and at times when I felt I was getting long-winded, redundant, or making negative assumptions, I encountered others of all stripes who felt these things must be said. What would history, her story, our story, and our ancestors say about our silences during this cultural swing toward pandemonium? If you aren't on your deathbed, you gotta say something, ask some questions, challenge some status quo, and demand the best for yourself and others. Artistry demands a hard look at reality, and at the same time offers a compassionate hand, an attentive ear.

We have experienced these transformative moments in history before: the Revolutionary War; slavery; the Second Great Awakening; segregation; lynching; the Harlem Renaissance; the Great Depression, the New Deal; the Cold War, McCarthyism; American Apartheid, civil rights legislation; Reaganomics, recession; the Bushes' war, the Audacity of Hope and Change. For nearly sixty years this society has invested in the shallow holdings of capitalization to build wealth. Now let's invest in souls and minds for the greater good and service of our humanity. This is the great new code we must write together.

Quite honestly, it's hard to know if anyone will read your observations no matter how many times you have had the conversation with yourself, or how well you may think things out. Doesn't matter how many pages you may take up expressing your views. But what's critical is that we all catch the spirit of human engagement in ideas and demand a moment to be heard. And even beyond that, the older musicians will tell you in a minute, "It doesn't really matter how much you know. What counts at the end of the downbeats is that the people experience what you feel. *That's* keeping it real."

This philosophy is, perhaps, not too high-minded at all. It provides reflective, balanced, and caring thought about who we are as creative individuals and what we want to share with each other. These kinds of considerations make life sweeter. But as I came to several points within this writing, I really wanted it to reach any person who was just interested in some music ideas. I wanted a reader to enjoy this and say, "Hey, I didn't know that about the blues. Maybe I'll check that out the next time I'm listening." But where do we go from here?

Something happened in the transfer of culture and power between 1980 and today. Somewhere in the presidential switches between Carter, Reagan, Bush 1, Clinton, and Bush 2, we got hit below the knees and our footing was slippery. We took our attention away from the weaker, more vulnerable communities. The perceived victories and voices of the 1960s and 1970s were on our minds, but we didn't continue to address the needs of our communities, and our society strayed further from a substantive definition of citizenry. That hopelessness was heard clearly in Grandmaster Flash's "The Message" (1982), but that message got hijacked to become a profitable, marketable concept. Instead of focusing on the message, the means by which it was expressed became commodified, co-opted into a glamorized concept of "hood life"—aka "ghetto," aka "thug life," aka "keeping it real for the peeps."

Why didn't we listen when Grandmaster Flash said, "Don't push me cause I'm close to the edge, I'm trying not to lose my head"? Many fell all the way over the edge and got trapped in the "jungle." Those of us who benefited from the gains in the 1970s rode into colleges or positions of influence, but there were not enough common folk to raise and rattle the message. That message was co-opted by a commercial culture where words and music and expressions began to lack vision. Somebody marketed that narrative, transforming that rage into a multibillion dollar commodity. And that narrative corrupted contemporary popular artistry.

John Coltrane said, "The main thing a musician would like to do is to give a picture to the listener of the many wonderful things he knows of and senses in the universe." We have to continue to work in several areas to influence cultural trends which should collide comfortably into each other. Engaging cultural theory (talk), constructing codes is important. Black people and their arts have clearly been at the center of American debates and dilemmas about itself, its industries, its markets, itself as a modern civilized nation. That historical fact alone makes Black destiny inextricably bound with what America is and will become. Many writers speak about the folks wrestling with cultural, social, political, and artistic meaning in society. That's because these are all sacred places where one can best understand the relevance and meaning of our exchanges, where our expressions and rituals are valued.

The Audacity in Hope: Post-Album Movements, the Jazz Urbane, Jazz Social Aesthetic (Soulive, Obama, and *Idlewild*)

No one is exempt from the call to find common ground.

—*The Audacity of Hope*, Barack Obama

In 2008, nearing the close of a chapter of this memoir, several inspiring, hopeful, and meaningful megacultural movements were in motion. It was the "Obama Call" to cement a new cultural identity and common ground that resonated with many. In the midst of war, terrorist attacks against innocent people, along with an encrusted ugliness and "polarizing rhetoric and politics of resentment" that pervaded our political social terrain, we could not have anticipated how the bar was going to be raised publicly in civility, intelligence, and integrity. Barack Obama was the man I told my eighty-five-year-old parents I wanted to grow up to be. The Obama Call was a serious cultural campaign which dominated the national political scene unlike anything my generation had ever witnessed. By 1978 we had heard about Kennedy, but in 2008 we were hoping for an "Obama-dy."

By 2005, neo-soul music had laid a new precedent for a real revival of a cross-generational, Black global aesthetic platform in music, film, popular culture, and cultural politics. This movement in poetry, performed as spoken word and exemplified by the hip-hop poet Saul Williams (seen in the movie *Slam*) was aided by the gluing of hip-hop with bebop and soul, the 1960s last poets rants, and from the art and visual work of Bearden to hip-hop's major visual artist, Jean-Michel Basquiat. In film, the movement took up the visual-cultural aesthetic of *Cabin in the Sky*, *Carmen Jones*, *Uptown Saturday Night*, *Harlem Nights*, *Boomerang*, and *Bamboozled*, and more recently in the frames and downbeats of the neo-soul hip-hop movies, *Love Jones* and *Idlewild*.

Idlewild, in particular, was a mainstream film produced in 2006 that brought all the pieces together in one document. It creatively mirrors what was hoped would be the aesthetic trajectory forward in terms of visual, sound, and movement. The movie is a masterpiece. Starring André Benjamin and Antwan Patton—known as the Atlanta-based hip-hop group Outkast—and released by Universal Pictures/HBO Films, *Idlewild* is the culmination of our postmodern era of pop culture which draws from the richest of Black films and music including the blues, jazz, bebop, hip-hop, and neo-soul, as well as Black dance and comedy. In feel, *Idlewild* hints at a Harlem Renaissance–like Black world, with varying degrees of vernacular, and Cotton Club–imaged nightlife scenes, But it also focuses on family relationships and the inner creative work of the principal character, an aspiring young composer-songwriter named Percival, played by Benjamin. The portrayal of this character offers a rare depiction of a value-cemented, sensitive composer who is Black and young. The film's breathtaking "Matrix-like" visuals pulsate in aesthetic conception and artistic spin, with a boldness of Black body movement and dance, modern music, bare-to-the-bones and edgy Black humor, depth, and an impeccable—and rarely seen in Hollywood—range of talent, from Macy Gray to Cicely Tyson. The interdisciplinary usage of mediums result in a modern visual uplift for Black people who, in Hollywood at least, are usually saturated in one-dimensionality. And that this piece was produced by two forward-moving hip-hop artists is telling.

⌒

"Wow, Mom, He Looks Like Me" (An Obama Poem)

Wow, mom, dad, what a treat to see a civil rights baby, potential president named
  Obama who looks like me.
Hey mom, look! He was born in 1961, the same year as me. Even ran the same
  college streets at my same time in Boston from fear to fun.
Hey brotha, a potential president of the United States whose grandmother is still
  African. God, Malcolm is dancing that we might be able to get to leadership
  through which Black people, all people, can be pride-full, again.
To feel the thrill for us post baby boomers, civil rights babies, get down momma to
  get a chance to hope for an Obama.
Hey cuz, could we have bet we'd this day get to see an American president who
  talked like me?
A generation of us now gets to work on a better plan and fix, we get to "take the
  red pill" like Neal, and finally bust out of the soul-less matrix.
Must happen I guess to each generation who gets to dream in a society run by
  someone their own age, now watching the world crack, burn and rage, we all
  praying there is a new vision to release us from this chaotic cultural cage.
Hey sista, he wrote his book called *The Audacity of Hope*, and claims we should
  pursue a philosophy of values in governing beyond tolerance and simply saying
  things to cope.
He said, "No one is exempt from the call to find common ground."
And while there are many with rhetoric these days all around,
I'd rather not, because their false rhyme
spitting sound bites, not as his, so sound.

Just think of it baby, that we'd escape "the Bushes" and get to dream. I really can't believe it, this post–civil rights child that in my day it possibly may come true. Must have been like this for you all, Mom, in 1963, to get the lift of a vision in the midst of divisions during the time of Kennedy.

Hey Dad, it doesn't really matter for me if another greedy and caring-less White man gets in again, just that Obama set new patterns of fresh approaches means ultimately we have the maps in these days of chaos, to have the audacity to hope again.

November 5

This morning's *New York Times* simply and profoundly read, "OBAMA."
  In his own words, "If there is anyone out there who still doubts that America is a place where all things are possible, who still wonders if the dreams of our

founders are alive in our time, who still questions the power of our democracy, tonight is your answer." I sit here the day after, having gone to my neighborhood main street where I purchased my *New York Times*. This is the same street I lived and walked in 1983. Back then I was twenty-two years old, and the next day Dr. King's holiday was announced. An elderly White man, right on the very same sidewalk at this same news-sharing coffee place said, to all who could hear, "Can you believe they gave a national holiday to that nigger!?" I looked at him and walked away, pained. But today as I bought my *New York Times* from a gentleman on that very same corner, who was that old racist's same age but some twenty-five years later, he said, "I saved you the last *New York Times* I had. Have a good day, my brother." Obama is the right one at this time and what feels right about this one—born in 1961—is that the times out of which he was born makes him prepared for the challenges we face together. He is someone who was birthed with the hope promised out of the civil rights era, and who grew up on the beat of modern urban America, who studied in college while being able to see regime changes, and who came to professional maturity to see the latest troubling of our noble democracy.

To watch people gathered from places all around the world to celebrate his winning of the presidential race was emblematic of the global outcry for meaning and the quenching of the dry throats we've endured. Nineteen sixty-one is a very good year.

Many of us have to look at this "Obama presidency" as a revolution—this bright new change of consciousness—to recognize our immediate joy and to appreciate what it has meant and what it will mean.

In the movie *The Matrix*, which I love, Morpheus asks Neo: "Do you believe in fate?" to which Neo replies, "No." When asked "Why not?" Neo responds, "Because I don't like the idea that I'm not in control of my life." Morpheus: "I know exactly what you mean." He continues, "What you know, you can't explain, but you feel it. When you go to work, to church, when you pay your taxes . . . You can't explain it, like a splinter in your mind driving you mad. . . . It's the world that has been pulled over your eyes to blind you from the truth. . . . That you are a slave . . . born into a prison for your mind." Morpheus offers Neo two pills, and Neo takes the pill for truth.

Truth is a journey toward discovery into the past and beyond the moment of pride. My deeper self knows of recent days in which lies, greed, hypocrisy, and political tyranny contorted the identity of this country. But this moment allows all of us the chance to embrace the "campaign for hope." This opportunity will not completely right the wrongness of our complex history and society, but it may encourage us to make a conscious effort toward changing the community, finding a new, worthier truth. At one deep level,

President-elect Obama is a key to unlocking some of those doubts that may have imprisoned so many hearts, souls, and minds.

One of the great challenges and charges of the twenty-first century is guiding people in our society to maintain our humanity. How may we once again become considerate, compassionate, and civil in our exchanges? Where we have fallen short, it seems to me, is in the cultivation of being humane and maintaining this principle of identity and character. Our societal "workings" that cultivate this kind of reflective thinking are bulwarks against a culture seemed destined to uphold problematic values and identities that look, lock, and push us backward again. I'm excited about the possibilities now of making good—great, even—on the hope that we can work toward pushing us to spring forward again.

CHAPTER TEN

Reckonings and Recognitions (2009)

Real stories are the best songs. You see the scene, you write that narrative. . . . You have to go with your gut, you have to have a knack for hearing the pulse of the marketplace. . . . We had the pulse of the world and we took full advantage of the situation, we were involved with all aspects, we used the same musicians, so we created a chemistry in our sound.

—Kenneth Gamble, Leon Huff

How Do We Reckon with the Opening of 2009?

This is at once a season of great optimism and bright beginnings, yet mired in the reality of a chaotic cultural mess bequeathed to us from both corporate conspirators and our own blind complacency. With the close of 2008 we saw the worst of combined cultural disasters in our nation's memory: two U.S.-waged wars raged simultaneously; assaults between the Middle East and Israel flared up; India and Pakistan heightened their aggressions toward each other; terrorist attacks and kidnappings continued; contemporary African pirates plundered the high seas; a man dressed as "Satan" Clause shoots and kills ten people at a Christmas party; and Americans were hit with the reality of the collapse of our economy. Now steps in the first Black president, a young man with integrity and vision, a leader imbued with a prophetic fervor not seen in fifty years, who inherits from George W. Bush and his cronies the worst American cultural-social terrain in history. Now what does that tell you?

White corporate greed and thirst for power and control eats itself to its own system's ruin. Our legacy of slavery in White America, as the old folks would say, is "cleaning up after White folks' mess." And yet we are challenged, and he challenges us to have the audacity to hope again. We shall work, and we shall see the work begin.

Alvin Ailey Dance Company and Sweet Honey in the Rock

Another year begins with a trek down to New York to connect and make art, and set things in place that should define the year. This time down is no different. The ride is gorgeous, as this must be one of the best train rides in America. I have written about the passing through Rhode Island, Connecticut, through New York to Penn Station and emerging onto 8th Avenue and 32nd Street. To get there, the train rolls through small Eastern Seaboard towns, across rivers, along the ocean, and through tiny urban and suburban area landscapes, which tell all about the way people truly live as you pass through them elevated in the air, voyeuristically gazing. It is an inspiring ride that always causes a creative stir in me. I always write as I roll through. I am here now to see the ladies of Sweet Honey in the Rock perform with the Alvin Ailey Dance Company. Seeing this cultural institution is a first for me.

I am also to meet with the Sweet Honey ladies to collaborate on a commission from several American symphony orchestras. The ladies and I actually met at the symphony hall in Boston this past November for preliminary discussions, which took place two days before the historic winning of the Barack presidency. At the concert the ladies emphasized the importance of going to make "the right" vote count. This is emblematic of the new responsibility we feel. As artists, we have been handed a torch that never went away, but we have been blinded by the ignorance and greed of the corporate mechanisms that have defined our culture over the last fifteen or twenty years. Of course, the exuberance and commitment of youth—namely in hip-hop, progressive rock, grunge music, spoken word, and technology—helped mobilize the Obama sweep. But besides this, there has not been much of a cultural shift to counter the barrage of stupidity that permeates our cultural identities, as experienced in TV, film, and popular music. So this is a defining time that perhaps allows us to take a more serious critical look at where we are headed and to define our commitment to the future.

At any rate, this new symphony represents that sense of commitment. Commissioned by the Baltimore Symphony and partners (though this could end up in Detroit or Boston), the work will center on music, performance artistry, and poetry/songs which point toward uplifting these kinds of ideals.

The challenge for me is to create a new symphonic work that celebrates the artistry of Sweet Honey in the Rock, traverses political and social pleas, and makes the mark of great music that can be performed many times and long after we are gone.

That's the trick, really. People are fond of representative works in theory, but in practice, people love music that moves them from the inner core, over and over again. This inner core idea, the sense that we are made begging to be made whole from the insides first, that is what I am committed to explore in artistry. And that, it seems, is what the last years have pointed many of us toward in terms of representing culture. What kind of expression and identity are we committed to, are moved by? Or my classic question: What's the right note?

I had never seen Alvin Ailey's company before, so I was doubly excited. I could see the crowd gathered outside in the street in front of City Center, which I had never been to. The "usual suspects" gathered around the entrance to the theater. You have to know New York and you have to know the ballet crowd to know what an event like this means to the Black middle-class elites, and "followers of culture" who are classic. This crowd has a long history, and you see them in every major urban center, whether it's Detroit, Chicago, Atlanta, Cincinnati, Indianapolis, Minneapolis, Raleigh, or Durham. Mud cloth wraps, dreads, Black culturalists who read Toni Morrison, listen to NPR, and those, too, who just came from church, even on this Saturday evening. The place was culture electric eclectic.

I was pleasantly whistled at by a dear old friend, jazz vibraphonist and composer Cecilia Smith, who had also come to hear Sweet Honey and Alvin Ailey. Coincidentally, we were seated right next to each other. She asked in horror, "You mean you've never seen Alvin Ailey?!"

"No, I haven't. This is my first time," I said too loud and proud.

Everyone seated near all looked at me with that same, "Oh, you deprived soul." But all were welcoming, and when the lights went down, we were all caught in that delightful spray of joyful anticipation.

They opened with *Firebird* by Stravinsky. Simply striking, gorgeous. Not long into watching the Alvin Ailey Company, you are aware that this is not simply an ethnic dance art troupe; this is one the world's finest professional dance companies in increasingly rarer form, they say, each year, now fifty in years. I sank with joy at every move, swerve, leap, and stretch, feeling almost as if I longed to curve and fly, but knowing that we were there seated for a reason: Dance is not a dreamt gift; it's a gift of extreme work and skill. The other thing that occurred to me is how this is the foremost Black arts ensemble in the world, again, fifty years old. We don't have an orchestra—jazz orchestra even—with any longevity, soaked in such tradition, history, and culture. I never thought about it. Not an orchestra, not even a Black choir of mention has this record and mechanism: touring, training, education. The Alvin Ailey Company and school is an institution. As children, we all have seen the pictures of Judith Jamison in that swirling white flowing gown, gracefully pirouetting through the air, those strong beautiful legs, and to feel that was tremendous. She was there, projecting her vision and Alvin's lasting dream into the bodies of those lovely young dancers.

They performed "Go in Grace" with the ladies, who composed and sang. Sweet Honey, without a doubt, is one of the premier performing ensembles in the world, and again a staple of our rich African American music cultural heritage. To see the performers interact with song, movement, and narrative—woooow. They sounded incredible. As I watched and listened, I began to envision ways in which our new piece could work with an orchestra.

Their signature work that night, of course, was the repertoire classic, *Revelations* (1960). I have seen sections, heard portions, and used in my teaching excerpts of that opening posture of the company—bent, hands raising to extend to bodies and arches, palms extending forward and swaying to "I've been 'buked and I've been scorned." And what a glimpse into the human experience in movement that is recognized and loved by everyone. Just as we hear Beethoven's *5th*, or Ellington's "A Train," *Revelations* is not only their classic; it is a dance classic and a Black art classic that once you have seen it, like the many seated around me, you expect this as standard repertoire. The woman next to me went on and on about how many times over the years she had seen the work. She recalled all the Black church members—dressed in those Sunday church lady hats that Black women wear—who would come out to hear the work, after church, and how during the performances the congregations would sing and hum along with the spirituals Ailey used the music to his classic masterpiece. I was motionless, stung by the grandeur and the grace of this great American dance company. And I saw Black too. I felt Black as I felt and saw greatness.

That is what I mean by representing culture—the idea that even the presence, mention, and the image of artistic expression engenders and excites within us a chord of meaning that cannot be bought; it is a magnanimity that preserves and inspires the best within us. This is what Alvin Ailey represents, and it was an indescribable resonance within me that now colors my memory of them.

I joined Ysaye, Cecilia, and the other ladies backstage. Several of us went to Sippys across the street after the performance. The next morning I got up and made notes about our previous meeting. On that occasion, we talked and listened to music for two hours—mine first, followed by works each lady loved. Completely artists in sharing, we dreamed of the new piece. We spoke of cultural, artistic, philosophical, and historical commitments and values, how music resonates, what it means, and how we "hear." I left having started what we hoped would be a completely rich, revealing, and rewarding collaboration.

Two thousand nine marks a time of moving closer toward clarity and putting specific pieces in place that will define my commitment. I believe this symphony, to be performed in 2011 or 2012, is one such manifestation.

The Jazz Urbane

The deaths of mom Banfield and big brother Duey in 2008 leave me numb and noteless in many ways. The Banfield family unit is now diminished significantly, and this really calls upon some inner reordering in profound ways. Your seeding in the world, your soil, is the place through which your roots are planted then expand and your work flowers. So what happens when the closest roots—a mother and brother—can no longer be tilled? You can't suffocate and die too. You must repot, redirect in some ways. I guess I'm trying to smooth over the bruised parts of my heart which ache from these losses by still believing that things can be better in a world without your mother there with you. She believed so much in what I believe in. I can hear her voice, see her finger pointing, share her convictions. I remember her scents, recall the wisdom of her stories, still cringe at her critiques and challenges, and most of all—even though she is gone—still burn inside with the same convictions she had about "putting it out there."

Artists are born with a creative desire to express and motivated by the responses we get from the many who hear, see, and feel those expressions. We live to be heard, as vain as that sounds. Each day, our purpose is recalibrated and retuned, as we make melodies, hum tunes, keep beats, or write the songs that keep the world singing. As corny as that sounds, it is really what we live to do.

I head into New York to find connections, start projects, shape the year ahead. There are ten areas (label, publishing, management/booking, concert series, scholarship/books, education, commission/residencies, radio/media, columns/publication, my college appointment) I have worked out that are helping to spring forward.

Grounded in all of this is an overriding idea I call "Jazz Urbane." I have been musing about this new identity in musical artistry, one to fill the current spiritual and cultural vacuum. With my connections and my commitment, I have been mobilizing everything to move Jazz Urbane forward. In short, this new musical sensibility captures the progressive new age culture but is sustained by old-school ideas of great music artistry, creating a market for both. A real musical artists' movement with a kind of "Harlem Renaissance" call and artistic celebration that traverses traditional lines and mixes music with media: old school meets Internet, but stays committed to giving people music that is not grounded in blind commercialism. In terms of entrepreneurial configurations, artists have the websites, Internet connections, but public radio is also of service. Education is our best investment, and the pedagogical ideology of caring for the inner soul. I also believe we have to make music in community. In other words, people need a place to hear and be in live music artistry.

All the great movements—punk at CBGBs in New York; early hip-hop in Brooklyn; grunge in Seattle; flower power in Haight-Ashbury; Motown churches, barber shops, and record stores; Minton's home for progressive bebop jams; and Harlem as a capital for Black and large progressive Black arts and identity—were grounded in this way. These were "place and people movements" and they were engineered primarily by artists' interests. While sometimes corrupted by outsiders, nonetheless these were important movements that inspired us by their lasting output.

My overt attempt to collectively engage in this way is in the creation of my own label called "The Jazz Urbane"—a "pseudo" subsidiary relationship with the label that has carried my work since 1995. Second, I have initiated two artists' music series (since Patrick's Cabaret and the Dakota in Minneapolis), the most recent in Boston: Berklee at Bob's (2006) and the Jazz Artist Series at Beehive in Boston (2006–2008). You must have a venue for people to come and hear the music. I have also tried to engage public radio with my shows *Essays of Note* and *Landscapes in Color* in the Twin Cities.

The other area is music publishing. I galvanized some business partners to better focus my company, BMagic Music, to better mechanize all these interests with the expectation that we could create some music, reach some people, and find sharing opportunities among artists and thinkers to engage our current culture in these various ways. I call this the Jazz Urbane, and liken this to the "manifesto" states: "Not really a new movement, just a new configuration of artists. The Jazz Urbane represents a rise with a frustration with "nonmusical culture" in the mainstream coupled with a progressive cultural, creative environment whose interests are sophisticated and that demand a difference.

I am also actively engaged in print media. With the help of *DownBeat* editor Jason Koransky, I have initiated a monthly column entitled "The J Word," which examines the culture of jazz through conversations I am having with leading artists. I also continue to work with Scarecrow Press as both author and series editor. My series, African American Cultural Theory and Heritage, examines contemporary living, expressions, and cultural critique of the Black experience.

These efforts sync with a notion that I have been expounding: Sophisticated and creative music—urbane, hip, noncategorical—can grow from cultural urban places and can thrive because they are produced by progressive and edgy musicians who are tapped into not only their music but also closely connected with creative music movements in other cities (Boston, New York, Seattle, Los Angeles, Chicago, etc.). These movements flower from the same urban excitement and creative commitment of musicians of all types (jazz, bebop, Mbase, hip-hop, techno, and now Jazz Urbane). It makes sense to capture this "swarm" of creative energy and talent and channel it into a musical "products" line. Such "products" are independently produced performances, radio broadcasts, and recordings, which specialize in the music acts exclusively. These acts could be developed and nurtured by a local music concert "series" that occur in regular venues. By recording these concerts and generating a campaign focused exclusively on these series—with local and national nightly/weekly radio broadcasts—we can promote a new "sound/art movement" and foster advocacy for new, creative music.

∽

Reflections

March 7

All is well as 2009 comes in with a swell. The music is moving, even as the economy is failing. Hope is alive, but so is the monkey of economic crisis that hangs on our backs. The news is filled with job losses, unemployment, declining stocks, closing businesses, and home foreclosures. Our culture is crumbling and from those crumbs a new batch of pies must be harvested and baked, because greed and irresponsible "me-ness" can no longer rule. It's like living in a "war zone" of culture and watching the generals in charge walk backward. Obama and his team seem to be working, but they must run fast up a greasy slide created by the Bush administration and the repressive Republicans who empowered the irresponsible.

Creatively, I don't know how we are to respond. I often speak of writing the "right notes," but even our best of those are thrown against a wall with no reverb—largely because the industry has changed and fallen, too. The once strong and forceful recording/entertainment industry has in recent years has become irresponsible, too. Now, record sales are down, and companies are closing up shop. We could hope this would result in less trash and greater investment in meaningful music—but we haven't seen it, in any significant way. There are still some very talented people and projects being released, but none of them represent new trends or movements yet.

I worked hard on the recording of my "Jazz Urbane" project. I'm still focused on the idea of bridging the divide between older and younger generations of musicians to create patterns of artistry that mean something. This concept is an attempt, as *Essence* magazine campaign purported, to "take the music back."

I'm feeling good about the potential to engage popular music, not so much jazz, as a potential "way in"—to share and make a case for music that moves people in some different directions. Even in a dismal, tortured world, people are still moved by the music. This movement can come from an eighteen-year-old or a fifty-six-year-old, and it will affect a retiree or a teenager discovering herself—doesn't matter. Songs and great music will never go out of being relevant, lifting, or inspiring. Despite the winds of a downturned economy, I teach, totally committed to making art. The push to stay creative continues on!

June 5

Much has happened, much is happening, and more will happen as we move forward. New York today was a blast. I had traveled there for one reason: to take a twenty-first stab at finding a manager. I met with manager/entrepreneur Charles Carlini. After more than fifteen years, beyond the times with Ramon Hervey in L.A., I found a guy, connected, and like me, a maverick sensibility, who sees me in himself. He understands. And he has clarity. I cannot describe how essential collaborations are in business, too. It is impossible to be in music and be out of business. But to find in this maze of music madness someone to steer you and stay with you is difficult. I am not a formula artist and my interests broaden—even as my waistline widens, my small bald spot spreads noticeably, and I want to fall asleep earlier. But I am still looking to turn my youthful wishes into realities.

I met Charles in the Time Warner Tower—58th and 8th Avenue—at the Bouchon. I had arrived by train from Boston about an hour before our appointed time. It was cold and rainy, but New York felt no less effective and lively, just sprayed with many umbrellas moving up and down and in and out over one another. I sat at a table which faced Central Park and ordered some tea. I took some time to go over my notes before Charles arrived. In researching him, I discovered we had several things in common. Besides being a guitarist, he studied philosophy because he felt as a musician he wanted to see more in the arts. His business ventures have brought him to a publishing philosophy.

After speaking with a potential manager, three things should stick out: (1) They know your work and have ideas for it; (2) They ask, "So what are we looking at now?"; and (3) They say, "I have an idea for us." When you finish your conversation, they say, "I'll call you in a few days." I have heard all of those phrases, in part or whole, before, and they can be misleading. I don't want to be too optimistic, but my meeting with Carlini felt both timely and really good. The search for the right manager can be a brutal journey of rejections, misfires, and misunderstandings about what you do—which may mean that no one will care *what* you do, and what you do can't sell. In this industry, you cannot get seen without someone bringing you in from the outside, with their insider's view of the marketplace. And reaching insiders takes an enormous amount of time, energy, and focus. Time equals money, and art has to make money to be well. After twenty-plus years experience, I know I have something to bring to the table, with a particular spin of my own, so we'll see. But I'm no longer hungry for this. Hunger works for the young. When you are older, being satisfied with who you are and assured that what you have done matters and is what really counts.

On Wednesday I brought Amiri in to help me look through the Pat Patrick materials, and to meet with his son, Massachusetts Governor Deval Patrick. Deval had asked Krystal and me to sort and catalogue his father's archives, which had been found in a storage bin, and the materials had been thrown in the trash several times. What we got from Pat Patrick, perhaps orchestrated from the grave, was a fantastic archive that he put together. He was Amiri Baraka's best friend. And so here is a story, a historical partnership, and a linkage to our great traditions that I cannot ignore history's call to help bring to light. So, I am hanging out for the past two days with the greatest thinker of our times for Black arts and its legacy, definition, and meaning. Amiri writes the book then sings into our ears; it's how we have defined our names as Black in music actually.

I get mentored by the great griot. And, as it turns out, through some discussion, a moment rising, the Q, Quincy Jones, invited me through our president, Roger Brown and David Baker, to co-chair for his foundation—a national effort to compile a curriculum on jazz education.

So tomorrow, I'm to get a call from Quincy Jones. Wow. Africana Center has now been officially planned, put in blueprint, and is being built. This

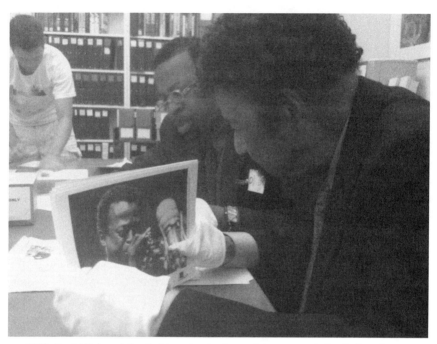

With David Baker at the Smithsonian Institute, doing research for Quincy Jones.

alone would make this move legitimate, long lasting, and laudable. My dean walked me through with the architect. I have built programs, and more programs, but never have I been involved in cementing a center. This is a great thing for our school and for these efforts. If nothing else at Berklee I can claim I—with my chair, Camille, and dean—put this in place. Very significant and exciting. Release of *Spring Forward*. The new record launched and is out there being added to some three hundred stations internationally. For the first time, I have been focused on releasing my music in a specific market. New for me.

June 9

On Saturday I had a conference call with Quincy Jones, and he invited me back to New York to have dinner with him. Now, let me start right here. I have worked all these years and one of my ultimate goals was to be just like Quincy Jones. And, while we have met before, never did he call me and invite me out to dinner. So, I guess it is safe to say, this is on another level. I have to ask, "What does this mean at forty-eight years old to meet on a mountaintop in your life your hero?" It's pretty nice. In some discussion over the last several months, my boss and mentor, David Baker, conferred that I should be a part of the national team Quincy is pulling together to write a new curriculum on American music—one he feels every child in America should have to have learn from. With the Obama presidency and a real sense of "we can now do," there will be rises in new ideas, approaches, and initiatives for many years to come. Innovators like Amiri Baraka, Billy Taylor, David Baker, Bernice Johnson Reagon, Quincy, T. J. (I mean it goes on and on) are now in their late seventies and eighties so it's my group's time to take the proper cues and clues and do the next right things. The current group, those a decade under me, isn't asking the right questions, nor pushing the right buttons for the right reason. They certainly have the pulse going, the time is theirs, but I believe the bridge group will be helpful. We are the last group to hold some pre-technology information values. Really.

My best friend Stephen Newby just called and reminded me of what time this is. It's our time to take the mantle, and much of my own work was tugging with destiny's call to be "blessed" by Quincy. It's my destiny, my calling, and time to, if nothing else, be able to hear from him, share with him my ideas, and be instructed how to think about what to do next.

The tie with Amiri Baraka, whom I'll also see tonight at another function, is exactly the same downbeat. Amiri Baraka was the first writer who seized my imagination, caught and kept my attention on what it was to speak about

Quincy Jones, Billy Taylor, and the author in New York, 2009.

Black music and culture. I am working on a project with him that will not only better define me, it will better ensure that I will do the right thing in his mighty footsteps to continue one more voice singing forward about the heritage, hills, and heroes of Black artistic culture.

It's raining as we pull out of the train station of Providence, Rhode Island. And I think of the idea of "springing forward," what that could be. The new record released last week internationally, adds new stations every day. That record is emblematic of a new moment for me symbolizing a new musician stepping forth, in new tones, proclaiming musically some new setting for not unique ideas, but a new call perhaps, to the humanity of our music. What will the music and the times and the new days ask us to value and believe in, as Baraka asks so wonderfully?

June 23

Letter to Dr. Ysaye Barnwell

Dear Ysaye,

So great to hang with you last night at Eatonville. Zora would be proud of 14th N.W. Coming into D.C. is always for me a fascinating journey. I think for "us outsiders" who visit, coming to D.C. is kind of like falling into a cultural-historic sandbox with four corners to dig through. On the one hand, there is the cultural-historic beauty and meaning of the city; on the other is Black people and their rich legacies; then there is the power of the contemporary cultural-politic and where it is and how the city resonates and is functioning on any given day as the capital. Then there is the global feeling of wondering what is the meaning of your place in the world? I mean, the danger here is of course like being in Rome. And Rome in its meaning is always about the potential rise or fall of modernity, and your mind dials that up, too. What does it mean to be in Rome, and when—or if—we are burning as we speak?

On the ride into Georgetown I was in the van with a woman who noticed that I was Black. She took this as an immediate invitation to share with me all the Black events I should go and see while I was in town. And that I should see the new photo exhibit that documents "extraordinary images we never see" of "the African Americans and their culture." While I am sure she thought her sharing was customary when you run into someone Black and that this chance was what I "needed" to be told, she had all great intentions and I listened appreciatively and patiently and pretended to be marveled at the fact that Black people actually had places where "they would go to swim."

Thinking about a recent trip to Oak Bluffs on Martha's Vineyard, I smiled. At any rate, this proud Washingtonian actually got me thinking about the tremendous value of cultural representation and documentation in D.C. before we had even gotten together for our meal.

So last night going to Eatonville and Busboys and Poets on 14th NW, wow! Again, only in D.C.: a restaurant designed and "arted" purposely to celebrate the idea of the range and depth of "Black people history," and the two restaurants—one for Langston, one for Zora—right across the street from each other. I couldn't believe the palpable depth of our legacy that was well represented in the murals, paintings, decorum, and, of course, the Black people in there, just eating. Forget about what was hanging on the walls! Oh my God. D.C. resonates in the neighborhoods with our beautiful, fully intelligent, and rich Blackness. The beauty and depth of all these sistas who greeted, seated, and sweeted us with the food, meaning, and relevance of the place. As we sat on "Zora's porch" I thought I had stepped back into all the places our grand memories of our heritage take us to, even living in a time where many of us never get to visit that place again. Sitting with you at Eatonville took me there. I had to have the catfish, grits, and greens! This brother of ours, Andy Shallal, what a beautiful thing he has created and documented in art, food and cuisine, culture, books, and the literary and functional framing of these the venues for music, reading, performance, and cultural ritual. Thank you so much for buying me *The 5th Inning* by E. Ethelbert Miller. To think he was in there that day doing a book signing! So funny, I am finishing a kind of memoir myself, called *Representing Culture*, and it too examines my own artist-reckoning with this time in our life and its meanings. Miller has a line in his new memoir that reads, "When a person becomes fifty or approaches the years that follow, his story is almost over. He can turn around and see the narrative he created." I don't think approaching fifty and these years is an "almost over" reflection at all. As a matter of fact, as we shared last night, we are at a critical time when there is a great opportunity to be at a new beginning yet again. That is exciting and full of promise.

So now, my dear friend, that you and the ladies in Sweet Honey did the first concert for the first lady at the White House was enough. Now you tell me you perform for President Barack! I can't imagine what you must have been feeling knowing he was feeling and breathing and enjoying the inhale of your notes. Amazing. Proud of you all!

I saw the website on your family archives, wow. This will be a great book. The documentation of moving, migrating, and the replacement of that meaning and it coming up—music that connects and then that is meant to cement our culture, is what you represent growing out of that. Your mom and dad and family's hopes are clearly being heard in the songs you teach and sing us and make us remember. We come better to see ourselves. What a song-story you have to make us breathe in. Wanting memories. I was chilled, too, by our own realization that those memories—even the want and reflection of what a memory brings—is lost to this generation. It's as if today there is another world we have fallen down into, a crusty deep and dark chasm that we are all scratching and crawling to get out of, back up to the surface where the light is, where the air is. But we are choked trying to get back up. And is it for naught, really? You can never say with young people, whether they are lost or it is lost. But you can certainly say if we don't do something really fast, it will be lost.

Again, though I am lifted by what you said, that we must make the songs that teach and reach, we too have to grab hold of the throat of this suffocated culture and breathe new air into its collapsed lungs.

This is our challenge.

Your story, "And they saw us . . ." is great. What a story! The idea that you could know that for the first time in history all those Black staff who represent generations of butlers—like Ellington's dad, and cooks, gardeners, workers—were lined up to receive the new president into the White House, and on that day, the Black staff were seen and loved for who they were and who and what their breaths represented—how Barack and Michelle, "saw us, knew we were there." Wow, Dr. Barnwell, you must, *must* write that moment. You must sing about it. You have to sing that story.

I will certainly speak to George Duke this weekend about your inquiry of him producing the next Sweet Honey project. You are right, this generation needs to understand that the new songs have to celebrate all they want to be and who they are, but they too must—like so many of us and before us—dismantle the cultural struggles that suffocate Black people, especially the greed of market forces that have kept the folks blinded and believing they are being and seeing themselves, this broken picture. "Nana's mirrors" (from the title of a Ysaye Barnwell song, "No Mirrors in My Nana's House") were meant to reflect a beautiful picture of the world and our identity we were to be.

Perhaps our new symphony with Sweet Honey could talk about doing that: how we can break the broken mirrors and recast the images and narratives that we must now step into, look into, and reflect forward where we need to be moving, and create the celebrations, the beauty and breadth of those reflections. We need the songs, Ysaye.

Love you,

See you soon.

June 25 and 26

Michael dies!

No one in my group could imagine what this day would be or what it would feel like when Michael Jackson died. I was expecting a visit from Jesse Taitt, a young pianist whom I have been mentoring. He had come over and was waiting for me on our back porch. When I got there he said, "Michael Jackson died." I opened the door, rushing in to get to the TV. Even on CNN, they were reporting only that he had been taken to the hospital, but even then, he was already dead. When the official word came, so came the shock, the overwhelming disbelief. How could this happen? First, you think what a gift in our world. Then you think: How will you really now be living in a commercial world without, despite his zaniness, without this principal icon-artist who defines popular culture? Then it hit me again as his music was played—that marvelous voice—how much of our identity was wrapped in and around Michael Jackson. The calls, e-mails, and texts I was getting were off the hook. It was as if the world had shaken and changed—especially the musicians of my group, who were devastated. Everybody was calling to share their disbelief: "Can you believe it, did you hear, Michael Jackson died?"

I called Amiri Baraka, the master griot who I often ask about such critical cultural events. "Hey Amiri, Michael Jackson died. What do we do?" He just said: "You move on. That's why Barack is here. Michael is with the past, you are in the now. So it's cool, just move on. I gotta run. My granddaughter is graduating." His granddaughter couldn't have known Michael Jackson like I did. And though Amiri couldn't relate to how I felt about Michael, he knew what it felt like to hear about the too early deaths of Charlie Parker and Eric Dolphy, of John Coltrane and Charles Mingus.

Krystal and I threw together an impromptu gathering, inviting over a few we thought who needed company to cope with this loss. We had barbeque, smoked salmon, burgers, and potato salad, and we played Michael's music really, really loud and cried. "Beat It," "Maybe Tomorrow," "Mama's Pearl," "Billie Jean," "Wanna Be Starting Something," "Don't Stop 'Til You Get Enough." All that great sounding music and we couldn't still get enough. Michael Jackson's music has the best sound. I can't explain it, but those Quincy productions just pumped and jumped out hugely. They were, as the kids say, "Way phat." You can never get enough of Michael, because he is us, and you can't stop being, so we need him to be. Now he doesn't live anymore. I feel old now, like when my mother missed Dinah Washington.

It didn't stop hitting me. I was preparing to leave for L.A., and put on more of his music. I just wanted to cry a tear with each song phrase, every note when I heard that voice. It was one of a kind and, again, culturally defining. When an artist dies, that sound in the world cannot be reproduced. If you can imagine a whole tone set that won't ring anymore—that's what it's like now. Michael Jackson was the shining image of art, popularity, stardom, and music for us. *American Idol?* Please! He invented the idea. I danced his Jackson 5 steps as a child, sang his songs as I, too, had a high "Michael Jackson voice" at age twelve. So, no it wasn't just Jimi Hendrix, but Michael Jackson who was my model of artistry as a performer, as a kid who grew up, almost alongside of him. All those songs from the 1970s, 1980s, 1990s—that's more than thirty years of music! In this sense, he is like Miles Davis, Duke Ellington, and Stevie Wonder: innovation, artistry, presence, and sound, but also, my God, the movement. These are the artistic attributes that help define the magnitude and depth of his work. He was the cultural icon that marked the making of my generation's identity. Besides trying to figure out what it feels like to live in your generation without the defining presence that symbolized your youth, what I am dealing with now is the meaning of such a loss in musical terms. There was not a more impassioned, craft-driven, and grounded performing entity before our eyes. Performance was perfection made in him. Without a live model of that, I guess you can only hope that new voices will come to make the music breathe with life again the way he did. That hadn't happened yet, and perhaps won't ever again. So where does this loss leave us?

A moment after reading the *Boston Globe* the next day, I did consider how bizarre his other life track was. The monkey, the chamber, the bones, the little boys over, the frightening "monster mask," the baby over the rails, the children born with various White parent partners, the fairy tale home called Neverland. But none of it obliterates the pride I feel when thinking about his work. And none of this takes the sting of sadness in my heart when I admit how much I miss his being here with us.

Michael Jackson's meaning is monumental, mountainous, and moving at so many levels.

We lost our commercial popular beat that made us feel young in culture. It must be like losing Marilyn Monroe or Elvis or Tupac, but even ten times more, because he was twenty times that large in culture, for fifty times more people, one hundred times more souls around the globe.

I'm flying across the country to Los Angeles, which was his home. Those who knew him also ask, "How did this happen?" I wondered if they were there as he was slipping. There was Quincy and Liza, Smokey and Madonna, Diana Ross and Liz Taylor, those who loved him. They were all there on TV.

We shall never know. Only his doctors know for sure whether he wrote the prescriptions for his own death. I go to play my new music for people in L.A. and I wonder: How will my music be heard against that great silence and hole in our popular culture resonance and meaning?

Michael, I miss you. Thank you, man!

June 27

I arrived at George Duke's home in Hollywood about an hour before I was to see him. This must be the fifth or so visit over the last ten years to the master's home and studio. But this time I arrived with a different mission.

This time, for the first time in my life, I came to play my music to his ear—to get instructions—blessings as it were—and he knew I was coming with my music.

Wow. George Duke must be one of the most loving, bighearted, and gracious musicians anyone can name. His gift is so deep and you can hear laughter and love in his music, and really in his playing. He and Mrs. Duke, Corinne, share an office space, both desks facing out toward the studio. After all kinds of pleasantries and catching up about Patrice, Terri Lynn Carrington, Billy Childs, my Boston crew, George took the disc from me and sat to listen. And Corinne sat there, too.

While we also discussed all kinds of topics—Michael Jackson's death, the myriad of distractions young people face, the sad state of today's music industry culture, and the disappearance of guitars in popular music, which I very much appreciated—this was a listening session for musicians. The disc of the new Jazz Urbane demo is well over an hour of music. George and Corinne listened and commented through the whole thing. Rare! They loved it, they got it, and they "blessed" it.

You can't know how it feels to meet the master on his turf—to sit there and discuss with George Duke a phrase, a groove, a lyric meaning, harmonies, changes that a soloist didn't "hear" or a singer "missed," a form, a line, counterpoint and lyric interpretation, and production values.

You can't know what it means to have George Duke hear a lick of your music and say, "That's funky." Now he invented the "Duke-ey funk" in jazz, so: Wow!

Time with George Duke was grand. I left there floating and understanding what I needed to do to step out here with my latest projects. It's got to be "funky"!

July 3–5

Martha's Vineyard, Oaks Bluff, 3:19 p.m. This is a lovely view of the world from the fourth floor balcony of the Wesley Hotel. This vintage hotel overlooks one of the marinas and bays off the ocean, and it's breathtaking. Views like these inspire and lift you, because it's a still life of the world. I can see the boats close up and far off in the distance, hear the medium-sized dogs with low voices barking from beneath, see couples sitting down in the galleys of their small crafts having coffee on the sea, the lovely homes nestled warmly along the shores surrounded in water and green. There was even a Spike Lee and wife sighting as Krystal brushed against them, rubbing shoulders as they passed in the crowd, heads turning, they, too, just taking in the Martha's Vineyard voyage. I have given into the romanticism and privilege of something like this, the entitlement of it all to sit in a place like this to rest, relax, think, and be away. Being away is something you pay for. Kind of ridiculous when you think about it. Being away is free, and the price is simply a thought to go away in your mind. But this is a different going away, it's the kind of thing only the adult, or privileged Whites would say and talk about in the movies. Now here I sit. I am looking up and down the main street at the boats, cars on the drag, people walking, the breeze blowing. This is life, I must admit. And I like it.

July 20

I returned from Los Angeles yesterday morning. Los Angeles this time was different. Largely because I'm older and I made specific visits with people who knew why I was there and were ready for my arrival. In the past fifteen to twenty years, the L.A. visits were always "introductory" ones: "Here is this young musician you may be interested in." Now it's: "Here's the older guy you may have heard of." The contacts were terrific and I made some major inroads. And the visits with friends were richer, like with Patrice Rushen and Billy Childs.

This view of the world is one of promise, for continuing the hope and idea of change, to meet the challenges of our cloudy-filled cultural climate. We are still in one war we have no business being in, fighting a possessed and persuasive enemy with many sides and faces and who now lives in many foreign places. Two crazy leaders in Korea and Iran are playing with fire, testing dangerous missiles as the world looks on in disbelief. And on this side of the world, we have a new president who was delivered on a theme of change. Okay, good start, but a rocky road ahead. Yesterday we received the worst reports yet on unemployment, even though on this island of fun, people don't seem stressed. I mean this is Martha's Vineyard, right? Which says something about the view from a side of privilege. You see the wounds in the world and you feel them, too, but you're behind glass or you're removed, so you don't feel the cold, sinister chill outside the window. Or maybe if it's all veiled, you can can't see it clearly either, which allows you to remain calm. But your friend down there on the street, you can see him coming and you see he's bundled up with a scarf and boots and is soaked by the falling rain. That's what it feels like: The rain is falling, the clouds are overhead, you know the weather is bad, and you're hoping the sun will come out soon.

We enjoyed seeing that political blunder called Sarah Palin, as it went down yesterday—a joke really—and she resigned from being governor of "the great state of Alaska." A surreal surprise. But she signed a multimillion dollar book deal which she won't step down from. And now we hear that Michael Jackson wished and planned a death like Elvis's. He got it and does that make us sadder now? Are we lamenting the meaning of Michael Jackson? His death is a sad symptom of living in a world you gained privilege to be in but came in through the back door and ended up going out again the wrong way. So those of us still in the room have to figure out how to live in the house and walk out as straight as possible when it's our time to leave the room. I know I'll have to leave the room some day, and I know not to exit the same way Michael did. The drug revelations to us are not surprising, alarming and sad as it is. Yet this cannot be the representation of all we have come here to be. We can't accept that. No way.

I spent two hours with Alan Kay, a recognized giant in the creation of a particular view of the world, of new horizons—and one of the pioneering inventors of the modern day laptop. So appropriately, I type on this electronic box with keys on my lap, as I look past the balcony at the ocean. Our conversation reverberated in me a philosophical frame I had held on to for some time, but echoes again now: We have to be invested in new views of the world. We have to pass on to each other and young people that it's not over and we have to create better spaces for ourselves and others. We can change the world because we're capable of transforming the conditions of the rooms we will be living in. Right now, I really believe in that.

August 5

I spent the past weekend in Bloomington, Indiana, with David Baker, another mentor, at his home. We are beginning the research for our book for Quincy Jones. It was great to be with David, going over our notes, looking

Dr. Billy Taylor gives me advice on voicings in Minneapolis, 2002.

through materials, getting our plan together. I also interviewed David about his life, about his philosophy, about being David Baker. And then I headed into New York again for Quincy to meet with Larry Rosen, famed producer and cofounder of GRP Records. He has created a fantastic film on American popular music, and we will use his film as a resource linking it to the Q curriculum guide.

I received a note from an old neighbor who was delighted to see me featured in the September issue of *DownBeat* magazine, along with a glowing review from Billy Taylor. It was quite a warming note. I didn't know I would be the focus of a feature, so it's that kind of thing that says, you are doing all right in the world; that moment of clarity can arrive if you can't see around the corner—when the fog surrounding you, even before you wake and notice, clears. That's what I'm moving toward as I approach fifty, I guess: clarity and clam.

Beer Summit: A President, a Police Officer, and a Black Professor Holding Down the Gates at Home and Who Be Acting "Mo" Stupidly?

I received a note from the chair of my department about an article first reported in the *Boston Globe*: "This was in the *Chronicle of Higher Ed* today. How horrible. I guess Boston Police still have a ways to go. Have you talked to Professor Gates? Best, Camille."

I couldn't believe what I read. Police had arrested a man for allegedly breaking into the Cambridge, Massachusetts, home of Harvard University Professor Henry Louis Gates. The man arrested? Henry Louis Gates himself. At first I felt sad, then I giggled to myself, not at the expense of our dear big brother, but at the absurdity of life. Our leading Black thinker, the head of the W. E. B. Du Bois Institute for African and African American Research, arrested in his own home for breaking in? It sounds like a script from MTV's *Punk'd*. But this was not scripted, not even a prank. It was for real. And it grew worse.

Let's recap and look at the cast of characters:

A Black Harvard professor of the civil rights age gets arrested in his own home, mistaken as a robber. He calls this an affront to "all people of color and poor people everywhere in the world."

A White cop who arrested the professor claims he was doing his duty and remarks that he didn't know Gates was "that educated."

The president, directing his comments to the entire Cambridge police, calls the arrest "acting stupidly," yet did he consider that inviting the professor and the cop to the White House for a beer might be considered by some not to be a good thing?

A Black Harvard law professor chimes in, claiming to be a champion of Black people and poor people whose experiences are everyday examples of what Gates went through. Right. They go through what he goes through every day.

The neighbor, a distressed White woman who made the original 9-1-1 call, then calls a national press conference and cries, "I'm not a racist. My parents brought me up to respect all people. . . . They are all just like us. . . . We were taught tolerance in our home."

Then a Boston policeman in American White backlash fashion sends a nasty racist e-mail to the *Boston Globe* calling the snooty Black professor something a bit more direct than the "n" word. After getting suspended, he goes on CNN and national press saying his comments that Gates was a "banana-eating jungle monkey" were just an example of his civil rights to express his opinion." The Boston mayor calls the policeman a "cancer to the city."

Next? A Black female police enforcement official gets on national television and says she supports her White cop colleagues, denounces the president, and says that as a Black woman she won't vote for the president again.

Let's see, any more characters here to note? Oh yes, in the same week, in the streets of Paris, Texas—what an oxymoron—White supremacists and skinheads engage in a war of words with the "New Black Panthers"—again an oxymoron—who have come over from Dallas.

Lastly, a Black policeman sends a letter to the president. He wants Obama to know he did not deserve to be called an "Uncle Tom" by Black America because he supported his White colleague. The officer charges that Professor Gates needed to be more responsible, that his reaction was overblown, and Gates too should be expected to answer for his behavior.

And how to resolve this name calling, blaming, and shaming? Alcohol.

So, a TV moment of the week follows for the world to watch: A beer summit at the White House garden table. A president, a policeman, and a professor chug some Miller Lites and discuss the experiences of real racial tensions that exist in American culture. What drama! And now the national polls are asking who acted more stupidly: Gates, Officer Crowley, or President Obama?!

Nothing like a few beers at the end of the day to derail a national controversy of race relations. Some say this was not a moment to waste, that it provided a "teachable moment," that the "beer summit" should have and could have prompted community forums. But for many, beer is something you drink when you want to forget something—not when you want to confront it and commit yourself to changing things for the better.

This was an American media tale that spun completely out of control: pure pop culture drama starring a police officer, a professor, and the leader of the free world. Professor Gates not only becomes the "post–racial age poster child" for police brutality against Blacks, but all people of color and, oh, the poor and wretched of the earth. He also gets death threats and has to change his e-mail address. Living in America!

Racial, cultural, and class tensions will never go away. It's American and it's human. But what people and the media do in these instances is fraught with human stupidity. Because the American way is to grab five minutes of fame and attention and squeeze that five minutes for cash.

The accomplishments and meaning of Henry Louis Gates for all he has done and contributed to and for us was diverted from a serious path. Gates's painful and undeserved moment of embarrassment was completely unfortunate, but it does not represent the real plight of everyday Black citizens. So instead of taking these important issues seriously or recognizing the significance of Dr. Gates's work, people will now remember him as the Black professor who got arrested in his own home by a White Cambridge policeman, and how the two of them drank a few beers with the president as they talked about race in America. What a legacy!

Great Ones Passing: Horace Boyer, George Russell, Hale Smith

Three of our greats leave us in a row. The great gospel music historian and mentor to many of us, Horace Boyer, passed July 21, then George Russell a few days later, and now another great, Hale Smith. All three of these great Black musical giants were mentors, teachers, and friends who I could call upon, especially Horace and Hale, before both were silenced with illness and then death.

Horace Boyer (1935–2009)

Horace gave me the final blessings and challenges on my new book, *Cultural Codes*, in an e-mail exchange we had:

11/3/08 12:55 PM, William Banfield wrote:

Hi Horace.

How are you all today?

Thank you for this, it's going in to my final edits.

Stephen [Newby] on his way in April, about the 16–19th or so, with his sixty-five-voice choir. I hope you are resting well, and enjoying your new year. All is well here, I hope you will consider coming down and being here with us and Stephen in April, he's bringing too his wife and little one!

I pray the best for you and Mrs. Boyer.

You are our treasure.

Best, B

On Nov 6, 2008, at 9:35 PM, William Banfield wrote:

Hi Horace.

How are you?

I was with the ladies in Sweet Honey yesterday, and they were thrilled to have seen you. This week I'm teaching Gospel Music Culture. Horace, I was wondering, this is a brief overview from my new book. What do you think, does it pass?

Much Love, B

On Nov 6, 2008, at 9:35 PM, Horace Boyer wrote:

Bill -

Thanks for letting me see your chapter on gospel—it's really quite good. It is clear that it is written from the prospective one who has seen (and incorporates) the entire gamut of the field, and written with a kind of present day rhetoric. I think that is important because you approach it without the prejudice of earlier writers for whom gospel came to them from something that was shameful, dark and barely deserving its place in the canon. At 73 years of age I can appreciate this because I remember its "laughable" position in the 1950s when my brother and I began to sing this music. Your first paragraph is very powerful and comes off with authority, understanding and a certain pride. Thanks.

I don't really have any serious suggestions but a couple of questions. I was going to ask if in the paragraph beginning with "Thomas Dorsey (1899–1992) is recognized . . . " if you should say, "But the emergence of Gospel music (inspired by the "sanctified" singing of the newly formed Pentecostal congregations) follows much, etc." you should not include my insert but you seem to cover that in the paragraph beginning "The emergence of the mid 20th century Black gospel music" where you give a good discussion of the singing in the Black church. You might give some consideration to specifying the Pentecostal church because fifty years ago it was thought of as "setting the Black man back fifty years." Now, of course, it is difficult to distinguish the Pentecostal church from the Baptist church; it was not always that way.

In the paragraph beginning "It's as if the ritual is a part of the music making" you are absolutely right to present both these because while gospel was certainly influenced by other Black musics, it always had its own "gospel style" and was not simply a "Jazzed up" Spiritual song, as you said. Good!

Now, I must present you with a problem: According to harmonies, to some extent rhythms, performance style (it was not possible to sing gospel with your shirt hanging out prior to Andrae Crouch), and the fusion of (gospel, R & B and jazz) style, James Cleveland is not in the same group as Edwin Hawkins, Andrae Crouch, Richard Smallwood. It is generally agreed that Edwin Hawkins began the contemporary era with "O Happy Day," by which time James Cleveland had temporarily moved Thomas A. Dorsey from the spotlight. He is really at the end of the Mahalia Jackson, Roberta Martin (she recorded several of his songs), Clara Ward era, and is thought of as traditional. He is really a transitional figure where he began in one era and ended in another. What do you think?

For an overview I think you have done a great job. Thanks for letting me see it.

HCB

George Russell (1923–2009)

On July 27 I sat with George and Alice Russell, a time for reflection. I have never literally sat at the feet of a dying mentor, a musical great. And so, as I sat there quietly, I was made more quiet by the enormous feeling of gratitude for the life of this artist, a tenacious champion of music. As I was there, I texted my teacher, T. J. Anderson, and delivered good tidings to the Russells from David Baker. Alice and I talked of this great tradition, speaking of Gunther Schuller, of Miles Davis and Gil Evans, and of Jimmy Guffrey. We spoke today, just Alice and I, George's spouse of all these years, about their lives in music, about making music at a time when the culture valued this great gifting, but who now seemed destined to be underappreciated by the callous and spiritual bereft of the times we live in.

We talked of the youth of this current generation and of the work we must do to instill in them the value, art, and history of the musicians who preceded them, to awaken them to the heavy responsibility of carrying on and how to move forward. Every generation loses its greats—that is nothing new. But it is particularly disheartening that in our day such greats are not being duplicated. Even though the present brings new flowering, the soil it grows in inevitably will harvest a different crop, a different generation of beauty for sure, but one pained by corrupted roots for sure, too.

So I sat there very quietly, at the feet of one of the last greats of that generation, born one year before my own father, in 1923. I held the latest edition of George's *Lydian Chromatic Concept of Tonal Organization*, taken from my shelf today. I just held it as I sat and talked with Alice, George heavily breathing near us. It will not be too much longer, perhaps a day or two, Alice feels.

Horace Boyer went home last week, too. I sat with him, Mrs. Boyer, and his mentee, my friend Stephen Newby. We laughed with Horace, even though he could not speak. We laughed and we "spoke" of music and times and it was wonderful. But these are also times in which we must watch our great pass on. And where do we take what we have gained from them? That is our perplexing question and our proposed task. It stares us in the face with a brutal reality of "You must now do." It's a curious place to be in, to watch a generation of your heroes pass on, watching and waiting for the answers to these questions.

11 p.m.: No sooner had I written this, the note came through that George Russell died tonight.

Hale Smith (1925–2009)

Hale had been ill for several years, stricken with a stroke, and could speak very little. He was, especially for us Black composers, the leading elder who paved the way not only with his bold music, but as a prominent publishing figure who had worked for many years in the industry, as a teacher, and as a forceful critic. My book *Landscapes in Color* opened with Hale Smith claiming that without the work of Black composers, American music would all sound like Lawrence Welk. He was something else, that Hale.

Hale Smith absorbed all American music. He knew it all and taught us all how to compose it and when it could be published. He made lots of noise with his giftedness and big presence which fell to silence, sadly, for many years before he passed away. In this state he did a most unimaginable thing:

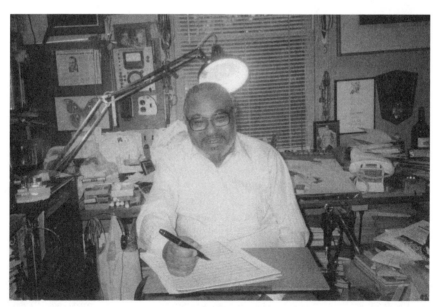

Hale Smith.

He refused to listen to music. Why? What did that signify? Maybe it meant that you should make your music to mean something while you still can, because when you can't make your own music, then all music takes on a different meaning, something you can't define.

Thanks, Hale, for making us serious about what music means.

We miss your greatness much.

September 19

Meeting Q.

I'm here in New York, leaving today after having spent eleven hours with Quincy Jones and David Baker. Quincy called this meeting to discuss our proposed plan for his QFoundation curriculum initiative. What a time. Berklee president Roger Brown told me that this is, "The moment you've been preparing for all your life." As I consider the work ahead in the next several months, he may be correct. The writing of Quincy's curriculum allows many roads to be traveled that link to my hopes. The least of these being just to sit and gain from him his generosity, industry wisdom, his great gift of love and encouragement that comes from him and touches everything. We had such an incredible time, David and I, with his foundation director whom we all adore, Madelyn Bonnet who orchestrates all this, and Q's business manager, Adam, a young man of great brain gift and humanity, humility, and sharp as a tack.

The meeting happened yesterday in the lobby of the Meridian Hotel in Columbus Circle, 59th and 8th Avenue. Madelyn brought David and me up and Q came in shortly. What a love fest. To see Q and David—born in 1931 and 1932 respectively—interact as old chums, while I, their "little brother," sat next to these greats was both awesome and humbling. They talked about gigs in 1940 this and 1950 that with Miles, Ellington, Monk. "Count Basie said this," and then "Frank [Sinatra] tells me to do that." But this goes even further with Quincy, who must be the pope of all music. His business and friendship tangles go from hanging with Humphrey Bogart to having lunch with President Bill Clinton, from speaking with Oprah yesterday to Colin Powell calling last week. And of course, he spoke of Michael Jackson, of how Michael's death is still so surreal to him.

Then we got down to the specifics of the curriculum. This meeting had been anticipated for months, and David and I had spent the weekend before, discussing how it might go before sitting down with Quincy. To hear Quincy's dream and to feel the passion flow out directly from him gave me yet another level of thrill—beyond what my limited words can convey. After a review of the philosophy, we asked, "Q how should we deal with the politics of culture on this?" He said, "I want the truth."

We all agreed this writing can be one of the new historical narratives that comprehensively address the development of American music. We also believe in the transformative power that this curriculum can exert on American youth, educators, and musicians. Nothing I've read in American popular texts inspires me to think differently about music culture. This way of telling that insists on its values, artistry, and innovation could release a new spirit, commitment that might move us to the next levels. For twenty years, I have been asking "What's the right note?" Similarly, Quincy again and again speaks of a "significant tone." That tone is about soul and humanity that resonates and connects. This is all about hitting the right note and knowing why the note merits a listen. Of all the things I am doing, this ranks high on my playlist for the next two years. There are dozens of figures, people at every level in this industry who will connect to this curriculum that is the jewel in Quincy's eye.

This moment is rather formative and forbidding, to say the least. It is the biggest assignment in my career, and Roger Brown may be correct. All my current projects—and there are many (the music series in Boston, my classes this fall, my residency at UCLA in October, the new Jazz Urbane record, the *Spring Forward* record to be featured in the Winter edition of Michael Fagien's *Jazziz*, the forthcoming philosophy book, the beginning of the Sweet Honey symphony/residency, the residency with the Boston Children's choirs, and the scholar/artist in residence at the Boston Arts Academy, and the spring 2010 release of my opera recording, *Soul Gone Home*)—connect with and to this work, and the Q narrative circles in and around all this.

Sitting with Quincy Jones, it is clear, especially acute, that the torch should be passed to our group, and if we do our work right, a new path could be set in place.

December 10

We started a little music scene at a place called the Bella Luna, in one of the city's neighborhoods that I reside in called Jamaica Plain (J.P.).

The Bella Luna was one of a number of hip places in J.P., where food and vibe are the thing, but the people who owned Bella Luna and worked there were our favorites. On the walls they hung fresh art, and the place was kind of funky Bohemian upscale, intellectual and down and swank urban all at once. They moved into a hipper complex, the Brewery, with a coffee shop and some other stores and a great location with parking (rare in Boston). I

BGKLS house band at Bob the Chef's, Boston, 2008: Lenny Stallworth, George W. Russell Jr., Kenwood Dennard, me, and James Cassey.

approached the owners and suggested a jazz series I would head up and we tried twice a month, with three sets of trios alternating. We started this past August. It blazed most times, fizzled and popped quietly others, but is growing a steady burn. My time last night was a burn and I was a demon. I had a great quartet playing with me and one my regular drummer partners here, Tony "Thunder" Smith, a seasoned veteran. The young man I believe will be one of our next greats, pianist Jesse Taitt, me, and Ron Reid on bass. I turned up the volume, closed my eyes and did what music has whispered in my soul and yelled in my ear to do, "play like a demon praying for understanding!" When you come out and open your eyes, people all around are enjoying themselves, eating, smiling, bopping their heads to your music. You feel salvation and redemption all at once.

I created another performance series in town. Monday's at Bob's Bistro, Jazz at the Beehive, Jazz at the Bella Luna, and now too, the Berklee Artists Series at Scullers. Scullers is the top draw jazz club in town, and the major agent there, Fred Taylor, is the city's veteran who has been producing music here for more than forty years. He and I created this new series. I approached him, he said "Yes," I got the school to buy in, and we began this fall with an all-star killer Berklee faculty and student lineup: Greg Osby, Gabrielle Goodman, Terri Lynne Carrington, Marc Rossi, Five Guitar Brothers (Dave Fuiczynski, Dave Gilmore, John Thomas, James Peterson, Thaddeus Hoggarth, and me),

Donna McElroy and my guys, BGKLS (Banfield, George Russell Jr., Kenwood Dennard, Lenny Stallworth, Stan Strickland), and the Jazz Urbane. This is the fourth music series I have produced in Boston since I landed here. We all agree that we must create the venues if we are going to be able to claim our lives as musicians, as no one will claim them for us. And as Johnny Rotten of the Sex Pistols exclaimed, "We had to write our own futures or die."

Music activism was all around the culture in the 1950s, 1960s, 1970s. Then, in the eighties, the corporations took over. Now we find ourselves with no recording industry, no venues to play, and a culture that doesn't know what music is. Music left or was left alone, shivering in a cold past. Of course, people like music, but they just don't know its true name anymore. So the musician—those of us who still know and hope to learn—must keep the music alive and in plain sight and sound of the masses. Musicians *must* create the scenes.

One night as we played, I saw a young man sitting in a booth by himself, with a computer, all evening. After our gig ended, after I had been playing like a demon praying for forgiveness, he approached us and thanked us for being there with the music. He caught word of us on the Internet, looked at my website, and drove out of snow-piled Worcester, Massachusetts, to listen. I couldn't believe it, because the music draws people to cling close. I thanked him, feeling that the demon playing was answered. Music leaves us and enters into another soul that is made whole because the music resonated within.

CHAPTER ELEVEN

Closing Comments on Culture:
Entries and Essays (2010)

January 18

We are in 2010, starting another decade, and we are still facing the cold winds of social, financial, and cultural meltdowns. Over the last week or so, Haiti experienced a huge and devastating earthquake, killing thousands. Much of the island has to be rebuilt, but the world has raced there to help; perhaps global relations is coming together soon. Human outreach also ultimately benefits more than just those in direct receipt of help because, despite the pain of all this death, companies and governments are lining up to rebuild and gain on new investments. Tsunami, Katrina, and now Haiti, even as two wars rage in Afghanistan and Iraq. This is the world we live in: suicide bombers, government spies, crazed Islamic fundamentalist shooting dozens on a Texas army base, and then for Christmas, a Nigerian student tries to blow up an airplane by detonating his underwear over Detroit!! Can it get crazier? The answer must surely be . . . yes.

I spent yesterday morning in a discussion meeting with my publisher here in Boston for a conference. Ed Kurdyla and I discussed the new book, *Cultural Codes* (2010), the newer memoir, *Representing Black Music Culture* (2011), and the business of publishing. Over the last five years with Scarecrow I have published as an author (*Cultural Codes*) and as editor (*The Jazz Trope: A Theory of African American Literary and Vernacular Culture* by Alfonso Hawkins; *Reminiscences of an American Composer and Pianist* by George Walker; Alexs Pate's *In the Heart of the Beat*; and *George Russell: The Story of an American Composer* by Duncan Heining) a total of seven books. These along with two previous books, *Musical Landscapes: Essays of a Musician Writing in a Post-Album Age* and *Black Notes*, were published in the last decade.

This focus on ideas compels and impassions me, and in the midst of trying to figure out the downbeats of a downward spiraling world, I'm feeling we must and can only do the best we can. Returning from the trip to New Orleans, Memphis, and the Delta, I have been immersed in writing the narrative to the history of American popular music, and feeling like this is the great charge of my life. With faith, I push to see this through because I know the result of the power of ideas and the joy and inspiration that happens when people are lifted by the presence of music in their lives. Those young lives must be lifted to be able to carry creatively what the world needs as we try and survive in a complex and conflicted new decade.

With George Walker.

March 27

Our lives are cluttered, even in our best attempts to dial down the everyday noises that besiege us. The volume in modern life and society is always on and up, filled with sounds and flashing lights. I've been writing this memoir for six years approaching my fiftieth year in 2011, threading together ideas about being an artist over the last forty years, what that means, what it looks and sounds like. I write a lot of music, a lot of words—and run my mouth a lot.

When I turned forty-nine a few days ago, I was on a train from Boston to New York, headed to the Schomburg Center for Research in Black Culture and to visit my friend, bassist Victor Bailey, who was turning fifty. On the way I listened to some of my solo guitar performances from recordings over the last six years. These pieces, performances stood alone. No full band, mostly guitar, some pieces with the beats of percussion resonating, and there was my clarity, my voice, my peace in mind, my expression. I thought, "Ouch, I can hear myself." There it was! It took me these last twenty-five years to enjoy hearing myself again. For me, clarity is hearing my voice, asking life's questions musically, making the cadences, finding and defining myself.

〜

Roots and Reason Series, Concerts Produced by Bill Banfield, Interviewed by Leslie Mahoney, Berklee Faculty News

LM: What does Roots and Reason mean in the context of Black music studies?

WB: We've tried to define Africana studies by providing ways for students to see the connections and development of American popular music. Our programming and course development consists of the history and culture of this music, and their impact on developing modernity; and the actual listening, performance, and discussion of those musical styles from the perspective and experience of recognized practitioners. We try to bring the world's best artists here and each year, these artists bring a thematic focus to a larger theme. It's very important for students to understand the roots of music. It doesn't come from MTV or BET or NBC. The roots of music come from people in communities who put music together and it ultimately becomes part of these larger styles. Roots and Reason is an attempt to show those larger connections and to show how artists connect to those roots.

LM: The term "reason" speaks to the context behind the music—the why. Can you talk about the circular notion that music informs culture and culture informs music?

WB: The term "roots music" is something you can interpret in a loose way. When you think of American roots, you think of bluegrass, you think of blues, you think of Native American music. It can also extend to something you might not think of as roots, such as Turkish pop. You can get very layered and philosophical about this. You can look at roots spelled r-o-o-t-s or r-o-u-t-e-s, and talk about the connectedness of all of this and the reasons behind that. To be completely culturally explicit, one school of thought is that all of American popular music derives itself from African American traditions. There are those who would hold that there would be no Berklee without Delta blues, Little Richard, or Mahalia Jackson. There is this idea that it all comes back to Black American popular traditions but more globally and honestly, it goes to Africa. And if it goes to Africa then it goes to the global world because all these ideas were routes to each other as well as routes to the vernacular form from every country. So these global roots connections meant that these Turkish musicians are going to do their vernacular forms, which are equivalent to our vernacular forms of the Delta blues and spirituals. But what connect these—besides coming from deeply entrenched traditions—are popular music traditions. And really America was the continent, the culture, that produced this modern popular culture. Even if you're a kid in Israel or you're a young person in Turkey or Brazil, you're going to want to get funky a little bit more and some, and you're going to look to Elvis, you're going to look to the blues, and you're going to look to jazz to help mechanize your vernacular form. In that way, each generation looks to American rock and roll and jazz to be popular. It's all a wonderful connection of roots that circle around and around.

LM: Why is it so important—for younger musicians and the general audience—to know the roots?

WB: This is an educational institution. It's our job to teach this. That fact that we are a leading institution in the world for American popular music underlines that role and responsibility. Fifteen or twenty years ago when I was coming up doing music, you were required to know the history and you were proud to know the history. Now there is another larger megacultural thing in place that has substituted that good old-fashioned idea of learning this. Technology allows you to bypass all that, go directly to the product, and skip the process. But in music and in arts, you really want people to have a skill set. In addition to what you sound like, one of the more important things is what you know from the inside. That's the education and the history—to know Muddy Waters, Mahalia Jackson, Chick Corea, so that you can learn the great lessons of the masters, and then create your own tradition. That kind of education is critical.

LM: How does tapping into the roots make for a richer product?

WB: It's not tangible but it's evident when you look at the end result of the product. If you look at Beyoncé or a star basketball player, and you look at what they went through to get to where they are, the process becomes obvious. The same for a great painting, whereby a great painter has studied texture and color, emphasis on light. When you look at a great singer or great performance or great band, you know the result of that is through hard work. That's what we want to do, that's our job, to encourage that kind of development that comes from hard work, experience, and culture. When you hear someone sing a song, you want it to sound like the person knows what he or she is talking about, that they want to convey an inspiring message or illuminate a certain cause or lift my soul a certain way. That's what we expect artists to do.

LM: How does the process of incorporating musical influences figure into the ideas of roots and reason?

WB: Musicians can take a piece of an artist and make it their own. An artist's sensibility is you listen to Kenny G and if you like him, then you go back and listen to John Coltrane and you like him, and then maybe listen to some India.Arie and then some great vocalists you like, such as Bonnie Raitt and you say, *Wow*. A young artist is supposed to combine all those things with life and experience and make a new thing. In that way, these are routes to the root.

The Warmest December

Chapter 10 of Bernice McFadden's novel, *The Warmest December*, opens with one of the most illustrative and truest accounts for me of the meaning of music in our culture:

> It was 1979. I was thirteen years old and rap music had a foothold on the Black youth of America. We all dreamed of spinning records behind the Sugar Hill Gang and Kurtis Blow. But my musical tastes stretched far beyond

the rhyming rhythms that filed the airwaves and pounded hard out of the boom boxes that sat under park benches or rested on corners while young men spun their bodies at breakneck speeds on their heads or elbows like tops on large pieces of cardboard for change and applause. Me, I spent hours in front of the mirror singing along with Natalie Cole, Aretha Franklin and Love Unlimited. . . . My microphone was a comb or a brush and my audience the cosmetics that lined my dresser top.

As a musician, I am easily drawn to what Black music represented to my generation growing up in the 1970s. Her account is a nonmusician's appeal to meaning, so I "listen" to her. On another level though, McFadden's writing here gives me an author's map, what I call her novel niche seven: (1) the "I"; (2) the "he said"; (3) the "human experience"; (4) "time"; (5) the "poetic inner"; (6) "character development"; and (7) the "space context." Almost every page of her riveting work taught me lessons about how writing takes hold of you, and places you in a narrative context by which you are led on a writer's inner journeys.

Chapter 1 opens, "Now and then I (1) forget small things that would not otherwise alter my life. Things like milk in my coffee, setting my alarm clock, or Oprah at four (4, 7). Tiny things . . . I hated my father, forgot that I even thought of him as a monster (6). . . . Come closer, closer, he said (2). . . . I smelled the whiskey (3). . . . I forgot how the sound of my mother's crying ate holes inside of me and ripped a space open in my heart (5)."

It's as if every detail of one's thoughts and actions—and the actions and thoughts of others—dictate a whole environment, a narrative around the human experience which we must engage in.

At a book reading sponsored by a local Black bookstore in Jamaica Plain, I approached her. I decided to go and meet her, hear her read. I was the only man there among a group of Black women—intelligent, well read, middle aged, NPR listeners and enamored fans who were knowledgeable of her many writings. I was clearly the white elephant with pink, polka-dotted fuzzy pink slippers in the room. I dared not move or say anything. It was scary, but she was not. Afterward, following a shy introduction, I explained that I was a local musician and professor writing my first novel. I asked, "What should I do to really define my writing, the steps to take to make it a *novel?*"

She graciously said, "The minute you define it, it ceases to be what it was meant to be. Follow the storyline of your characters and it will define itself." I had been given my novel writing lesson.

Her advice is not unlike that of my less-comfortable-with-sharing buddy, author Alexs Pate, who was not as warm and fuzzy about this—perhaps because authors value the novel terrain as sacred. Pate's advice was that an author has the key to create any world she has in mind, a world that the reader must be invited to live in."It's the only time a Black person can name his characters, his own name and decide how the world must to be," Pate advised. And that this would escape me as a musician is odd. Music's content always overrides the restrictive nature of the rules or the parameters of expressions within form. That's why Ornette's free jazz is free, and why funk never fit the radio rules of commercial R & B.

Despite my artistic formalist needs, these were met by my many months of polemic rants, but it was McFadden's novel niche seven in her writing that became my "rule of the lines" as it were, and I needed the rules. You must hear how to feel and tell a story. It has to be an experience your reader can feel attached to at the heart of the tale. Empathy, rage, wonder, speculation, attention to the humor—these details all paint, dance, and sing the novel narrative.

Ms. McFadden's chapter 10 held for me another important meaning beyond its elegance: It was the way people could see what our music did. As a musician, like Ralph Ellison, I have fallen into the spider's web of writing as an identity. When my music cadences for the day and my fingers ache, it is the tone of words on a page that begins to sing of my soul's need for connection with aesthetic companionship.

This was how Ellison became our sharpest voice, creating the tone for us to hear in *Invisible Man*, harmonizing those crude social dissonances his character faced in finding his identity. In McFadden's chapter 10, I see Black people's relationship to music. In this context the character sings for hours in the mirror as if onstage, imagining herself the star who everybody loves. But what would happen if the music stopped? It becomes "too quiet." In that quietness, the music delivers us, buffers us from life's brutal beat, the unloving reality of a chaotic world. In music's "delightful distraction," we are allowed the moment to maintain sanity of the soul. This is how the opening of chapter 10 speaks to me.

In my own novel, my principal character claims, "We are all caught in the inescapable thrill that lights and counts for everything, if you are open to the art. And that's it, the musicians are channeling something and they know it. Now when that's blocked then the people can't get to the well man, you force them to go dry at the throat, they become course, cut throat even. So we don't want the music to stop."

I write as a musician attempting to tell the tale of artistic experience, about art as an expression that points the way, that dabbles with meaning, that hints at truths and provides an experience of inexpressible joy in us which mysteriously mends us. For inspiration, I look to the poets, the writers who lovingly embraced music. Toni Morrison wrote that music was, ". . . a sustaining force, which healed, nurtures and translates Black experience into above all else, art. My parallel as a writer is Black music because all the strategies are there. . . . It makes you hungry, it slaps, it embraces, music is the mirror that gives necessary clarity . . . and literature ought to do the same thing." That music gives all the strategies, as I had found in McFadden's novel for me was instructive, as strategy. In McFadden, Morrison found the novel to be, "Searing and expertly imagined" (quoted from Paul Gilroy, "Living Memory: An Interview with Toni Morrison," from *Small Acts*. London: Serpent's Tail, 1993, 175–182).

Many months after that warm spring day at the bookstore signing, I found the inscription Ms. McFadden had written in my book, which I hadn't seen or read before. She wrote, "To Bill Banfield, keep writing, the world needs your voice."

Wow, thank you, Ms. McFadden. I shall always appreciate and remember your encouragement in helping me find my voice in writing. I will continue to follow the storyline.

∿

Don't Use the J Word: Jazz Connections to Culture and Meaning

Discussions with Dr. Billy Taylor, Geri Allen, Lenny White, Stanley Clarke, Esperanza Spalding, Wynton Marsalis, Lee Ritenour, Don Byron, Billy Childs, Michael Powell, David Baker, Nnenna Freelon, Chuck Wilson, Christian Scott, Anthony Kelley, Morris Hayes, Kendrick Oliver, and Maria Schneider

If you wanted to use a term representing a music culture that is relevant, contemporary, and connected to the people, please don't use the "J" word. I raise this idea within the important cultural debates about our music, our artists, and the cultural contexts they work within. I suspected I would get good information, sharing from this great group of artists. We are all living similar tales in culture, drinking from the same rich well, and yet simultaneously watching the stream being potentially poisoned with corporate dictates which always affect artists. What begins to flow back, no matter who was speaking, are the "natural" inclinations when artists talk and that edgy expression that comes with the territory of jazz artistry anyway. The exchanges were like a community, family, cousins who are reunited at the family reunion feasting and watching the barbeque burn on the fire and feeling, "Should we pour more sauce on it, save it or must we savor the flavor of the moments or sanctify the memories?" A discussion about the identity, place, and meanings around jazz (the J word) today looms large, because we care about this music, frankly. There is across the board a real suspicion of market forced, corporate-dictated stuff, the need for an American jazz re-education among the masses, concern about the dislodging of jazz from Black identity and the need for musicians to rise up and take back the music. What does it mean to use a word as a movement in art and realize that word has no real connection and application to the culture it's applied within? In recent discussions with contemporary artists, critics, educators, there are thoughts to share on these issues. I interviewed, hung, jammed with friends from both coasts. For example, making a very interesting point to consider, bassist Esperanza Spalding noted that unlike "my group" that has anxieties and questions the "place of jazz" in the market, her generation is ". . . in a better position to not be burdened with that question of what it is or will become, because being in such a period of cross-pollination, I don't know what it [jazz, the J word] is now . . . and that may be a good thing." Musicians regularly talk about the meaning and practices of music. This is ultimately what establishes music, guards against corporate control, provides interpretation and growth, and safeguards against erasure.

Right off the RTF (Return to Forever) international tour, drummer Lenny White said, "All over the world and here in the States, a key phrase from the tour that was consistent from people was, 'Thank you for doing this again.' That's the difference, we are filling a void." Billy Taylor lamented with me in his Riverdale apartment that the thing he notices the most is, "The lack of camaraderie and community among the players . . . that that's either gone or being blocked. Mary Lou Williams would invite both Monk and Budd Powell over to her place and say, 'You guys have to play piano with more finesse.' They would do this, share with each other." So here are as a start, reflections from three different generations, each born thirty years apart from each other, all doing jazz in our culture, and all feeling the relevance of at least the questions addressing what this music is meaning in the world we live in today. This jumping off into the exchanges framed our many subsequent talks during the summer of 2008.

Is jazz the American art form under the radar and currently the invisible art form?

For artists, aesthetic, philosophical discussions usually outweigh market speculation, categories on record bins, and audience tastes. But in a real economy where market forces dictate culture, the hearing and placement of recorded or downloaded music, "new artist" signs, festivals to the now fewer live venues for performing, consider: What does jazz mean today and how and where does it "count and cost" and matter? Has it become again the American music that is under the radar and an invisible art form? Given a competitive market for commercial/art dollar, how will it maintain its distinctive voice, character that was once needed to define what it was, or how the culture saw and used it? And who gets to decide what face jazz puts on a corporate executive or on contemporary artists who want their voices to define the substance of the culture of the music?

The reality is, you can't really talk about the J word in the abstract, but you must deal with it in real form in connection to "culture," TV/media, fashion, education, radio, movies, and other forms of popular culture. Jazz is definitely not dead, but where are the spaces that it lives and connects, and how are artists truly making those public connections? Jazz music may be like Ralph Ellison's *Invisible Man* in the music world today as he put it, "You [the J word] ache with a need to convince yourself that you do exist within the real world, that you're a part of all the sound and anguish, and you strike out with your fists, you curse and swear to make them recognize you. And alas, it's seldom successful."

For the first time in many years, jazz music is not only absent from the common person on American streets, it is an "invisible identity" because we rarely see or reference what the J word is in mainstream popular culture. As a matter of fact, most people don't relate to the J word musically in our culture. Nothing new really. While working in residence from Duke University in New York, composer Anthony Kelley responded, "It's been co-opted. It's a dangerous word [the J word]. Because now it has the same implications [real or imagined] of the C word—classical music. It carries the same shame of cultural poisoned identity classical music has, "esoteric and irrelevant." These are harsh words from a twenty-first century Black American composer who uses jazz to inform his classical symphonic works.

But the problem here is at the larger cultural level, in that the meaning of music usage overall in the public market has been switched out and replaced by a huge media and entertainment monster (DVDs, video games, reality TV) that is eating our young people instead of feeding them. Jazz will find it harder and harder to survive, unless it makes itself responsive to this culture crisis. Because if we don't prepare our youth across the culture, there will be fewer and fewer places for it to be acceptable as a contemporary music form, and will be of little use to a culture that doesn't know what it is. Some of the blame Anthony Kelley speaks of has to do with the way in which art demands self-consciousness more than not. It may be that we turn a deaf ear on society's problems because we find so much of our time focused on "our work." Young people are not using jazz in large enough numbers to tell their creative stories in tones anymore, and that's reflected in the general culture and it shows up in sales. Our work may need to lean, too, toward a bit more of an educating focus, filling a void left in public schools and popular culture.

The Jazz Band in Culture

After seeing these four recently—White, Chick Corea, Stanley Clarke, Al Di Meola—playing as a source fusion band, it is clear they truly helped to create the models for this new approach to jazz. Five major bands emerged from the Miles Davis experiments of the 1960s: Return to Forever (RTF), Mahavishnu Orchestra, Headhunters, Weather Report, and Tony Williams Lifetime. Tony Williams and Joe Zawinul have passed on and true to Lenny White's comment, RTF is the only remaining seminal band of this movement and this was only a reunion, not a re-fusion of the band or return. Gonzalo Rubalcab's new Cuban quartet, Hiromi's Socibloom, are refreshing fusion ensemble-music twists in the missing piece of this jazz band puzzle. Missing in action is Bob James and Lee Ritenour's Fourplay which along with Pat Matheny represented a new wave of the progressive jazz band formula countering more commercial formulaic smooth jazz configurations of late that followed. While there is the Yellow Jackets and Mike Stern recent collaboration, Bella Fleck currently holding up tradition, Soulive representing a new hipped-hopped twist, if in the search for the Ellington and Basie traditions, and even if we had to stretch to look over the record bin fence to neighbors like the remaining Rolling Stones, Mint Condition, the Roots, one has to wonder if the long-lasting touring bands in jazz and popular music culture will ever again be a defining entity of jazz performing culture?

Lenny White

WB: You just finished a tour where you have come back with a band from the seventies with a repertoire of recorded works and the same guys you played with twenty-five years ago. What's the difference in the musical culture between then and now?

LW: Before, what we did was a movement, a part of something with a whole lot of different artists. Now there are not that many. We were sources, we were originators of a new thing. Nowadays it's all about copying the source. All over the world and here in the States, a key phrase from the tour that was consistent from people was, "Thank you for doing this again." That's the difference, we are filling a void.

I also spoke to two reigning contemporary J word artists in this area (jazz big band orchestra), Maria Schneider and Kendrick Oliver.

Maria Schneider

WB: Tell me what it means to be a jazz big band leader today. What do you walk through to "get there" and how are today's audiences responding? Do you feel okay with the cultural marketplace as it relates to your art, or if you could, would it have been better musically, existing in another musical time? What are the advantages, disadvantages today?

MS: I would say I'm happy to be making [jazz band/orchestra] music now because that is all I know. I once spoke to a Basie musician about this and he noted that at the time they were working constantly, he wasn't aware that he was living "an era." He said they were just busy making music. What's most important now is to take what we have around us, the whole landscape, the world, present-day questions, and search for new answers, expressing who we are, now. And this is an interesting time musically because we don't have one kind of music or cultural movement that everyone rides on. The world has become so eclectic and so diverse. The new reality is global, and it could be daunting and confusing to find your place within it, but I find it exciting, because through music in this present time, one can also experience a sort of citizenry of the world.

Differences in American, European audiences? I can't know or judge how anyone would perceive my music, but generally the outer reaction in varying places, Brazil, all over Europe, and the U.S., is one of openness. My music has elements from many kinds of music and I think most people listen in relation to what they themselves know. So maybe they are responding because they see it as having a piece of their world in it. I think that's partly how my music connects. But my personal hope would be if people most connect to my musical world by feeling humanity in the music. I know that's what I want to experience when I listen. That's where the power of music is. My feeling is that jazz [classical music, too] went through a phase where everyone was trying to press the music further and further in terms of harmony, rhythm, complexity, but in many cases, to my ears, it often loses its humanity amidst that. I sense that many musicians are trying to get back to the place where music, even if highly detailed, complex, and intricately constructed, still communicates with people.

Kendrick Oliver

WB: How are you managing your identity as a jazz band artist?

KO: I personally feel very comfortable, and I considerate it an honor. Wherever I see Roy Hargrove he calls me "the maestro." To have musicians recognize you as such is great. I think the jazz band is a profound tool of entertainment, because it has the size of the symphony orchestra and the hipness that can reach a larger audience. The problem is not with the consumer or having an audience connect to this. If kids get to go see a show of a jazz orchestra, if you are grooving hard and if it's done right, the kids have a blast.

I went to a clinic with the Lincoln Jazz Orchestra with Wynton. All these kids were there, and Wynton had them swinging. And these were kids with no musical background! The problem comes in when they hear the words, "jazz orchestra" or "jazz orchestra with conductor." The problems really though come with the promoters. It's the jazz promoters who drive the market or if it's going to be too expensive. You hear, "How big is the group?" "No, no . . ." before you can even quote them a price. But if you put together a swinging program, it will be successful. It does get frustrating financially sometimes, so you have to find alternative ways to do the financing. It's a part of having a large group. The big band though is a terrific art form, and people always ask, "How do you do this?" It's only difficult in your mind. If I said, "I'm not going to be able to do this," then of course I wouldn't be around. I love doing this. It's something that's in me.

This is something I look forward to doing when I wake up, and I'm generally thinking about it when I go to bed. It's a beautiful art form and while it's not as popular as Beyoncé or hip-hop, everything has its place. I honestly believe we are in line for a huge revival. I watch the subtle things. We live in a star-driven society. It's funny how if one person does something everybody else jumps on the bandwagon. Natalie Cole's record—before you knew it, everyone is trying to do it. Rod Stewart was trying to do it, then Queen Latifah was doing a record with a big band. Imagine how many people would do this if a Beyoncé wanted to get involved. It's a profound art form. It takes a lot of skill to play in a big band. And it takes a special musician to do this.

Not only do you have to be selfless, you have to also be talented at the same time. I think at some point players are going to be rewarded for that kind of sacrifice, of being a part of such a significant art form.

WB: Does this—sacrifice, working hard—translate to something that this generation wants and values?

KO: Yes, if they are given a chance. I had a terrific high school in Houston, Texas, the high school of performing and visual arts. We all had different ideas of what we were going to do. I had no idea that I was going to lead a jazz orchestra. My high school director said, "Pay attention to everything you do in the industry because you never know when you are going to need all these tools." I respected how the big bands were run. I thought it was amazing how all these people had to work together to get this one sound. If you look at it, these are the same things coaches are asking football players to do; all individuals working to get to the same goal. Financially the reward hasn't been there for the musicians like it is for athletes. But if you get a young person who is a talented musician, it's a rewarding experience and I think it's very sellable. We sell our young people short. I do clinics where there are great music programs, and where they don't have great music programs, and we get an awesome, awesome response.

WB: You don't do just pop arrangements, right?

KO: We have a program called In the Pocket. We take all these different styles, swing, New Orleans, gospel funk, and put them together. We did this at a small college in Rhode Island and I invited up Kirk Whalum and it was bananas, the response!! People who have never heard jazz before, if they hear the groove, it connects. The groove element is always the key. It was the type of show that everybody could appreciate.

Culture, Innovative Voices, and Corporate Dictates

Innovation among instrumentalists was always an identity that marked the J word movements. While numerous young new artist signs flood the traditional and smooth jazz markets on radio, are there any real new innovative, distinctive, original voices who have changed the approach, sound of their instrument? Visionary means culture, game change, like a Hendrix approaching distortion and revolutionizing sound, or Bill Evans's complete new way of harmonizing, or a Miles Davis inspiring a generation to go a new direction. There is nothing "new or visionary" today. In a conversation with bassist/composer Stanley Clarke he added, "It takes certain ingredients for people to understand what we do. There have always been players, musicians out there on the fringe, and that was not popular. Jazz is virtuoso music. We are on the fringe edge man . . . we are the 'fringe benefit.'" Perhaps with the exception of bassist Jaco Pastorius, or the innovative approach to guitar of Stanley Jordan, jazz has produced not a single instrumental voice of this kind of retwist or remaking of an instrumental approach. While Kurt Rosenwinkel, Stefon Harris, Esperanza Spalding, Christian Scott, Miguel Zenon have dynamic presence and voice, no single trumpet player, saxophonist, pianist, drummer of major distinctive "instrumental voice changing significance" have really been projected. Donald Harrison, Christian McBride, Terrance Blanchard, Roy Hargrove, and the Marsalis family are all the "traditional icons" now and can't really excite the marketplace as young or new. In the vocal jazz tradition looking back to now, Al Jarreau, Bobby McFerrin, Take 6, Cassandra Wilson, Dianne Reeves, and even Norah Jones stick out. It would be very smart for jazz to claim Erykah Badu and Jill Scott, who are original voices with heavy roots in jazz.

Billy Childs

WB: What has happened in your estimation in the marketplace as you have watched things change?

BC: Audiences have been separated from jazz, and there are a number of reasons for that having to do with corporate shifts. Jazz is a music that requires what I call "active listening." Listening that engages your mind, you have to imagine things and have your brain working while you're listening. In the eighties a lot of things were created that are the antithesis of active listening. One thing, MTV came on the scene and now it became necessary to have a visual image while you listen to the music. Nothing was left to the imagination. Your mind doesn't have to think about anything; it was told what to think about while the music was playing, that and technology encroaching upon us.

WB: Given that you've watched your music as a jazz artist grow from the late eighties, through the nineties, now twenty years later, what does it feel like, is this an identity that even has sense anymore?

BC: Jazz is part of my vocabulary. It is what I do. I also do classical, and all kinds of music. I have had in my whole career, been doing music that I've never been ashamed for. I have relative respect in my field from my peers. I have always been unto myself, and I am going to do what I do, and however popular that is or not, is beside the point.

WB: That is what any jazz artist says, they don't care about being famous. But you are rare in that you won a Grammy award for jazz! What does it mean for a jazz composer to win the Grammy for best jazz composition?

BC: The Grammy is a great thing to put on a resume, and it was a great honor when I got it, but it hasn't helped my jazz career a lot. Yes and no, I guess. Because I got nominated so many times in one year at the same time, NPR then got interested in me (for the first time) and they did an interview on me. Then I got a lot of record sales and recognition. NPR! I had no idea how powerful they are. The Grammy win had a great impact on that. It was another thing that helped me produce my music by myself without any involvement from record labels. [Childs, now with Artist Share.]

WB: Working with Chris Boti, the lead selling contemporary jazz artist today, comes with pluses. What are the challenges, how do you navigate this "jazz identity" within in a more "commercial jazz label prescription"?

BC: Well, it's "jazz pop." With the Chris Boti gig, and I must say, it's a very music fulfilling gig. I love that gig because the band is so great: Billy Kilson, Bob Hurst, James Genus, Tim Lafey, Mark Whitfield, and Chris on trumpet. But for my own "jazz thing," the bottom line is this is a means to an end because it's a way to gather income so that I can do my own jazz chamber music. He works a lot, and I have gotten identified now with his sound. This is not a bad thing because it's not a bad sound, it's a good sound. I don't really care if it's a pop sound; the bottom line is when I do my music, it will be real because it's mine, it's what I want to do and I have the capital to do it and I'll be able to do it now on my own terms without any interaction from any corporate interests.

Nnenna Freelon

I asked Nnenna to give me her read, definition of jazz culture, what's real, and what in her mind defines "voice."

NF: Jazz culture for me represents how I was brought up in this culture. I was taught by older musicians.

I came up in the [Black] church, where there is a family, a community, a lifestyle and there is a sensibility, right things to do. Things that are wrong, invisible rules, and things you observe, a decorum. You don't run up over somebody's solo. When someone asks you to sing in church, you might expect payment, and your answer is always "Yes." You stepped up to the plate. All these things existed in a larger community. It was not a thing where the music is over here and culture was over here. These emerge from the culture, it shaped, fed the culture, and reflected back to us who we were through the performance of it. We learned "Lift Every Voice and Sing," Paul Lawrence Dunbar. And you might think Paul Lawrence Dunbar had nothing to do with jazz. But we had to learn all this as a part of the cultural puzzle from Langston Hughes to Miss Smith's cornbread. It's all a part of the understanding of this music.

When I came of age as a young singer the older musicians told me who to listen to, challenged my notion of what music was all about, and this really helped and encouraged me to get better.

Ellis Marsalis, Milt Hinton, Dr. Billy Taylor, these are people who took me under their wings. Ellis said, "You sound pretty good." That was it. "Now, you need to listen to Little Jimmy Scott, Dinah." He led me down the path. He could tell from my voice what I did and did not know. He didn't praise me, as praise can stop you just as quickly as criticism does.

"Everything you hear in culture should be a product of all you are. I can hear the people who are hearing truth. The "passers" are obvious. But if it represents falsity it is because it's not approached in truth. The human voice speaks and sounds like life experiences. It took me years of listening before I understand that and could hear my "voice experience." Dinah's voice cuts you like a sharp knife. Or a voice like Shirley Horn's that wraps itself around you. Andy Bey, a voice full of earth and dark blue, purple, a night voice. Like the griots' voices, God gave him that voice and he learned to use it. Billie Holiday, she invented herself. She was an articulate singer with a life experience edge.

Freelon's idea of life experience is what seems to be missing today. I can hear my mother's voice in the speaking of a saxophone, and the prayer rants of Deacon Jones there too. This cultural connectivity is what many miss in the commodification of this art form and what we claim and fight as the root of the problems.

Despite all the recent hoopla over today's "new generation of new jazz visionary players/singers," beyond the "George Butler Columbia youth up-surge movement" in the eighties with Wynton Marsalis and crew, or Steve

Coleman's Mbase configurations, jazz as a movement among young players has been silent on these points as an independent contemporary musical movement. We are sure that the gene pool did not dry up, but is it within the "industry thinking" that no longer values such idea as innovation, distinction enough to seek, find, record, and finance such "new original voices" in jazz? But given the fact that "original" voice has now been co-opted to mean, how many of the "same voices" can we put out there, what could a "new configuration" of voices look like, sound like? I wondered and questioned if this was due to the public not being able to take this innovation, or if the industry was involved in dictating audience tastes, and how jazz artists respond to this corporate shift. Maybe we can find another word to describe innovative artistry which symbolizes daring originality and perhaps the J word is not the term we use any longer for this. A peculiar predicament for this art form.

Christian Scott

I asked trumpeter, band leader Christian Scott if he could trace the lineage from everyone he listened to and shaped him, what would that list look like, and secondly what is Christian Scott bringing to the table?

CS: I would start with Buddy Bolden. When I was a little boy, my grandfather would sit me on his lap when I was two or three years old and sing a song about Buddy Bolden. So I knew about Buddy Bolden before I knew about the trumpet.

Of course next would be Louis Armstrong. Then, Roy, Dizz, and Clifford Brown. I'd probably get a little "fat girl" in there (Fats Navarro), then Lee Morgan, Kenny Durham, Freddie Hubbard, Woody Shaw. Then I stopped, because I was told not to listen to guys who are alive. So, it stops around Woody Shaw.

I don't like to read the press. But someone said that there was a quote where the writer said, I was one of the "architects of the new sound in jazz." But, I'm just a cat. I'm just trying to get my point across in the music. People are definitely starting to hear things stirring. What my group is trying to bring to the table, to contribute, is we're not the type of band that edits ourselves. If I hear something that ties into my sound, I'm not going to discard that sound, because someone else might consider that as less valid than jazz. I'm not an exclusive person. When you start to put labels on things, like for instance, Max Roach called himself a creative sound architect. These ideas are starting to translate to our generation, which is why you have guys like Aaron Parks or Robert Glasper who take these chances and have these different palettes. It's not that the palettes are so different from what's going on, it's just they are listening to what's out there and not editing out of their music because other people condemn it. Right now for this music, it survives, just the same as it's always been, you have to assimilate every texture and palette that comes your way. Because this is about being the best you can be, it's not about being only as good as the times dictate. You need to learn everything, listen to everything, and be prepared for everything, because if you don't this music will not survive because it's been deemed to be something that is not commercially viable.

I love my band because they are fearless. When we get on the bandstand, I have no idea what's going to be coming at me and I love it. It could be coming from Satch to Nine Inch Nails, or something from a 50 Cent record, and processing all of it. And if we want to get into the game, we have to be the best like that. We can't have another generation where people have accepted the kind of insincerity that is requisite in a musical survival in the context of jazz. We can't have any of this, that is done. I was talking to slam poet Saul Williams, and he was actually talking about how hip-hop has become republican. Cutthroat capitalism, "forget you, I got mine," "I'm not worried about you getting yours." And I look at jazz and it's very similar. We have to let go of this notion that we do whatever it takes to "get on." That's not how it works. You make the music that is most compelling to you, you have convictions about what it is you are going to do, and whatever happens happens. We've gotten a lot of flack about how our music sounds. But if you listen, it's just the blues. It's the blues, that's it. The blues modernly nonedited.

Jazz and Education and Mentorship

A reality check: In 1975 as a fourteen-year-old eighth grader and aspiring guitarist, I attended a regular Detroit public school in everyday urban America. We had music programs then. My musical heroes were George Benson, Al Di Meola, Stanley Clarke, George Duke, Lee Ritenour, Earl Klugh, Patrice Rushen. I still have those record albums today. The sad story, ask any kid who attends public schools in American cities who they are listening to? My other friends coming along also attended these same urban middle and high schools: Geri Allen, Gregg Phillangaines, Dwight Andrews, Regina Carter, Carla Cook, Kenny Garret, James Carter, Mark Ledford (deceased 2005). What are our schools teaching and what new future jazz artists are they producing? Of course they are out there, but . . . in what concentrations and numbers? Teaching at one of the leading jazz institutions in the world, Berklee School of Music, our students are understandably unlike the students who came twenty-five years ago exclusively and passionately to study jazz and jazz icons. Today you have to wonder if any could even name a Duke Elling-ton standard or be interested in whistling a Charlie Parker head. Miles Davis, for many students, may be some old jazz dude who has a gravelly voice. We wonder if the J word conjures up excitement about the dream of innovative playing for many younger players today as once practiced? Jazz, we may have to accept, is not the only model marketplace to find the next great innova-tive voices and there's nothing new or strange about that from examples of Jimi Hendrix to Macy Gray to Raul Midon. The Berklee College of Music example here mirrors perhaps not a J word cultural and musical ignorance, as much as what is at play are wider interests these days, accessibility, cross-style pollinations, the influence of global culture, more fluid use of technology, and increasingly more approaches to the idea of diversity in the mainstream markets; perhaps purists not allowed. The differences are the cultural climate and context which we as musicians must change. The problem with the media industry projection of jazz culture is its selling the culture with ads but doing little to cultivate the culture of the music. Musicians always care more about the health of the art, not the industry.

That point was raised here with Geri Allen, as I asked, How did music matter in Detroit growing up, and how did it shape her, and do these differ-ences matter with current "jazz meanings"?

GA: Well today, especially in light of the loss of IAJE, this is key right now; music should be at the center, the creative mechanics have to be at the helm of where we are going. Dr. Taylor mentioned that while the organization might be gone, the people are still there. My take on that is there should be a touring mechanism that would support the bands and musicians. That's what makes the music self-perpetuate. Because people would be seeing it all the time. Like Ravi Coltrane, for example, after repeated tours, we are looking at the choices in personnel he has made. People would be watching this, seeing who he might choose as a pianist, drummer, the new faces, etc. In all respect to IAJE, the musicians felt their place was on the back burner. The performative aspect of this is about the player's or the musician's process which has to be at the forefront. Perhaps we could rally with local businesses to support this touring idea as well. All the things we musicians don't have, we have to create access to these services. We should go after these things to allow musicians to be a part of this.

They [businesses] could take on these bands as patrons, so that musicians have the benefits of health care and these kinds of things that we must be thinking about now. This is just my take on how or what we should be talking about more. It's as well an apprenticeship, mentorship kind of thing. The musicians passed this on. They were able to do this through touring and attach themselves to these mentors. The musician needs to be the focal point as a true representative of the music. This is the way we all learned. Myself and Kenny Garret learned this way. I met Marcus Bellgrave and Donald Byrd, who did a residence at our high school in Cass Tech [Detroit], and because they understood the mentorship aspect of this, that's how we got this.

Cultural Contexts: Meaning Now . . . ?

It would be culturally irresponsible to be asking what does jazz mean and represent and where does it live, and deny a critical discussion about social-racial and cultural politics in America. Jazz is a music that was uniquely formed to voice very specific actions, needs, and that is why the music sounds and means and communicates the way it does at its core. Further, politics and policies actually shape some of the market meaning, value, messages, symbolization, and imagery of this music culture. In late August, I attended a Harvard Du Bois Institute forum/ town talk, "Does Race Still Matter?" And while these baby-boomer concerns press hard upon the identity of the several hundred gathered, this current generation looks oddly at our ruffled brows. But their "entry in" is still dictated and navigated by White executives who are less likely to be concerned or caring about Black identity or cultural climate and connections. But with jazz, you have to care about the history of the music and the costs of carrying on with this legacy as the way artists are projected, how many get advertised—promo-dollar spin and time and airtime, page time, and artist-signs—matters.

Further, when does jazz represent in its current configuration or connect within the contemporary contexts of Black people, its founders, or "originators and sources" (to use a Lenny White reference)? Rarely do we say and deal with the big white elephant question in the room: why is jazz not associated more directly with Black people today?

Are we not concerned that young Black people whose grandparents and great-grandparents were accused of "dirtying" White American teens with jazz and bebop in the 1920s, 1930s 1940s, 1950s, that today these same teens would discard jazz icons, neither claim nor recognize these artists? Bebop was the music of the young Black progressive musicians who championed a free innovative expression that ensured today's youth could have the right to play what they wanted and to say what they wanted to be, sit at a lunch counter and be counted as free in America. Nina Simone, Charles Mingus, and John Coltrane certainly represented these connections. In all respect to the argument for "European jazz" artistry, which to this writer's definition does not represent the same historical distinctive approach or context to the origins of this history, there is no jazz that today is connected to dance or fashion or a people's cultural identity and story. And that may be okay, just don't call it the J word anymore.

Wynton Marsalis

In terms of the issues of art and racial identity, politics and what to teach, Wynton had this to say:

WM: Don't call it Black music. Many people have a perspective on this. I had a teacher who did and he called it "White music." And that would make me cringe because that would mean I couldn't play it. I grew up endorsing it [a culturalist labeling], but now I don't. So I would teach it as American music. The greatest people who created it were a great people. It was Black people. So why isn't it that that's the achievement of America? I ask all of my students three basic questions:

1. What is the difference between improvisation and jazz improvisation?
2. Where do your melodies come from?
3. How do you construct your style, what are the components of your style?

Apply these questions to any of the things you and I are talking about, and you'll get your answer.

Now my students do just fine with the first question, but they don't do well with the second or third question because they don't know how to. They don't know what the cultural questions are, and they certainly don't have enough things going on to define what their style is, or what it's made up of. Your melodic information is your musical identity. It comes from folk people, folk materials. Charlie Parker is the only person who could make a fast line, a melody line. We are all from that line of playing, and none of us can do that. Bach couldn't do it, and his stuff wasn't all that fast. Today we play runs, but he [Parker] was the only one who could take fast lines and make them a melody.

If you must, call it blues, African American, music in the African Diaspora . . . and you get to the root. Ask the questions what and who has the music produced, then you answer all the questions. We can't duplicate what people did. There is no other music that is American, but this music. White folks cannot be removed from jazz either. Teach the music right, and you don't have to worry about it. Racism is still abundant in jazz, but I haven't seen evidence that we need to worry about White people being scared of the music and where it is from. They are usually the ones who invest in it. Black people don't.

If you look into the future of this music, it will not be these nationalities warring about this or that. It's American music. The pressure and meaning of what America means, Negro musicians actually playing this music pressed and defined these issues much more than we are dealing with these questions now. So there it is.

Don Byron

Don Byron adds still another layer to the questions about, this J word, and Black and other identities in the musical world we live in.

DB: I have always skirted around jazz, because for me it set up certain business limitations. If I wanted to play rock I could play with rock musicians, but could never be one. Rock musicians feel intimidated by jazz musicians and, of course, if you're Black you must play jazz. When classical musicians meet me and find out I play an orchestral instrument, they jump to jazz, disqualifying me from what they do. For me, the J word is often used to tell me what I know, how I know it, and which music I'm supposed to play professionally. If I write a concert piece and the harmony is thick, a classical reviewer talks about jazz. The music may actually be coming out of Stravinsky or Satie, but it is reduced to "jazz." And although these things seem trivial, it affects product placement, grants, and marketing. If you make a classical record will the audience for that music ever find out about it?

During the Mickey Katz period, the jazz press insisted that my playing that music was jazz and somehow it was troubling to them, while it was really klezmer music played by someone who'd worked legitimately in the idiom. The folks already in klezmer music insisted that what I was doing wasn't real, despite its actual authenticity. In the assertion that the music was jazz, I was often disqualified from world music venues, or even getting product placement in stores with other klezmer music. Even now on Amazon, the Mickey Katz recording, one of the most influential recordings in that music, is never klezmer music, always jazz. No one wants to admit that Black and White jazz musicians have different paths, and the competent White jazz musician is doing a range of things—commercial, ethnic, Broadway—while Black jazz musicians depend on a single economy. The jazz skills are how lots of music gets done. People that know jazz artists do film scores, Black singers in Las Vegas fill out the ethnic, Latin bands play pop. Somehow jazz—the institution—does not admit that.

Unfortunately the major reality affecting the work life of Black musicians is racism, not jazz. Ultimately, White musicians are accustomed to a kind of trade deficit: they work in Black music; Black musicians don't play [in significant numbers] in the "White musics"—rock, country, classical, Latin, polka, etc.

I really hated all the 1980s and 1990s negativity about fusion. I never understood it, and it was a negative criticism disproportionately applied to Black musicians. In this case jazz—the institution—kept Black jazz musicians from making music that appeals to Black people, particularly younger Black people, yet a few years later the jam bands do exactly this for a pointedly White audience and everything is hunky-dory. Jam bands are never critiqued in that way the jazz moniker does refer to concrete skills that other musicians are not required to have. I think most American musicians should understand jazz, and I am always shocked when the same ignorance that both of us experienced in school resurfaces so many years later. I believe in having those skills, but the music is not a fixed status quo music. Jazz is one of several important manifestations of what African American musicianship looks like. Gospel is another, the AACM [Association for the Advancement of Creative Musicians] and BAG [Black Artists' Group] are others. The world needs all of these sounds, supports these sounds.

The J Word Living outside of the Context of Jazz: Pop Culture?

There was a time in the 1960s, 1970s, and 1980s when most musicians cut their teeth on jazz, even in R & B recording sessions (Motown's Funk Brothers, Stax's Booker T. and the MGs). Many of these musicians were still essentially jazz cats doing the sessions. This cross-pollination is evident for us to see as Marcus Miller produced Miles Davis and Luther Vandross. But I wonder, what is the common music language dynamic among this generation's mainstream pop session players? I was interested in how great musicians were adapting in the straight up pop field and if they looked lovingly over at the J word. I asked Charles Wilson (who plays with Justin Timberlake, writes for Timbaland, and is currently on tour with Rihanna) and Morris Hayes (long-standing keyboardist, programmer, band mate with Prince, also currently recording and on tour, and who is a consummate bebop pianist, by the way) how they intersect musicianship and marketplace? How do audiences respond today to this question of musicality and industry prescriptions? Their comments were consistent.

Charles Wilson and Morris Hayes

CW: We are the beat generation. We are concerned with the feel that keeps you moving. We don't build from the harmonies and the melodies, we build from the beats up and float the melodies and harmony second, because that's what the people are tapped into. But I study all that music, I know that music and I flip it. I give you all that tradition, but use it to bring them in a new way.

MH: You have to consider the bottom line at the end of the day—what do the people want? I don't mind the word "commercial." It's commercial, it's commerce, you are selling something, in that, music has to sell. But Prince has figured out how to meet the people, that bottom line, and the corporate midway, and he does it his way musically, and it's [his music] always going to fill a stadium, and I have watched him do this all over the world from London to L.A. to Japan. He figured it out.

George Duke

Duke is a master performer, composer, producer, and is an icon in the jazz field, respected as someone who sits squarely in the middle touching all traditions from rock to swing. Having worked with Cannibal, Miles, Frank Zappa, and Diane Reeves. George. George Duke in a recent NPR special-feature interview affirmed, "Many of my fans asked me to do another funk project [Duke Treat/Heads Up]. There are not a lot of new R & B records in the traditional sense out there. . . . This record is wrapped in a jazz bed. This record is about fun. There is a balance. I wanted that reflected in the album. I wanted to touch on the subject of everyday people. . . . I believe artists have a responsibility to write, play, sing about the problems that are going on in the world today. Artists have always been the reflections and the healing of society. . . . I was inspired by Earth, Wind & Fire . . . they had the perfect ingredients: great lyrics, great music, and still were popular artists."

Michael Powell

In 2009 Michael Powell was finishing work on Anita Baker, a major recording artist figure who easily tracks her paths from Dinah Washington and Sarah

Vaughan and Billie Holiday. Powell's production in the 1980s revolutionized popular music radio as he introduced live session musicians again, with very "jazzy" arrangements that broke us literally out of the disco and robo-produced electronics on the Madonna stronghold and "saved us." I asked him in the beginning of the new projects in 2009, how he was managing this balance between jazz artistry and popular market expectations at the label?

MP: The first thing is, quality never gets old. For her, the approach is to try to keep it fresh and new. Anita likes a lot of dark chords, keys. There are a lot of sonorities, progressions, we don't hear anymore. I tried to incorporate those changes for the new younger listener. We are trying to stay pop, but at the same time keep it musical without being "too jazzy." The hard thing about that as a producer is when you work with a certain caliber of musicians, the hardest thing is harness, hold back, be careful with voicings. Like Greg Phillangaines, he can take it there. No ♭9ths, no altered 13ths, you are trying to achieve a popular palette. Keeping it nice for the listeners, if you do use those extended chords. You really have to make a conscious effort to hold out. It's the musicality that we are trying to go for.

WB: Did the label exec give you any restrictions, or definitions?

MP: They don't know what I am doing yet! But I'm just doing my old formula: just great songs and melodies, and surround that with really great music. When the audience hears this, they should say, "Wow that's a great song, great voice, with great production." It should come all together.

It's like, "Damn those ribs look good, smell good, but it's pork!"

They want us to deliver a great record. When you get to this level, I want to approach it differently. This time it's with live horns and live strings.

We want to take her musically to another level than we did before. I think the questions are: "What is she going to do now? What is Mike Powell going to do now this time around?" It's funny how certain chord structures take you there, but you have to sprinkle it with a little flavor and you can get away with it. And it comes out as something people will appreciate. I always try to do something that will stand the test of time; you really have to trust your ears and your heart. Jazz may just save us again!

Lee Ritenour

Spending time jamming and hanging with Lee Ritenour, I asked the industry veteran, one of the brains of the highly successful Fourplay, what was the conceptual thinking behind the formation of this group and how did it compare to classic fusion or Grover Washington or Kenny G, how did they distinguish their brand of more marketable jazz from "smooth jazz's" identity, and did he take seriously the complaint that this form is watered down or selling out the soul of the music due to its commercial acceptance?

LR: I've had a very interesting experience with the evolution of contemporary jazz, especially when it comes to the West Coast players who were there at the start of this: myself, Patrice Rushen, Dave Grusin, Abraham Loboriel, Harvey Mason, Ernie Watts, Alex Acuña, Anthony Jackson, Al Jarreau, George Duke, Tom Scott, Larry Carlton, the Crusaders, Joe Sample. Many of us played in a place called the Baked Potato every Tuesday night for five years, starting around 1974. The kids were lined up around the block starting at 5 p.m., but we didn't start until 10 p.m.! But we were all coming from a jazz point of view. We had all studied jazz seriously, and were respectful of what had come before us. We were in a period where Miles had just done those few albums including *Bitches Brew* and started crossing over. We were all coming out of this cycle where in the late sixties we had this incredible rock music like Hendrix around. People like RTF were touring, Mahavishnu with McLaughlin was forming. Herbie and the Headhunters. So there was a fusion already of funky, church-oriented Latin fusion we saw even in someone like Horace Silver. We were all evolutions of this process along with David Sanborn, Bob James. This was a great period, and all very natural. Motown had moved to L.A. and we were session players too. It was a natural thing for us to incorporate all this music.

Now cut forward, and we began to be accepted on a radio station here called the Wave, around 1985. I could hear my music next to Steely Dan or Paul Simon. This was fresh, for the moment. The corporate powers actually termed the phrase "smooth jazz" and all of sudden we were all "smooth jazz players." Pretty soon they were calling us up and saying, "We love your record but can you take that high part of the sax solo out where he climaxes the phrase, because those notes are too shrill." It got worse and worse and more diluted. I was invited several years ago to do a radio interview, and this guy was very hostile and said, "Don't you feel guilty and bad about being the creator of smooth jazz and destroying contemporary jazz?" I said, "I didn't do this. Those corporate guys did that, so that it's become a 'jazz muzak.'"

Fourplay happened in 1990, and by this time the smooth jazz thing was entrenched. The way this came together was the most beautiful experience, because we did it for fun, no pressure, and we were given a budget. We decided everybody would write, and we picked the best tunes for the record. It was a million-seller. Then we started to get the pressure. Now it was to make a hit after that, to fit the radio programming format, to repeat a million-seller. It was the dynamic of the label guys. Most of these guys have retired or are at smaller labels now saying, "I wish I had let those guys do their own thing." But organically, that was just the music we wanted to make. When you are honest with yourself musically, you are going to hit a chord with audiences who agree with what you do musically.

Where Does Jazz Live Today?

Given we have these various entry points and are simultaneously vying for some of the same audiences, same marketplace, and same desire to reach people with music, how does and where does jazz connect and live and mean today? There is again an incredible amount of product out there, almost too much. How does one distinguish between talent and just another pretty or cute face or sound? Is it time being out there, sales, or critics liking the true measure of music that counts?

On this day, August 30, 2010, I've just spoken with veteran Marian McPartland, attending her ninetieth birthday celebration at the Tanglewood Jazz Festival in Lenox, Massachusetts, the summer home of the Boston Symphony. And this speaks volumes about the home and company of jazz culture today. The festivals boast of the exuberance of excitement and support from the jazz cruises to street festivals. Sitting in Ozawa Hall (named for famed Japanese conductor Seiji Ozawa) listening to contemporary jazz pianist Mulgrew Miller and icon Ms. McPartland play, one has to consider the vibe of the environment. Jazz lives today in a variety of venues from concert halls, clubs, cruises, in the fingers and breaths of jazz ensembles in high school and college bands, on the radio, in record collections, and in the hearts of jazz lovers. In this setting though you sit quietly, no "yeahs," "get down," or "go man." This would be inappropriate. This harkens perhaps to Billy Childs's criteria that jazz requires active listening, but here you are engaged in cerebral sharing. One notices Ms. McPartland's artistic performing shelf life and more than sixty years of service, and the performances of repertoire too that have held up over those sixty artful years. Beauty, taste, elegance are terms that come to mind. But watching these two is like watching old friends play choice games on a musical playground. Taking turns with melodies, and tunes, and pushing each other on the swing, following each other's new harmonizations, sliding down circular slides, quoting, and covering tunes, showing each other sand castles and destroying them together, laughing all the while through their fingers. The applause comes by their appreciation of all this, and it takes all this to "get it," really.

David Baker

WB: David, what do you make of this question of defining, understanding jazz and where it is and going, in your mind what have you seen?

DB: The problem with the J word is all the baggage that it brings with it now, that is what is different or what has changed over the years. I'm not sure it's justified that we have this baggage, but it's there, whether we want to admit it or not. My first response to you is in a question. People can only communicate based on the words upon which they can agree on its meaning, and the meaning is the same when they use them. So what is the composite word, words, that would divest the stigma? I mean like the cat who invented the term "rock and roll." It may be that whatever words are being used are not worthy of evoking the cultural landscape that you are referring to. The problem is we have allowed the entrepreneurs to frame the problem in their terms, and you know what that means, whoever gets to frame the problem gets the say in what directions this is going to go. And so for me one of the things again is that the music now is seen almost like technology in the ways that it is propagated, the shelf life is so brief. When we [musicians] talk about music, it's in completely different ways because we understand that music didn't start yesterday, it didn't start in 1917, or when Europeans started playing music. Unless we are able to frame it so there is a consensus that transcends the notes on a piece of paper, and these names. It must embrace all the cultural aspects that we deal with. Right now the music gets vilified because a record producer says this is going to be this way, and that's what "it is." We've never been allowed to set that frame for what it is.

The music is also reflective of how the people perceive it.

I remember in the 1940s, when all of a sudden there was Little Richard, but instead of Little Richard, people [mainstream culture] bought Pat Boone. It was because of whatever was going to be more profitable for the people who make the rules.

Then you also have Baraka on the one hand and Stanley Crouch on the other turning it into a boxing match between the two of them. So this is a perfect time to be talking about what does this music mean, what do we stand for? How can we reach another generation if we don't even agree on what this music is? We have to get people in the same room because there is something that is lost on the telephone, e-mail, and even in a book. But if we can sit down, have conversations and hash out ideas, and say, "Well, look, this is what I see is wrong with that." It doesn't matter who writes the book, by the time it's in circulation, it's already in past tense. There needs to be a forum to deal with the vibrant and volatile ideas. Somebody has to take the bull by the horn and say, "Let's do this." We are deeply concerned about how things are being misappropriated. So does it start with a renaming of the phenomenon? What controls any movement in culture is about naming, because that's how we communicate with each other. So I'm wondering is there something we can do? Duke refused to use the term "jazz." And Miles was very upset about the term "jazz" because of all the baggage that it draws. And the fact now is that it has been turned into so many different things. All these things were a part of what it was, but not enough to get a full picture. It's like somebody pulling out a piece of a jigsaw puzzle and saying, "What is this?" It's a question of finding a language that people can agree on. There is no consensus today of what the music is and then there are all these fights over words, not ideas. This is the other reason that reinforces why the J word is such a problem.

WB: What changes have you seen over the years with your students, and how are they relating to music, both from what they come in knowing and where you take them?

DB: Yes, I have seen a change but it's a regression rather than a progression. They come in already with their concepts about what the music is, without any experience about how all these interactions have affected the original forms. And when this happens it's like not being able to see the forest because of the forest. I'm now restructuring and narrowing my classes down to the specifics and the important people and the important ideas, instead of trying to take care of everything and everybody that's out there. So it seems to me we have to start with a reframing of what we are looking at. And the minute you connect the two, music and culture, then you set up benchmarks that reflect the culture because the culture was there before the music.

Take the words "soul," "smooth jazz," we have to be able to draw distinctions between these, among Grover Washington, David Sanborn, or Kenny G. They want the trappings of jazz, to play "jazzy," but they want to play jazz. But they are using the jazz, but the words are mispronounced, the wrong meanings, and over time when it is used this way then it's assumed it's the new meaning. When I say soul, I mean Aretha Franklin, James Brown, and the people who come out of that tradition.

But when this has been covered by people who have grafted onto it something that wasn't there from the beginning or something that changes the meaning of it, that's a problem. I mean do what you need to do for evolutionary purposes, but don't destroy the original while you do this. And without knowing the original how can you know the benchmarks? Ninety percent of the problem here is how we use words. What this is about is considering a change of the language.

Billy Taylor

Jazz lives in places outside of the United States. Because they have come to respect the music and all the aspects of it as a means of communication, a way of making a point, the freedom to say what you mean, musically. When I think about my race, who invented this music, we have taken very little and made a world-renowned classic music, which speaks to people all over the world. Jazz is the kind of music that shows people who aren't allowed to speak a way to say things that are meaningful. And jazz is one of the ways to do this. African Americans developed a music which spoke of freedom that was beautiful and that the world wanted to have this, to be spoken musically. That's not happening, generally speaking, today in jazz. There is nothing comparable to a Coleman Hawkins taking *Body and Soul* and playing for three minutes, and people listening to that and playing it over and over because it was meaningful to them. Jazz does not have the same relevance today because it's manipulated by people who don't care about the music. The industry is doing things that are harmful to music. If you move to where we are today from Ellington, to Oliver Nelson, then to Quincy, just these, music was meaningful to a large amount of people, because it spoke of who we were, how we thought, something we could all share in, even if we didn't speak the same languages. Jazz is not dead yet, but it's very close to it because there is no way we can compete with volumes, availability, in terms of the way the water has been muddied.

WB: What must we do to be saved?

BT: There are many who are doing things to keep the music needed and valued. We are all having the same problem and we have to go back to save our souls, but it's how we are going to have to take the next steps to putting the music in front of the people like they are doing with *American Idol*. Now that aspect is also what is killing the music. But, they know how to do this over and over again although it seems to serve no useful purpose because it's just the presentation of the same old things, duplicated. We have to do this better. Coltrane, Miles, Monk: They were trying to do something that reached the people, and they were saying something that was musical. They were also trying to take something but offer it down the line a little better, a little further, that's what the artists did. We have to take and find better ways to say this music to larger numbers of people, and not just copying things but making other people believe as we do. And we have to create programs, boat rides, festivals with the same fervor of excitement; we can't paint ourselves into the corner anymore.

Cadences

What we notice in periods like these (Harlem Renaissance, bebop, social protest, soul movements) with "the stakes so high, do or die, sell or fail, newly find, now redefine," that true artists are deeply committed to expressive work that conveys who they are, the conflicts, the angst, and the triumphs of the human struggle for good and worse, music that matters. This (what meaneth the J word today) is a relevant question at a critically defining time. And that could mean being signed, on the charts, "in the mix," and commercial or liked, too. It is the art we hold to as blood, and what we in marked significant ways respond to in the long run, and what is required of jazz, art in this "commercial products/faces period." One might say jazz today is not redefining itself, nor filling a void, and not providing for musicians an artistic space as it had done and needed to do in the past. That may be, as Esperanza said, "good" as this culture may not require it to " have a name" or provide community or be the only source material for new progressive musical art in the public commercial spaces. Jazz is a huge cultural form regardless, will always be, we guess because this is great music, and artistry, no question. The questions certainly are not "Is jazz dead?" or "What is its future?" It is the wrestling with the place of jazz in the marketplace, and its slighted identity as it lives in its own hard-won present. Where does the J word live to be a music that has connectivity in our times? Looking away from radio lists, or pop polls, jazz is our creative music art form and its story is heard from one place consistently: among the many players in the fields. The participants are both new players in the game: old school, those who use turntables with a mojo, and those for whom the deepest meaning resonates only from the bottom pitches of a wood bass. The artistry of jazz today is as varied and in this varied voice comes its present, reflections of its past, and certainly its future. There is clearly a range of exciting and new artists participating in mainstream jazz today. But jazz has never been about the work of a single art-ist. One community and its aesthetic movements have never single-handedly reigned at once, but crisscrossed in a sea of artists and audience approaches and likes. But the definitions have come from many musicians working the language, the culture of improvisation, blues, to modern sonority and themes, connected to American living. Or as Maria Schneider so aptly put it, "The new reality is global . . . through music in this present time, one can also experience a sort-of citizenry of the world."

It is clear that all these artists agree that the critical ingredients of jazz are culture, history, mentoring, heroes, traditions, finding your voice, and the defi-nitions lie primary in the priority to make music that has no restricting labels, but holding onto traditions that have value. And that music has real meaning in our culture especially when it connects to the world we truly live in. Every-body here seems to agree as well that jazz music cannot be moved, taken from its culture and that the real enemy of jazz may not be solely commodification, industry dictation, or label fabrication at all. Our own separations from the knowledge of the core root of jazz, meaning tied to its history, is what pains us.

Seems we have to find ways to dislodge the blockages in our culture that prevent young people to feel and see examples of creative artistry that is iconic, relevant, and challenge them to use that language to decode and explain the world they fit in and live in. For many of us, that would be the J word. And maybe, as Spalding hinted at, this is a great time to be shedding old burdens of definition, justification, and unnecessary anxieties of its survival rate.

But lastly, we should consider creating new environments, culture, audi-ences, musicians, institutions that the J word can plant itself in; the loving soil of the souls of new listeners. The J word has to be wrapped around the peoples' moving, celebrating feet, and it has to be whispered, sung lyrically, and shouted meaningfully as the music that means the best of who they are and the beat to accompany where we are headed.

～

Bicycling in Bangkok: Considering Condition, Context, Challenge, Conflict, Change, Charge, Cash, Comfort, and Complacency

With the increases in the demarcation of the haves and the do-not-haves, times have gotten tougher, even more for the ones we keep stepping over and on. These dynamics in society never change and are seemingly getting worse. The heat just shifts to different days of the week, but every month and every year it's the same: people are "hit." It seems the poor in every city, culture, continent are less and less likely to be thought of, served, given advantages, seeing and being themselves as "worthy," and receiving the blessed societal fruits of normalcy others benefit from. If you don't see yourself as having the "goods" (looks, cultural stuff, and goodies), what then do you do to be? You live perhaps the poetic blues life, that is, your lines of song are constructed in a tonality that sounds, exists, and allows expression in the darker keys, modes of modern life, meaning; you ain't got all the shit everybody else got, what you're supposed to have. This to me is universal, wherever folks are oppressed in societal cultural systems from Baghdad, to Georgia, both in Russia and the United States, and China and the Sudan.

I began to reflect more deeply on the meaning of being poor and powerless as I begin to feel more empathy and understanding of what I was seeing all the time, but sat silent about. You come to places in your maturity where you can't be quiet about injustice, because social rotting stinks. Why are people acting so desperately, I asked myself? It is clear now, as it probably has always been; the context and the ensuing conditions of peoples' lives in a difficult economy and culture, show up in all the conflicts one encounters. But we have to consider what will it take to change all this and who will be charged with our tasks to make our world better for everybody?

Condition

There is no doubt in my mind that the powerless and poor are this way because someone else set and controls the social conditions we are born into. Your own elevation out of this condition, if you're lucky, is ushered in by all kinds of operating factors like, being lucky, getting your blessings, having a will to survive, ingenuity, smartness, resolve, or figuring out the game. There is no way out of the conditions of poverty and powerlessness it seems, to pull away permanently from the grasp of the social cast of economic and societal poverty except by cracking through these social barriers, through human enterprise when people are empowered and self-determined, inspired and refuse to accept their threat of death.

And this breaking away can't be inevitable for all or most. My observations do not grow from knowledge of social theory. I am seeing this from living and growing up, encountering the powerless and watching shifting cultural or social divides that are static in places all around the country. Riding in South Central L.A. and visiting a cultural center set up to empower young people and keep them safe provided me with an experience that broke me out of my own bubble, that people, young people are faced with seemingly insurmountable social odds that will probably in my time never change. I don't think anyone wants to be poor and feel "less than," nor have less than others. I know now that the social condition we see is the result of powerful and prevailing presets of class, social, economic equations which are permanent at worst and normative at best, and bent at times but never broken. Rags to riches are stories and not reality. Yet riches rule. On my plane ride in today, I overheard a woman lamenting that her recently graduated college child was making up her mind over what she wanted to do with her life. Her friend asked, "What is she doing now?" The distraught mom replied, "Oh, she's bicycling in Bangkok. That's what she wanted to do until she figures it out." Her friend raised concerns about this choice and her safety. The lamenting mother replied, "Oh, it's ok, we're paying for it." The reason for my reflection is due to my desire to shake my own complacency, find understanding, despite the reality that exploitation of the powerless will never cease, nor the social conditions that plague us and disturb and rub our sense of deep concerns for our sisters and brothers who are deeply locked in this struggle. So the question becomes, what can we do to reach out to influence change in the reality of this whacked situation?

Contexts and Conflict

Another reason for my own exploration of the conditions of powerlessness I see so rampant is my own sense of frustration and powerlessness to absolve the social contexts of my own people here in America, and everywhere I see us living in the world. But you don't have to be in South Central to find it. I can start in my own neighborhood where I grew up. I traveled recently to my old block. In the days when I grew up there, we thought it was a protected Black bubble where we were to spring from and rule the new world. On that block this year alone there were fourteen homes abandoned as a result of the housing crisis in mortgages in the United States in 2008. That block is devastated. In the neighboring areas close to my current block in Boston, the social reality of financial and social anxiety is so palpable among people, you could cut a chunk of this "mist of living funk" out of the air, and if you could cook it up and serve it we would fix hunger in the world. Anxiety over housing, jobs, crime, and cultural chaos is rampant and raging more than I have ever seen in my life. And yet this identity that thickens into another generation's permanency is owned by Blacks, Browns, and people of color I see everywhere in this nation. It is impossible to be separated from this human spiritual sadness and disappointment I feel from the fallout of social cultural disparity that is prevalent. In travels throughout New York, California, Boston, and the South, there is another century of Brown peoples, who are taking care of White children, mopping hotel floors, cleaning motel rooms, and serving in our service industries. And I wonder: Good work or a system of entrenched powerlessness at work?

Herein is a social, class conflict worn around the necks of many people I know. I wrote in 1999, some ten years ago as I was visiting Utah, a poem called "Wearing Afros in 1999." Here I speak about the shame I felt to be privileged, to be near snow-covered mountains as the world around, even then was cracking up on crack, and we all were feeling social anxiety all around. I spoke and wrote on the conflict so many of us were in, as to what must be done to reach out and help contribute to a change needed to free and clear the world of the social stronghold of depressed social states we were in. That was ten years ago and I am even more deeply conflicted. Because the reality is that once you have tasted the success of your sweat, of the privileges of your stations in life, it is not easy to look in other directions toward the devastation you run from, and to have your luxuries or accomplishment. The poor blues tonality becomes not the music you ever care to listen to. Poor and powerless peoples' problems have become "theirs, not yours" and more absent from the comfort of conversations you are having with your friends about your next deal or project or vacation or investment or whatever. The blues life and poor peoples' shit—their "condition"—is a social context that is best remedied if they got it together, fast. "Their challenges" will become a conflict of my best interests if I bend and be "over there." The inevitable changes and shifts in this situation more easily become a social change that is fixed by a charge given to us by our ministers as, praying for someone, or our politicians who run for office while imploring a theme of change. I wonder what change will really bring, and that is the conflict so many of us face because the world shrinks because of space, and as the room is crowded the resources decrease, and my comforts too. I am thinking a lot about our busted roles and responsibilities in reversing the rampant roll down the hill, now backward and downward of our failing and falling communities. In this blues, of all of ours, we must deal with this our locked static modality when addressing the social realties we see daily, yet stand on our stages and sing so silently about.

Cash and Comfort

I'm sure it is cash and comfort that is the buffer that keeps the silence and the balance between our concern and our sanity. This comfort makes it difficult to move into some kind of commitment to change the social conditions we see daily around us as we drive through or by or around. There is a program in South Central L.A. called A Place Called Home. Visiting there brought tears to my heart and eyes, just as I am dealing with my own charge about getting off my "fat butt" of complacency around powerless peoples' blues. This center is a compound of comfort and stability, a safe place for young people to enjoy music lessons, dance, and ballet from African to modern, participate in jazz, rock ensembles, art, computers, produce and record music demos, mentoring and family counseling, health and fitness, peer advising, literature and poetry, resource center and library, serving two thousand kids from ages thirteen to twenty-one for the big fat price of free. The environment is busy with love and caring and commitment as every kid has to swear to live by something they call "habits of the mind and heart," and ethics, and positive image and commitment to focus and skill building to contribute to their community.

In an earlier piece, I asked whose call is this to accountability? Mom? Dad? Community, churches, schools, leaders, common people in the streets? The media megacultural industry? Here with this is a model of societal success which is immediate, attractive, valued possibilities and can be seen and sustained visibly. We have to be courageous and innovative like the people here to help reposition a balance of visible and real options. Here are values, payoffs presented where there is a lack of resources, there is a commitment to imbue these South Central youth with a desire to seek higher goals that make them independent, self-propelled, creative, innovative.

Time and time again over the years, it keeps proving that in our culture creative arts are powerful and effective expressions that change peoples' lives, and sustains those identities and ideas. Creative culture for sure must seek deeper commitments and engagement to affect people to be empowered beyond powerlessness. This kind of program is an example of how we can commit to fight the bombardment of problematic chaos that we are forced now to accept, by erasing the definition of nonworth from young people and empowering them to redefine themselves as worthy, and providing tools and encouragement that are missing and disrupted and corrupted.

One very pervasive block of the potential for people today to be moved beyond powerlessness and be empowered internally is the external bombardment of images and messages of "others." And those "others" never look like the people who are powerless. So the conflict again is that there are many messages about what is the good life, the desired normalcy. Mega media commodified televised messages are hugely part of the problem. What blinds the beauty in us is the external projected commodified ideal that cash will give you comfort, as opposed to defining an image of yourself that does not bend to the dictates of greed and selfishness that comes with the territory of getting cash and purchasing your comforts. Self-worth prepares and propels people for greatness and social, spiritual, and economic normalcy. People don't need to be rich, but they need rest from social destruction—a result of the race to obtain goodies. Powerlessness and poverty then become a context not a condition of your genes, lack of intelligence, or a desire to be inhuman.

The discomfort we have in moving away for these locked identities is that these social states are so entrenched in our definition of society, culture, no side can agree on how to fix the problems or find the remedies. Who you calling poor? Who says I'm down and out and powerless? Who are you to be saying? When did you begin to have your conversation about changing my condition?

What has happened—unlike the poor in the 1920s who were impoverished Americans suffering from the Depression years, or the droughts of the Midwest in the 1930s, or the social dissatisfaction in the 1960s—while there were cultural revolution voices, protest and countercultural movements, what we have now is a super commodified status of what is called ghetto Fabulous, urban identity, keeping it real. There is here a celebrated mythology of heroism generated from perceived prison power identity, being "gangsta" and the idea that one proof of your worth may be a trip to the penitentiary. This is real. Turfs for what becomes your playing field are fought over in communities, and our children are caught in the war field and games. So we have now competing ideas of our truest culture, comfort, and both of these are realized and mechanized by one thing, getting more cash.

Charge and Change and Challenge

How would change come and what would it look like? Who would be so noble and change, and what do you want me to give up, give into, and how long will it take for this change to be my reality?

The Beverly Hillbillies didn't change shit. And we liked that. As a matter of fact, we delighted in watching Granny grab her rifle, aim to shoot Mr. Dry-ass-dale right in his stiff behind. The one thing I am noting is value construction and definition. We will never all agree on these terms like, values, "the good life," self-worth, what is normal, comfort. Because most assertions of what the problems are is an indictment against the best that you, I, and them over there have come to be. And then you have invested so much into the definition of your worldview, whether it's "mainstream, Pleasantville, America," Wall Street or Walmarts, or "the common real and ghetto fabulous urban." That's just three competing identity world-views, we didn't add in a Catholic version, Muslim version, Jewish ver-sion, a call for gender and sexuality definitions, ethnic, regional, and race revision, and versions of values! So the charge of change for everybody is clearly challenging.

What kind of living, values would be normative, comfortable, and bring to the table an equal number of participants to discuss what needs to happen to maintain a society where everyone would be empowered to see themselves as valued being there at the table? What would that equation for equality and a normative definition of balance look like?

I have no idea.

That is the challenge. That our discourses lead us to what it would take to dismantle the societal matrixes of play to prevent people from slipping into permanent casted boxes. And who among you is willing to give up the comfort or cash necessary to provide the balances needed in moving toward this? Who cares, and who's listening? The challenge also would be to listen to someone tell you her story. That challenge is to take the time to engage with the plight of someone else's circumstances, to gain clarity on how she got there, because inevitably each one of us is tied in King's definitions of "the inescapable network of mutuality." We'd have to find a few songs in keys that everyone could sing, and we'd have to agree on the tempo, and we'd have to agree upon what the agreed cadences could sound like.

Many of the questions pondered here will remain a challenge to answer adequately, I'm sure. The charge though is more basic and doable. We have to slow down and take more time to think about and invest in caring more for others and not just our own possessions. I often share that being actively involved in cultivating our culture is one of the investments we can make to ensure we are always the best we are becoming. The safeguard to social chaos at this point, so close to our edges of incivility, is a careful and caring concern for one another.

The human response, the artist response to create a poetry of a blues to illuminate the broken condition and sing through it, or as in jazz, "play through the changes" is a useful idea. The poor and powerless in all of us makes it necessary and important to consider these conditions we know are all around us. Just having an eye and concern on the least of us, having em-pathy, being aware when the power systems suffocate people, and having the courage to speak up and not step on or over helps illuminate the inequities that our comforts and complacency blind us to. Bicycling in Bangkok won't be an option if we are seeking most days to consider doing the right things, being useful of and with our time while we're figuring it out.

It is in this context that any change can come. The decreasing of the demarcation of the haves and the have-nots, and the stopping of stepping over and on people, these are the human interactive dynamics in our society that must change. Every time you sit and speak to someone and share where possible, a piece of your day that is lifting to the next person, this action raises greatly the potential of the other person to be a bit more powerful. That person's job then becomes sustaining that idea of empowerment, and as we hold each other up, each one of us can be building on a shared definition of our valued worth being possible.

∿

Payoff: Investing Yourself in a Multi-Toned, Voiced, Angled, and Cultured World (May 29, 2009)

Delivered at University of St. Thomas, Fortieth Anniversary of Multicultural Students Services Celebration, St. Paul, Minnesota

What an honor to be here. I am so very appreciative and honored to get a chance to share with you on this fortieth year celebrating multicultural advocacy, programming/education on this campus. Denise, so proud of you, your office, and the efforts of the administration to provide, a garden, to grow these wonderful students toward a place and into practices of academic and cultural excellence.

Given our recent struggles in the world markets, and following our president's advice to "invest wisely, with accountability, and moral and ethical choices," multicultural truth, reality, and the beauty of all the people, all the time is, really "staying it real." Make no doubt about it, God did not paint the world one color, or perspective or view, all White. White Out is not our cover nor correction, but there is from the beginning an equal blending of beautiful colors, a rich and textured many-scented garden cultivated in rich soils. I like to think of a multicultural world as a beautiful garden we walk through and among. God is the ultimate planter who asks us not to kick through the soil, step on the roots, pick inappropriately, but rather thankfully gaze in its beauty and wonder.

We ought to just marvel in our investing in a multitoned, voiced, angled, and cultured world. To our academic cultural side as it relates to living in a multicultural world, author and social theorist Manning Marable has written very powerfully on this point. He states in his article, "Black Studies, Multiculturalism and the Future of American Education":

> We must rethink old categories and old ways of perceiving each other. We must define the issue of diversity as a dynamic, changing concept, leading us to explore problems of human relations and social equality in a manner which will expand the principles of fairness and opportunity to all members of society. . . . Culture is the textured pattern of collected memory, the critical consciousness, and aspirations of a people. . . . The national debate over "multiculturalism" assumes such critical significance within political discourse, as well as in the structure of the economy and society. . . . Our nation's cultural heritage does not begin and end with the intellectual and aesthetic productions of Western Europe. Multiculturalism suggests that the cross-cultural literacy and awareness . . . is critical in understanding the essence of the American experience "from the bottom up." The criteria for educational excellence must include a truly multicultural vision and definition. (Quoted from *A Turbulent Voyage: Readings in African American Studies,* Collegiate Press, 1997)

Don't you love Obama, just the thought of it? He's not going to change the world, but he sure does make it look like the world wants to change. There's no way, no matter what your political blending or bending is, that we are going to talk about multiculturalism and forget we have the first Black president, and a beautiful, brilliant, and charming African American first lady. They are just truly representing.

I watched the whole affair for a year with my parents, nearing ninety. And my dad said to me, "This is the first time Black people could really feel that maybe, after all these years this is something they could get behind and their vote could really count for something they believed in."

For me, this is the first time that I am the same age as the president of the United States. They were always old White guys. Now maybe this is not a snippet of multiculturalism at all, but really just me getting old. But, I'll take it either way. It is meaningful in this way, and that can't be belittled, it really cannot: We have a Black president.

Obama for me felt like he was a right one at this time and what feels right about this one is that the times out of which he was born makes him prepared for the challenges we face together. He is someone who was birthed with the hope promised out of the civil rights era, and who grew up on the beat of modern urban America, who studied in college while being able to see regime changes, and who came to professional maturity to see the latest troubling of our noble democracy. Someone whose cultural, racial, geographical mapping ends up being from Kenya, his father a revolutionary and brilliant mind, having a Muslim name, deep in Christian beliefs, a deeply American praxis, committed to communities, and upholding the principles of integrity, hard work, and prideful in educational excellence.

But to watch people gathered from places all around the world to celebrate his winning of the presidential race was emblematic of the global outcry for meaning and the quenching of the dry throats we've endured for a sense of sanity in our societies. This global equation, this multicultured, textured garden growing all more resonant and fragrant, is what this program models at St. Thomas.

I think many of us have to look at this "Obama presidency" revolution, this bright new change of consciousness, both on the surface to recognize and appreciate our immediate joy, and as well deeply to address what it has meant and can mean. And I think that's what Marable from the quote I read earlier is referring to when he says, "We must re-think old categories and old ways of perceiving each other. We must define the issues of diversity as a dynamic, changing concept, leading us to explore problems of human relations." The recent overtures, attempts with Cuba, Mexico, South America, Canada, Europe, while at this point only symbolic, may represent a world that is global in its sharing of power, global in its reach to extend across human relations, and global in new celebrations of culture and people.

One of the great challenges and charges of the twenty-first century is guiding people in our society to maintain our humanness. How must we become again considerate, compassionate, and civil in our exchanges and ideology? Where we have fallen short, it seems to me, is in the cultivation of being humane and maintaining this principle of identity and character. Our societal "working(s)" that cultivate this kind of reflective thinking are bulwarks against a culture seemed destined to fall into upholding problematic values and identities that look, lock, and push us backward again. I'm excited about the possibilities now of making great and good on the hope that we can work toward pushing us to spring forward again.

And we don't live in a world destined for divisions, but our destiny is harmonious, continues and builds polyphonic, polyrhythmic and resonates best deeply with rich colors and hues, and marked with the blues, and as beautifully constructed as Bach lines and Zora Hurston's ethnic ties. There is great payoff to explore the market measured in wider colorful meanings and to be a contributing member of the human as God and nature intended.

So the other day I mentioned to my dear colleague here, Dr. Kanishka Chowdury, "What's up with this difference and tolerance stuff you all talk about here?" I wrote him. "I don't like what either term implies, but rather, I like, singing and sounding together, music/arts as a model means you and I, we, are together. While we attempt to harmonize, and we reach downbeats, sometimes there is syncopation, and we create, jazz, soul, funk, blues, and bebop. Sonorities are nonhierarchical different melodic fragments, stacked and sounding together. Here there are no notions of hierarchical pronouncement of 'difference or who tolerates who,' but just all together, it sounds. We sound, and sounding in the earth is a reality."

The burden of difference and tolerance is what many object to. One question becomes, "Why am I burdened with examining, relating my difference within your normative gaze?" I have to accept the burden of feeling your tolerance, as someone who has been given the entitlement to tolerate, put up with me, others. And, different from what and why am "I" being asked to tolerate "you"? And who are "you" to "tolerate me"? And who says anyway that there is difference and tolerance to be represented? Who defines my difference? You?

Tolerance assumes you have the rightful place, and you are holding your breath, adjusting to me until you are comfortable. In this way a temporary accommodation. And difference, makes me have to bear the burden of distinguishing myself for you. Next, I have to say, how and why I'm different, then the discourse follows about my differences. In the end we all just want to be "me," and all I need you to be for that, is for you to be "you."

As a musician I hear this as a many pitched chord, with a sonority sounding together; that's the model. Or a walk in a many fragranced garden that best celebrates and recognizes diversity.

Well, that's how we ended up, just like we left when we had fun all the time fussing five years ago. Tolerance and difference needs to be unpacked to in my mind end up only meaning and representing terms of convenience, not power, solely for the act of speaking and naming relative qualities, not assigning hierarchical relationships.

Now, in terms of the work you all, these bright students gathered here, are doing out in this new global world of new relationships and the promise of hope; you have to be proactive with your reach toward excellence, and yes, you have to be proactive orientated with hatred and evil. Gain for yourselves personal worth, dignity, move toward excellence, and put yourselves at the buttons of power and racism, classism, sexism, other-isms will be seriously undermined. You can dismantle the debilitating bite and sting, hurt, humiliation, insult to your intelligence, and the affront to your humanity these isms cause, and secondly, you can change your "non-access to power." Two things will seriously dismantle social-isms: it's lessened by your excellence and then putting yourselves in position to have access to power by being there at "the button." The biggest reason why there is racism at institutions is largely because you are not there teaching, administrating, and making decisions that effect change. That's what is meant by power, having the means to execute decisions that affect people and meaning. Excellence is the best weapon against this kind of stupidity from people or from an institution. And by creating solid patterns for success, this wave creates an impenetrable mind-set that ensures motion and looking forward; history is full of examples of this.

When you know your history, you excel in excellence, you know your craft, you are "bout it, bout it," you then create images, ideas, creative activity that lifts you above the snarls of the fantasy of White superiority, dummy-male dominance, greed, and racism. To evoke a Malcolm X affirmation, "Once you change your thought pattern, you change your attitude. Once you change your attitude, it changes your behavioral patterns, and then you go into some action." That's how you first deal head-on with hate. That's how you come to your White, Asian, Hispanic, Muslim brother and sister and bring something to the table about a shared humanity of greatness. Your issues of being Black, or Latino, Asian, White male under attack are not more important, though it may be more pressing than other problems in the universe of issues. Because really, today's reality is that we are less divided by Black, White and more diluted, derailed by the inhumane mind-set of greed and power hunger that is exhibited more brazenly and bold than ever. Today, you have to come together on what are common strategies. The statue of John Ireland stands and reminds us of his commitment to tolerance and understanding.

What is uneven is that inequality is not equally visited upon the greedy. Today's issues megaculturally can be seen heated by the continual rapid rise of greedy, power hungry men, societies, and cultural enterprises that dominate, exploit, then constrict human capacity. That insanity is sold as reality in culture: radio, literature, music, news and media, and especially popular culture commodifications. These become mythologies, preferred because they are strategically placed in view as normative, standard, and then redescribed as culture. The reality is that God is the planter of a huge garden we walk through, and there are so many varieties of beauty, scent, texture. All grow in the garden.

So we come here tonight to raise up, celebrate, give more rise to leadership, significance of this program in forty years of service to St. Thomas community, for the advocacy of diversity initiatives, work done on behalf of students, work being done by the students, this strategic, safe place garden, called Multicultural Affairs, we say, Thank You! for it, and be moved to greater places because of it.

∽

The Baking of American Music Culture

When you are dealing in print about music and cultural creative history in the academy, education, and pedagogy, even in the popular press with music culture, it has been written traditionally by non-Black writers. These writers have leaned and tended toward a culturally biased history narrative that has missed highlighting Black intellectual creative invention, innovation. This leaves us following a narrative that artistry molded by mostly western European traditions and the industries of technology provides all the "best and worthy" American music culture.

But in fact the viewing of the histories suggest Black bards, plantation singers and musicians who were mixing creativity by necessity, and knowledge of "forms" were the first true creators and users of the forms and styles that came to be recognized and celebrated as "American popular" culture music.

You have to begin with slave spirituals, the reports of missionaries who found these "slave renditions" and slaves singing by themselves into the night, and their gatherings in slave quarters, the famed Congo square to be the first real blending of all of this. They were the ones who "stirred" things up and started the controversies and complaints among White "insiders" way before F. Scott Fitzgerald talks about the Jazz Age starting because White teens were dancing to a Black composer's Charleston, or any writer rambling on about ragtime infecting America, or White southern groups complaining about the immorality of Black songs as in the 1950s. Those early slave inventors never get the credit because they are dead and never asked for it. Broadway, Tin Pan Alley, march music, popular song and dance first get aesthetic, stylistic, and certainly rhythmic roots from this slave performed stuff, field cries and spirituals.

Taken steps further, blues and jazz roots come from this also before they can be traced to European harmonic conventions. But even this "twisting" can be traced too to Scott Joplin's "intention and inventions" and the way he cultivated a school of younger players to refine this in sheet music and jam sessions way before the Kansas City jams or Tin Pan Alley or the Brill

Building writers' publishing machinery even gets started. We can't forget Louis Moreau Gottschalk's fascination with Black dance, song forms which he heard done by Black singers and dancers in New Orleans at Cong Square which he then composes and publishes as the *Banjo and Dance of the Negro* in the 1800s. These, it seems to me are clear examples of this creative invention that sparked music copy-ation and is on record!

In band culture, the record of Black trumpeter, band leader, composer Francis Johnson (1792–1844) and his Johnson Celebrated Cotillion Band of Philadelphia was heralded then as rivaling Europe's best wind bands. Frank Johnson's leadership and unique artistic accomplishments in this regard has been well documented. The most remarkable musical sound invention introduced to the world at yet another time in the 1870s was the work of the Fisk Jubilee Singers. This was a college educated group of young Black performers, singing Negro spirituals. Europe had never heard anything like this and the musical world was changed forever.

European composer great Anton Dvorak makes the first global outcry to not forget about the Black writers who are your most original voices: "I am satisfied that the future music of this country must be founded upon what are called the Negro melodies." This was published in a critical article as a letter to Americans in the *New York Herald* in 1893. Dvorak had been recently employed here to head the National Conservatory. White critical press and the academy openly denied and dismissed this, arguing that Blacks had created nothing that was modern or American in music. A joke, yet completely in line with current racist thinking that drives historical debates in the academy which consistently undermine reporting on the inventive, intellectual, and cultural contributions of Black people in general.

Even taken toward another direction, American popular culture—dance, theater, comedy—which led to Broadway and Hollywood, maps were drawn from an equally powerful series of cultural inventions: the early nineteenth-century minstrel shows, both White and colored faced. These began with Daddy Rice, who "exploited and commercialized" a common Black man's dance movements, called it Jim Crow, and made the preeminent American cultural theater form, the American minstrel show from which all American entertainment comes. I am as well reminded of the comments of nineteenth-century author J. Kinnard's comments in 1845:

> Who are our true rulers? The Negro poets to be sure. Do they not set the fashion and give laws to the public taste? Let one of them in the swamps of Carolina compose a new song, and it no sooner reaches the ear of a white ama-

teur, than it is written down, amended (almost spoilt), printed then put upon a course of rapid dissemination to cease only with utmost bounds of Anglo-Saxondom, perhaps with the world. Meanwhile the poor author digs away with his hoe, utterly ignorant of his greatness. (Quoted from Eileen Southern, *The Music of Black Americans: A History*, New York: Norton, 1977, 93.)

Just from these accounts alone screams the question: Why has the American music story been drawn incorrectly with roads and conclusions pointing mostly toward European American invention, while celebrating Black energy and style, leaving out Black creative critical conscious invention and innovation?

Quite another important issue besides the proper documentation and qualification of these contributions is the public marketing and dissemination of information/culture. In every case this is an issue of the power of culture communication. In other words, he who has the power to "put it out there" has the power to exploit, control, claim ownership, and give it the spin. The question of who benefits from the cultural commodity in market sells and culture capital seized upon is crucial and must be examined.

There are four essential basic elements in my view that distinguish American popular music from all other music in the world: (1) the experience—unique historical/cultural narrative; (2) the music and beats—blues melodic mode, beat patterns, forms, rhythmic drives; (3) the meanings—rituals, church, jam sessions, marches, and social dances, philosophy of expression; and (4) the stylings—artistry, approach, aesthetic. If you took Black culture and artistry as a contributing voice in contemporary popular music out of this mix of elements, American popular music would, as we know it, cease to exist. The narrative exploring American popular music culture deserves other framings of the questions, other tellings of the history, other considerations that help to draw our critical attention to the many and varied ways that American music got stirred up, mixed into the mix, and got "out there."

More importantly is the exploration and documentation of what overall effect these contributions have had on American cultural identity and in its "people meaning." These great and wide cultural implications must be always documented newly before again mass media and the scholarly world forget and further disseminate narratives about origins and historical implications. This is a more complete baking of American music culture.

CHAPTER TWELVE

Tag and Coda

Mama Said Knock It Out: "Plan Your Work and Work Your Plan, Baby"

July 2009–July 2010

When my mother died, I saw that my father was an old man for the first time in my life. So I had to decide what to do, how would I see the world now and live my life with this new reality. My assumptions and my priorities changed. I had some clarity, but I still had to work through some fog about this. The loss thing in death is bad because you can't bring them back. When my mom died that summer (2008), we had not gotten over the loss of sleep due the six months of blues we'd been suffering from as my eldest brother had just died. Anne wasn't very sick. There was no family drama over her passing, no issues with the usual family squabbles over money, possessions, and we had no pain in the funeral rituals associated with her death. My mom had an incredibly warm and uplifting memorial on Friday, June 20, 2008. It was a warm day, actually beautiful as if the sun had opened up just for the skies to be warm and bright to symbolically receive her. The mausoleum at Evergreen Cemetery Chapel at 19807 Woodward Avenue in Detroit where we had scheduled her memorial service was open and available early in the day for setup.

The problem with the death piece though is that after it's over you can't go on the next day and fix it all and start again, reboot to work on the plan to bring the person back. Unless your family person's name is Lazarus or something, she is gone forever. That forever and not coming around again

221

was what I found most troubling, deeper than the pain of what the cry was meant to get to. That emptiness, my mother's "gone-ness" was on many days a permanent and conditioned context unbearable. There's nothing I could do about it, despite me thinking for the best that I would wake up and say, "Damn, that was a horrible dream," and smile. The wake-up never happens. I'm an insides guy. I feel and internalize; my logic centers are there. Loss felt deep from within is deeper than pain; it's disturbing, which resonates as a loss in your brain, your being, and the deeper part of the core in the heart. There's something missing in your life when someone you are connected with dies, especially a mother, I guess. I mean I've never lost a mother before but I sure hope this "shit" never happens to me again. And when death approaches undetected, taking hold to take someone out you can't slow it, as it grabs and the person is snatched away. I had to fly in on a plane knowing my mother was dying in a hospital bed, and that the family was waiting on me to get there.

So I didn't have enough dirt left in my stomach to dry up any more tears. I was dry. But I find it just amazing when I think about it now, months later that my mother is gone. She actually died. This I find for some reason an amazing reality because death is an incredible finality. Once a life stops beating, that's it. It reminds you of how incredibly precious a human person is and added to that, the worth of the human person who brought you into life. Wow.

Soul Gone Home

The opera Soul Gone Home (released June 2010, Albany Records) framed my mother's going home. How musically fitting. I hate death and as I have become older, I have lost sooooo many people whom I lived to be here for and to check in with. These were all people who gave me definition and shaping and told me I was not there yet, and were there with me when I had not yet arrived, and as I arrived they opened the door, turned on the lights, and explained what was now in the room. I can hear my mother's words of instruction now still so crystal clear, "You gotta plan your work and work your plan, baby."

My Spring Forward record, released in the spring of 2009 (Innova Records) was my requiem record, first to my uncle, friends, Mark Ledford, Bill Brown, then my cousin dies, then my aunt. Before that my niece Brooke Banfield died, then Regina Carter's mom dies. The very aunt, Aunt Nelle whom I spoke with as I was returning to Boston in 2005, dies, then my brother dies in January 2008, then bam, six months later as I am recording my opera *Soul Gone Home*, my mother dies. In the making of the *Spring Forward* record during the year in 2005, I had to stop everything, creatively. I couldn't play so I canceled gigs. I couldn't write music. I couldn't write words. I just stopped everything because the pain was so deep. I was creatively paralyzed. But I got over that because I had to grow up and accept the fact that people die, and I would never stop again or be so low that I couldn't function in life due to death. In a very twisted way, I was preparing myself without even knowing it for the death of my big brother, then six months after, my mother's. It was not a plan I had intended on working, and I'm still working it out. But again, my mother always said, "Baby, plan your work and work your plan." I believed in that. I remember this sooooo vividly. Mom would sit at five in the mornings having her coffee, just sitting there quietly thinking to herself. I would come down the stairs as a child and say, "Mom, what are you doing?" She would say, "I'm having my coffee, baby." That was it.

I always thought that was her way to let me know she had clarity. It seemed all right for the moment. She would later show that having her coffee was a moment early in the day where she could sit quietly and put her day together before my dad went off to work, before the children got up, and before she had to go to work too. That image of purposeful contemplation has stuck with me today. And as to a shout-out to the rap song, "Mama Said Knock You Out," I have always believed my mother's charge to stay focused on your work, your plan for life, and to knock it out. That kind of value in committed focus and following your plan faithfully is a value from her that cements, sticks, and stays in me.

What We Do

I am sure my identity speaks to a corralling of experiences shaped by all these incredible connections and sharing what we do as artists. We inspire and challenge each other as we do what we do in the world. The work of artists is always connected to a song, dance, poetry, and painting as we are moved with striking brushstrokes all at different times and at the same time all at once in many colors. It's a very dynamic thing, but we feel each other and we smile. Most of what I wanted to reach toward I am still reaching for and those triumphs I'd hope fifty would bring are within a finger's reach. And what's significant about this is that all any of us do is never solely the result of just our doing. All this resonates with the connections we have with others, and are representations of the culture we live in and out of that are we found.

Final Cadence: May 26, 2010

Nassau Street, Princeton, New Jersey
Living and loving out loud is a beautiful thing."

> —Cornel West, *Brother West: Living and Loving Out Loud, A Memoir*

> The republican party and hip hop benefit from the same mentality and human environments which have lots in common . . . keeping people ignorant, death and destruction, being distracted from truth, keeping people aligned to military actions mentality, gangsta' fear, and upholding a poisoned status quo.
>
> —Anthony Kelley, composer, Duke University

WB: What does that tattoo on your arms really mean for you?

Millennial tattooed young lady from North Carolina (born 1990): It will mean that I'll have something to remember that was significant for me, that was important for me now. I'm taking that risk with these, that I would have marked myself and that I'll have that, to value.

For me representing culture at this point in my life, 2010, is a full immersion in the living with the stuffings that fill up your life and the grappling with what that means in the moment, the times we live in. Because to represent is to live, to matter, to have meaning only because you "stand in" for that which is the what and the real of our existence. That's a hefty charge if you take it seriously. This generation, now called the Millennials, born from 1980, those twenty years younger than I, take "representing" very seriously. They "put their foot into" that step and claim, "I'm represent'n," marking their identity. Millennials with "their" text messaging, listening to, obtaining, purchasing music only through a computer or a smartphone, and seeing performance mostly on MTV or YouTube, how does that factor into music meaning, worth, and representing? The Millennials (Rihanna, born 1988), Generation Y or Google or the Techies, those born from 1980-something until now, then there are the Gen Xers, born from later 1960s through 1980s (Tupac), then there is our group, the bridge, a hybrid morphing of the classic definitions, the last tip of the baby boomers perhaps, but having their formative years shaped in the mid-seventies to eighties which I call, boomer-Xers (Barack Obama), then there are the "old people, the baby boomers" (1940–1954), and then the traditionalists, my parents' group born (1920s) at the start of the twentieth century. Even through my definitions here, with discrepancies in how I am marking these divisions in decades or ideologies and cultural value imprints, the most impactful defining markers are how each group sees themselves being represented, participating in the culture they live in and value. The classic generational worldviews: job done well (traditionalists), getting ahead through hard work and contributing to the great new society (postmodern baby boomers), survival (Gen X), and lastly the desire to create, innovate, and make your identity, and being heard now by creating your "own personal branding" (Millennials) have been put in place. (Information cited here from Lynne Lancaster and David Stillman's *The M Factor: How the Millennial Generation Is Rocking the Workplace*, 2009.) These are the kinds of representations that generally have marked generational thinking patterns in larger cultural society.

"Living and loving out loud is a beautiful thing," says Cornel West. It is also the title of his latest memoir on his life which he gave to me on a visit, during the late spring of 2010.

I end this memoir here in Princeton, New Jersey. I began my intellectual journey making an assessment of the parts of my spiritual, academic, and musical mapping by the encouraging words of Dr. Cornel West in 1988 or so when I began my doctoral studies in composition, at the University of Michigan, Ann Arbor. Cornel West encouraged me then to stay on this path and seek out another big brother, Jon Michael Spencer. It was that beginning of associations that grew my mind of ideas in this way. I read everything he wrote, watched him giving lectures, conferred and checked in for twenty years as he graciously always made time for and with me, teaching and always wrapping his deepest talks in the deepest tradition he too respects, Black music culture traditions. Cornel West came and inaugurated (with Sweet Honey in the Rock, Black Music Matters concert) the newly began Africana studies music programs I direct in Boston at the Berklee School of Music. Having dinner with Cornel that summer evening, hanging and sharing about music, rap, and hip-hop, Obama and hope, fears and doubts, and more hope, and most importantly, the critical importance of art to caress and correct the human spirit, given these days to chaos is timely.

While I handed him my then recent book on the philosophy of Black music, *Cultural Codes* (Scarecrow Press, 2010), it was in residence at Bowling Green University, being with another mentor Ray Browne, founder of American popular culture studies who died last year, that I completed *Black Notes: Essays of a Musician Writing in a Post-Album Age* (Scarecrow Press, 2004). From these starting points, I want to "shout 'bout and be properly representing rightly."

There is a challenge we have as public artists and scholars who represent the people, but the people don't really walk on the campus of Princeton or Bowling Green or Harvard. But here's the interesting identity that our group has: We are truly from the street, hood, and communities, but we glow and grow in many soils as "conscious select eclecticism" that happens to be our generational coding. We all pull from the best of many sources, and not unlike the Millennials who patch identity from many places. We do it differently. Cornel's *Living and Loving Out Loud* speaks to this idea of being "loud with love."

And as we sat and dined and hung, then walked the streets of Princeton meeting people, he strolling confidently and comfortably in his own deep and beautiful Black skin, "shouting out" to folks, and very common folks like the cab drivers, confused looking young brothers ("How are you doing, my young brother?"), encouraging dissertation students, bowing to women we passed by crossing the main Nassau Street from 6 p.m. until nearly 11 p.m., it imprinted further the way I too want to live my life representing as an artist who lives loudly with the spray of my expressions dripping wet in love.

Adding more to the sweetness of this cadence, I left Cornel that day to join Amiri Baraka in Newark. We met at the main Penn Station train terminal. This was literally meeting "da major" of Newark, poet beloved of the people, as Amiri's son, Ras Baraka, had just won the city's vote as a council representative (2010). As we walked over through the station to the downtown Hilton, everybody wanted to give a "shout out" to da' mayor of Newark, the poet of New Jersey, and to the thinker who for so many years gave us the cultural card to call ourselves Black, boldly, beautifully, and "badly."

Amiri and I are writing a book together on Pat Patrick, his good friend the great musician who played with Sun Ra for nearly forty years. We have his personal collection which I have the responsibility of archiving in Boston. Wonderfully, both *DownBeat* (July) and *Jazziz* (summer 2010) magazines did full feature stories with pictures of the opening and dedication of the Africana Studies Pat Patrick Archives. Both of these are powerful illustrations about what we mean by artists meeting in the streets of the worlds we live in, and that has to be represented as one example of what we do.

No ideological linkage at all, but we have to be cognizant of the representations that mark our times. Indifference and silence in our world is particularly inexcusable, especially for artists. But values change as you mature; that's what I shared with the tattooed young lady. We don't live only with what we want to remember, or lived and did, we value the way we live in and live through the world as we become. Becoming is as much about representing and more important than what you did.

A profile of me in *Jazziz* magazine.

What if that kind of representing, taking full ownership of what you mean to people, what you value, how you mark yourself, how you stand, how you connect with community in love, could be our end goals? So in this way, all we do should be focused on the serious engagement we seek to share with others. In this way we could not stand without the others' legs and heart to breathe.

With composer Anthony Kelley and author and professor Mark Anthony Neal at Duke University, 2010.

Given who we are in this modern way in 2010 and beyond, what must we do to be sane? We watch, we work, we wait, we hope, we pray. Still, I am as I was in 2009, inspired by hope. I guess now I just have hope in hoping as a coping mechanism.

We don't stop the work; we keep moving. With still the greed, hatred, wars, social decay, and the downward spiral of the larger megaculture we live among in contemporary society, with the funk that's all around, we simply learn to live in the stench, knowing in reality the stink will not yet go away. Perhaps we are just deodorizing and opening the door when it will, to allow the joy of the refreshing breezes to rekindle the faith and allow us to take another deep surviving breath before stepping in and out again.

I can return now to a theme I introduced earlier in this book where I stated that pouring what you have into someone is an act of purposeful giving. This idea of love and giving to one another, our ideas, values, who we are to one another really means even more to me in the light of the great loss of my mother, my own maturing into the realities of knowing our representations are not always a harmonious cadence. Art in my mind is always about representative and giving expression. There is no other reason why artists create other than to represent and to share. To represent culture is to engage in the living of connective, representative living and then, at the end, to have "a concert of the sharing," to honor the gifts and the enjoyment of what that kind of living means to all involved. That's what artists think about a whole lot. That's what I want to be focused on in my years fifty to seventy, twenty more "arts years of being" with and celebrating that incredible gift we are given for seeing and giving and being in the world. We as artists want to be representing culture and that is a life marked by giving actually.

All my best,
Bill Banfield, 2011

PART III

WHEN AGAIN?

Thirtieth anniversary of Boston's John Coltrane Memorial Concert, 2007. From left to right: Stan Strickland, Tim Ingles, John Lockwood, Eric Jackson, Bill Pierce, Leonard Brown, Carl Atkins, Emmit Price, Amiri Baraka, Ravi Coltrane, Syd Smart, Bill Thompson, and Larry McClellan.

CHAPTER THIRTEEN

The Artist Photo Profiles

The most important aspect of this book is the illumination and visibility of the work, exchanges among Black artists working in American culture during these important thirty years, 1979–2010. People rarely see this documented outside of the frames of mainstream media which are usually only drawn through the suffocating pens of stardom. Artists work and live together, fueled by a common gift to give expression to ideas and experiences, and they inspire and collaborate with one another. Music for musicians is about love, collaboration, development, sharing, fun, and focus, moving people, about "who you be" and "what you be about" deeply committed to, being seen on the scene with the song to sing, about styles, grace, and moving a soul up in this place. These ideas are represented here through the workings of more than 170 contemporary connected artists, hanging together in these thirty-plus years, growing up and developing contemporary art practice and culture. These are pictures I took with a variety of cameras over the years, pictures of musicians, artists, teachers, poets, dancers—just hanging. There is no more significant act done by musicians than reaching people, hanging out, making music with other musicians and artists. All the shots of friends were representative of the many spaces and places we artists work, onstage as well as in between the curtain and the downbeat, during meals, in clubs, on tour, in rehearsal, teaching in class and in their studios, lecturing at and attending conferences, at public art installments or contemplating creatively alone, recording sessions, over meals, mentoring, reading scores together, passing on info from father to son, auntie to niece, or from artist to audience, these are many of the ways artistry gets represented and put out there. Most of these are people I consult with weekly and have been most supportive and inspirational in shaping my life as a musician and artist; this is my artist family, my group.

T. J. Anderson

T. J. Anderson is my musical father. He is the great master who birthed me into thinking seriously about the depth of musical creation, process, structure, and being a composer. He headed the music department of Tufts University, served as composer in residence with the Atlanta Symphony, and was the composer who brought to life in orchestration, the Scott Joplin opera, *Treemonisha*. T. J. Anderson is the leading Black modernist composing figure today. He and his wife, our big sister Lois Anderson, have been colleagues to the biggest minds and artists, particularly in contemporary concert music circles for decades. T. J. is on the board of the American Academy of Artists.

Victor Bailey

We were all about nineteen years old when we heard Victor Bailey was called to go on the road with Joe Zawinul, Wayne Shorter, and Weather Report—the world's greatest jazz band at that time—to replace Jaco Pastorius. Nothing else need be said! Victor Bailey is the great bass virtuoso player of our generation. Born into a musical family, his dad was a musician and writer, but too, uncles, grandfather, brother, and mother all were musical. It was in his early college days at Berklee and hanging out in New York that he heard Joe Zawinul replaced the great Jaco Pastorius. Victor spent the next twenty years defining the next "sound directions" of electric bass, and as a recording artist, producer, and sessions performer he played with everyone from Sonny Rollins to Mary J. Blige and toured with Madonna.

David Baker

My brother, teacher, and great friend. No one living has defined jazz education more within the academy for players than David Baker. People don't just sing David Baker melodies, they sing David Baker exercises. That's deep for musicians, that somebody can teach you exercises that shape your development. One of the greatest teachers and program developers in American academy, he has done it all—Grammy nominations, Grammy awards, NEA Jazz Masters award, serving on the Pulitzer Prize Committees, writing books, running major training camps, composing everything that can be possibly written for instruments, instructing choirs, inspiring thousands of composers and performers. David Baker is a living legend in American music, never to be matched.

Amiri Baraka

Our Black artist consciousness. He taught several generations everything that mattered about being Black and being an artist in American culture. The foundational books, *Blues People, Black Music: The Autobiography of LeRoi Jones*, the plays, the musicals, the poetry, social criticism, music reviews, the Black arts movements, and every political speech, social consciousness poem, and play, were the strongest literary and philosophical treatises ever written about Black expression in America, its history, meaning, and artistry. Amiri Baraka is the indispensable voice in the history of modern art expression. I modeled everything I wanted to be as a thinking artist from his work, and to this day he is a part of my every conscious conversation and writing about Black music and its impact and meaning in society.

Dr. Ysaye Barnwell

Ysaye is a great artist in our time. Besides being the distinctive bass voice of the world renowned Sweet Honey in the Rock, she is its principal composer and guiding leader, after Bernice Reagon retired. Known too for her arresting and captivating workshops and lectures on "singing together as community," her work is uniting generations of people around the most common ideas of connection through singing, to reflection on the state of world affairs.

Marcus Bellgrave

Our Detroit great Jazz teacher. He is a musical institution in Detroit. The Detroit master played in the 1950s with Ray Charles, Charles Mingus, Tony Bennett, Sammy Davis Jr., Dizzy Gillespie, Ella Fitzgerald. Marcus inspired us all young Detroiters, through his incredible education and jazz mentor efforts from which Geri Allen, Kenny Garret, Rodney Whitiker, James Carter, Bob Hurst, Regina Carter, Carlos McKinney, myself, and many others all came through in various forms.

Composer John Costas, Stephen Newby, Leonard Bernstein, the author, and composer Denise Ince.

Leonard Bernstein

No musical personality fired me up more than Leonard Bernstein. No American artist of any shape, besides Quincy Jones, has accomplished more. Leonard Bernstein was a giant in the world of music. He sat me down and said why it was important to be an American composer.

Terrance Blanchard

Terrence Blanchard and me.

How many Black musicians get to compose film scores for major movies? One from my generation: Terrance Blanchard. Terrance is a great New Orleans musician, great trumpet player, band leader and recording artist, and Spike Lee's go-to-man for music, an industry leader.

Bill Brown

Ron Crutcher, me, and Bill Brown.

One of the greatest Black concert singers in the world. No performer championed Black classical contemporary composers more by not only singing works in concerts, but commissioning them as well, than Bill Brown. He was our Black music solider. He had the most distinctive voice you will ever hear. Again, Bill Brown championed our music as composers and made people listen to the sophisticated songs of contemporary Black composers. His gift and vision for artistry in this way could never be matched. The first thing out of his mouth to every composer he met and admired was, "Where's my music?"

Dr. Rae Linda Brown

The author with musicologists Dr. Rae Linda Brown (left) and Dr. Dominique de Lerma (right).

Rae Linda Brown is the leading musicologist of our generation. She has authored, edited, and championed the work of African American composer, Florence Price, and helped lead the way in Black music history studies as a professor in music for decades. Currently, she serves as vice president of undergraduate education, Loyola

Marymount University, in California. She taught us all in the ways of the academy, at every level. Many of us passed through her courses in African American music as doctoral students at the University of Michigan, Ann Arbor, in the 1990s, but she was our big sister, friend, and academic career counselor to this day. These musicians at University of Michigan include: Guthrie Ramsey, Louise Toppin, Kyra Gaunt, Timothy Holley, Stephen Newby, Jethro Woodson, Gregg Broughton, Tiffany Jackson, Anita Johnson, Joshua Hood, Rachel Williams, Darryl Taylor, Timothy Jones, Charsie Sawyer, Albert Howard, Ray Wade. Most of these Black artists are professors of music at major colleges and universities across the country or are performing with the likes of Metropolitan Opera and major symphony orchestras. This is amazing, and all of us are mentored by this fabulous woman.

With Ray Browne.

Dr. Ray Browne

How do you create a way of appreciating and studying the world differently? Dr. Ray Browne created American popular culture studies and championed well into his nineties.

Don Byron and me.

Don Byron

Don Byron is a fantastic musician! And too, every jazz generation has a clarinet performer and while Don plays and writes all, we first knew him as the greatest jazz clarinetist of our group. Like most of the artists in our post–civil rights group, Byron is an eclectic, as his change of hats is fluent, as jazz artist, arranger, composer, and contemporary musical thinker. We attended together, along with Najee, Regina Carter, and Rachel Z, NEC as young undergraduates. Don went on to become a leading new music jazz artist with more than ten albums on Blue Note and Non-Such record labels. Always leading in most respected jazz readers polls, feature stories in *New York Times*, in 1992 was named best jazz artist in *DownBeat* magazine, as a wind player his music languages again are vast from jazz to klezmer, classical, funk, hip-hop, and new concert music, being commissioned for concert works and festivals. He is known well, too, as an artist's social critic, one with edge. For our group, Don Byron is the artist's progressive.

Regina Carter

Simply put: She is the world's leading jazz violinist. Regina Carter is today recognized as popular culture's violinist. A recording artist, cultural icon for the instrument, a MacArthur Fellows "Genius" Award recipient, grew up in Detroit, worked on her craft, art, sought her mentors out and learned from them, then went out and took hold of the music world her way.

Billy Childs

The single most respected jazz composer of my generation. A world class jazz artist too, began playing with J. J. Johnson, Freddie Hubbard, and working close with another mentor of his, Chick Corea. Billy was notably carried as a signed artist for many years on the Windham Hill, Stretch, and Shanachie jazz labels, and most recently, ArtistShare. His incredible Jazz Chamber art was awarded the Grammy for Best Jazz Composition in 2006, for his *Lyric* album, and earlier Grammy nominations for his arranging *Fascinating Rhythm* for jazz vocalist Dianne Reeves. But it is his work as a composer that is most original and inspiring, as he has forged through his work one of the most unique compositional voices, a blending of serious composition and form with jazz improvisation. His work defines jazz's best next directions compositionally.

Ornette Coleman and me.

Ornette Coleman

How do you write a new way to play?
How do you play a new way to hear?
How do you hear a new way to say what music is?
How do you tell music making to be another way so players can be more deeply absorbed?
Ornette Coleman did all of that.

Carla Cook

One of today's most distinctive voices in jazz. Carla Cook, in the hardworking way from her upbringing in Detroit, schooling in the East, and gigging, established her craft and following in New York, went on to becoming a recording, touring artist upholding and representing the work of jazz vocal artistry. A recording artist with several albums carried on MazJazz label, her distinct voice and lyrical-soulful approach to song interpretations has made her a favorite in New York and national circles and among friends.

My father William Banfield with Harold Cruse.

Harold Cruse

Harold Cruse was my great culture thinking teacher and mentor. I taught his classes at University of Michigan, Ann Arbor, and sat at his feet being trained about how to think about culture. He wrote the greatest book on academic identity for Black thinkers, *The Crisis of the Negro Intellectual*, about and on our identity which we have still not corrected nor recovered. I love this picture of my dad and him strolling as Black gents after having coffee in Ann Arbor, Michigan.

With George Duke.

George Duke

Nobody is more funky.
Nobody's palette is wider.
Nobody has produced more great
recordings and been a mentor for
more artists than George Duke.
The great musician.
I just call him the master.

Marcus Bellgrave, Douglas Ewart, and me.

Douglas Ewart

Multi-wind performer, master
musician, award-winning performance conceptualist, recording
artist, and an active member of
the AACM, Douglas works and
records locally in Minneapolis
and around the world.

Jon Faddis and me.

Jon Faddis

The tradition of Dizzy Gillespie
continues in my generation through
the performance, big band directing, and artistry of Jon Faddis.

With John Hope Franklin.

John Hope Franklin

The great African American historian. He told and lived our stories. There will never be another
to write and keep the story as high
and meaningfully erected as John
Hope Franklin.

My wife Krystal and Nnenna Freelon.

Nnenna Freelon

There was for a generation, a line of defining and distinct sounds/ voices: Bessie Smith, then Ella, Billie, Betty, Nina, Aretha, Phyllis. Today it is Nnenna Freelon. Nnenna is a major defining voice of jazz performing artistry of our times. Six-time Grammy Award nominee, she has performed with Herbie Hancock, Al Jarreau, Count Basie Orchestra, and Take 6. A recording artist who has performed at arts and jazz festivals, in musicals and opera, and headlined clubs all over the world, her delivery, style, depth, range of repertoire, detail, voice command, and stunning beauty takes your breath away.

Henry Louis Gates Jr.

No one has done more in the "public mainstream" eye for championing at such a populist level as a professor and scholar than Henry Louis Gates. He built one of the most visible and powerful African American studies departments at Harvard. Few Black writers, besides Ralph Ellison, John Hope Franklin, Amiri Baraka, and Toni Morrison, have written the definitive books on thought, expression, history in an area. Everyone who speaks about Black language refers to his work,

The Signifying Monkey. He, like his great idol, W. E. B. Du Bois, is our Black academic institution builder of the modern age.

Berry Gordy and me.

Berry Gordy

Berry Gordy is the founding father figure of Motown, which at its peak was one of the largest Black-owned businesses in the world. In music, publishing, film, and music talent–management/development, Berry Gordy was an entrepreneurial visionary, a musical symbol of Black urban music creation in America. As a Detroiter, he helped to brand the city as the musical sound of young America with an almost endless array of artists, including Marvin Gaye, Stevie Wonder, the Temptations, Smokey Robinson and the Miracles, the Four Tops, Diana Ross and the Supremes, the Jackson 5, and too many others to mention.

Herbie Hancock

Herbie is a master. His contribution to our music culture is legendary. He is one of those child prodigy geniuses who didn't stop being a prodigy genius when he turned twenty. Every decade from 1965 to 2005, he created and innovated the music, and then doing what none had done, won the Grammy for, not best jazz record, but best record in 2008. He is the great example of humanitarianism among artists—not just in deeds but in his humble spirit, generosity, and character. A musical angel walks among us.

Donald Harrison

His resemblance to and resonance of John Coltrane is scary, as great spirits in art never leave our presence. Donald, after graduating from Berklee College of Music, teamed up with fellow New Orleanian Terrance Blanchard, both performing with Art Blakey's Jazz Messengers in the 1980s, and formed the then-modern recording equivalent to Bird and Dizzy. Donald Harrison is one of our giants in music as an incredible musician, mentor of young artists, a great New Orleans big Indian chief, a searcher of wisdom, and keeper of the soul. He is the great example in my mind of genuine moral, spiritual, and artistic greatness.

Morris Hayes

Morris Hayes is today Prince's main music tour, production, and musical director of his NPG bands and a part of his musical team since the 1980s. Morris is an amazing pianist, keyboard electronic synthesis master, recording sound and production engineer. His work has stretched across every kind of popular music including jazz and he has worked with everybody from Prince to Lenny Kravitz, Maceo Parker, Mint Condition, Chaka Khan, Erykah Badu, Sheryl Crow, will.i.am. He wears all the hats of the contemporary recording, performing, producing musician.

Jon Hendricks

Jon Hendricks and me.

Known to many as the jazz singer who lyricized classic bebop music in the 1950s, '60s, '70s, Mr. Hendricks has become one of the leading figures in vocal jazz culture popularizing "vocalese" styles. His numerous associations with leading artists such as Dizzy Gillespie, Max Roach, others and as an arranger, made him an articulate advocate and "speaking artists" for Black music practices. Principally associated with the vocal trio Lambert, Hendricks, and Ross, he recorded numerous jazz works and set the standard for vocal scatting, harmonization, and modern jazz approaches. He is a vocal giant in Black music.

Gary Hines

Gary Hines standing behind me at the piano.

Gary Hines created and produced a sound, a band with full touring choir, called the Sounds of Blackness. He is a giant of a soul and deeply committed to our music. Everybody loves Gary Hines—he is one of our greats in upholding great Black music traditions. The Sounds of Blackness was created as a Macalester College group from Minnesota and Gary nurtured that community and introduced an all encompassing choir/band ensemble that sang gospel, R & B, jazz. He created a top charting community model that embodied those critical principles of Black music practice, and was a critical member of the new wave of sound in the 1980s and 1990s from Minneapolis that included Prince, the Time, and Mint Condition.

Harold McKinney and Milt Hinton.

Milt Hinton and Harold McKinney

It's ironic that I have this shot of Milt Hinton, the great bassist and widely appreciated for photographing many of the great jazz musicians of his generation, here seen with Detroit jazz pianist great Harold McKinney. As a younger composer I was commissioned to write a piece for five bassists to honor Milt Hinton.

With Quincy Jones and David Baker.

Quincy Jones

The greatest accomplishments in music ever and the deepest human commitment to seeing those accomplishments represented the best we can be and become.

Mark Ledford

There are few as naturally and critically gifted and focused on their skills as was the singer, trumpeter, guitarist, writer, producer, arranger Mark Ledford. From Detroit, a graduate of Berklee College of Music, he was the voice of the Pat Matheny Band. Mark worked with everyone as a New York session backup singer and producer too from Mary J. Blige to Steve Winwood. He was a super talent who left us way too early. Our group from Detroit (Regina Carter, Carla Cook, Terry Connelly, Jeff Stanton) will never be the same because of this great loss in our personal and professional lives and growth as musicians. We miss you more than madly, Mark.

Spike Lee (second from right) and me at the University of Michigan, c. 1990.

Spike Lee

Spike Lee is our cultural scripter in cinematic form, at a time when the visual imagery of this generation was beginning to be the defining aesthetic component. We hadn't had an Oscar Micheaux or Melvin Van Peebles for our generation until Spike Lee burst onto the scene innovatively and powerfully with *She's Gotta Have It* (1986). Mars, his alter ego, as is Alfred Hitchcock's funny insertion of himself in his own films, was a character who represented a comedic seer antecedent response to the filmmaker's serious plunge for us into the questions of modern Black identity, sexuality, race relations, violence, and cultural coding not before seen. Because of his brilliant work we marveled as he championed our narratives, issues in an "up in whitey's face way," about being a progressive Black person in racist American culture. He said powerfully and beautifully all we wanted to say—in music, politics, literature, TV, and magazines—in his films, from *School Daze* (1988), *Do the Right Thing* (1989), *Mo' Better Blues* (1990), *Jungle Fever* (1991), *Malcolm X* (1992), *Crooklyn* (1994), *Clockers* (1995), *Get on the Bus* (1996), *Four Little Girls* (1997), and my favorite, *Bamboozled* (2000). With *When the Levees Broke* (2006), in which he documented the devastation and irresponsibility of the Bush regime to adequately respond and help the area and residents, he continued the great legacy of people like Langston Hughes and Ralph Ellison in tying social critique in other mediums with the sacred care and canon of our music and musicians. Spike Lee's work for my group is monumental, and the most representative media model of Blackness in all its splendor and complexity.

Lionel Loueke

A leading innovative voice of my generation, West African Benin jazz guitarist Lionel Loueke has been hailed as the new voice in contemporary jazz guitar. Lionel creatively combines African vernacular approach, sounds, rhythms, and harmonies to blend a unique Afro jazz art. Herbie Hancock, a frequent collaborator, has called Lionel a "musical painter." The *New York Times* called him "a startlingly original voice and one of the most striking jazz artists to emerge in some time."

Marsalis Brothers

Those Marvelous Marsalis Brothers: Branford, Delfeayo, Jason, and Wynton. The royal musical family of my generation.

With Branford Marsalis.

Delfeayo Marsalis.

Jason Marsalis.

Wynton Marsalis.

Portia Maultsby, me, and Hale Smith.

Portia Maultsby
(Indiana University)

The great ethnomusicologist who pushed and pulled a generation of us to examine more thoroughly the history and culture of Black popular music. Portia and the crew at Indiana University, along with David Baker, created the longest and most prominent Black music and popular music studies paradigm in American academic history. We are all more knowledgeable and informed about Black music studies because of this school, the University of Michigan and U Mass Amherst, all of which created and maintained through the late 1960s and 1970s through 2000 or so, the most dynamic academic scholarly research, centers, archives and prominent artist/scholars' collectives anywhere in the world. Many of today's leading thinkers came through, knew about, and collaborated in the mix of this wave of training connections.

Bobby McFerrin

I call him the walking note. Bobby McFerrin is the most illuminative example we have today of pure genius artistry of undeniable singularity of sound, approach, and impact. No singer alive today has more innovated musical singing artistry than Bobby McFerrin. Bobby's musical legend as a performer, innovator, conductor, musical conceptualist, and recording innovator has made him one of the most sought after modern artists in the world. He also is a great husband, father, and human being.

Marcus Miller

No one has seen this photo of Marcus Miller with an upright bass (I'm particularly proud of this shot). He is the most well-known and respected bassist of our generation. His musical genius and leadership have shaped Luther Vandross to Miles Davis and beyond. He is one of the best and most visible examples we have of a great and famous musician who symbolizes as in the past what the finest of our musicians do.

Mint Condition

There are six bands left standing: Rolling Stones, U2, the Roots, Dave Matthews Band, Earth, Wind & Fire, and "our band": Mint Condition. Mint Condition is the greatest Black band living and performing today, and everybody from our group looks to them to be the model.

Undine Smith Moore

Of all the great women composers, Undine Smith Moore stands out as one of the great teacher mentors and one of the most performed.

With Undine Smith Moore.

Yusef Komunyakaa, Toni Morrison, Krystal, and me.

Toni Morrison

Our master American novelist is the great Toni Morrison. She commissioned an opera from me, hired me to teach as a visiting artist/professor at Princeton, and put me together with the greatest poet of our generation, Yusef Komunyakaa.

Najee

Najee, known to many as one of the first waves in the 1990s in smooth jazz, is one of the finest musicians of our generation. Widely respected, but highly "under discussed" as a major saxophone voice, he is as influential to Branford and Donald Harrison as older great masters. Najee was influencing everyone who heard him in Boston or New York in those late seventies, early eighties years. He left Boston performing first with Chaka Khan, before being signed, recording, and going on to be the premier "smooth jazz" modern jazz saxophonist. But to the musicians, he is a great saxophonist. He is my big brother, the first musician who literally took me to New York and said, "If you want to be a musician, you have to learn to get around New York circles, so let's go."

With Stephen Newby.

Stephen Newby

My best friend in the world, Dr. Stephen Newby—"Newbsky"—and I grew up together in the same hood in Detroit, Russell Woods. We began making music together in the sixth grade, completed our master's and doctorates and lived in Ann Arbor together. We've gigged together, toured in Africa together, produced concert series together. We've watched each other be married to women we love. We talk about everything together. A supremely gifted pianist, composer, vocalist, educator, choir director, and a "classic PK" who grew up in the Black Detroit Baptist church and writes symphonies, gospel, and opera. Stephen Newby is a complete twenty-first century musician. He serves as professor of music at Pacific Northwest University, Seattle.

With Gordon Parks.

Gordon Parks

I stand here next to a legendary artist who took pictures, wrote books and essays, composed music, played, and gigged. He is our quintessential Race Man and Renaissance Man, our model.

Dr. Willis Patterson

The great Black dean of music, University of Michigan, who brought more Black musicians into the academy than anyone. Black musicians could name him the Willis Patterson Conservatory.

Michael Powell

Michael Powell and me.

Michael Powell, guitarist/producer from Detroit, via Chicago, simply saved music in the 1990s by bringing back for a moment real, live playing musicians on records—not multi-tracked, but playing together. Michael Powell was the musical mind behind the sound of Anita Baker. He wrote, produced, and played guitar on all those hit albums, and hired the best musicians around. He was our second Berry Gordy. Michael Powell's work brought integrity and musicality back into the music industry by again reintroducing "live performing" musical records, a radical move in the middle of programmed dance/synthesized drum beat led productions in the late 1980s. His work was nothing less than a revolution in popular music, and he continued to produce many of the major, respected singers of the day throughout the 1990s including Aretha Franklin, Patti LaBelle, Jennifer Holiday, Gladys Knight, James Ingram, Oleta Adams, Grover Washington Jr., and Aaliyah. His sound is great music sound, and his musical integrity set a new precedent for popular music not matched since.

Guthrie Ramsay

Guthrie Ramsay and me.

Guthrie Ramsay is another important voice in contemporary musicology in our time. Professor of Musicology at U Penn, author, and a gifted Chicago born pianist whose fingers speak fluent Bud Powell, gospel, and funk. He wrote the leading Black music book of our generation, *Race Music*, and is helping to define what Black culture holds and means for the next generations to do something with it.

Max Roach

One of the greatest jazz drummers and renowned musicians from the bebop era. He is honored here with a drum concerto with the Atlanta Symphony, by composer, Dr. Fred Tillis.

Patrice Rushen teaching the author's Africana studies students at Berklee College of Music, 2009.

Patrice Rushen

Among our group, no one has done more in the professional field of music as the pianist, composer, recording artist, performer, singer, jazz performer, arranger, musical director, film scorer, and producer than Patrice Rushen. Patrice Rushen is the model that musicians in the industry looked toward and were measured by. She has worked, produced, and been musical director for everybody from Janet Jackson, to Prince, to being the music director of the Emmy, NAACP, and Grammy Awards shows, to being composer in residence with the Detroit Symphony. Patrice is a seminal figure in our development in contemporary music. She is my "big sister."

George Russell and me.

George Russell

The great jazz theory educator. The great visionary who challenged Miles Davis how to think new ways in music, Dizzy Gillespie, new ways to write music, and taught so many of us new ways to approach jazz improvisation and music as a sonic approach.

Christian Scott

Makes us proud. The legacy has not stopped. Christian Scott represents in approach, attitude, style the new directions in jazz artistry. His records and his multiangled approach to the genre earned him a Grammy nomination for Best Contemporary Jazz Album in 2008. Nephew of jazz great Donald Harrison and a native New Orleanian, Scott consciously forges new definitions for jazz, and one of the few who never separates nor distances himself from hip-hop and contemporary popular culture.

Grammy winner Esperanza Spalding.

Esperanza Spalding

Wow!!!! She arrived and made us believe in genius again, redefining bass approaches, and redefining the presence and impact of modern jazz artistry. I love her humanity too.

Bill with members of Sweet Honey in the Rock.

Sweet Honey in the Rock

The leading, defining, contributing and living a cappella voice ensemble of our generation who have clarified, documented, and sounded the meaning of our social and cultural expression for nearing forty years. There have been twenty-plus female artists who have made up Sweet Honey in the Rock, and these six (Ysaye Maria Barnwell, Nitanju Bolade Casel, Aisha Kahlil, Carol Maillard, Louise Robinson, and Shirley Childress Saxton, their sign interpreter) have held the posts the longest. Founded by master griot Bernice Johnson Reagon in 1973 at the D.C. Black Repertory Theater Company, Sweet Honey in the Rock has been a vital and innovative presence in American music culture from Washington, D.C., to communities of conscience around the world. Their work and repertoire is steeped in the sacred music of the Black church, the street calls of the civil rights movement, songs of the struggle for justice, youth empowerment, and sometimes just the fun and meaning of being Black women in the world. There exists no other group like this with such stunning vocal prowess and presence that captures so completely our music; the complex sounds of blues, spirituals, traditional gospel hymns, rap, reggae, African chants, hip-hop, ancient lullabies, and jazz improvisation. Sweet Honey in the Rock is a world treasure.

Members of Take 6.

Take 6

The most significant and innovative sound and group that our generation saw coming up in the 1980s and 1990s. Take 6's emerging and virtuosic vocal artistry set a precedence based on the best of Black American, jazz, gospel, doo-wop, American vocal, and song traditions not matched since.

Dr. Billy Taylor

The towering senior figure in jazz music culture today. No person has done more to represent this legacy of great American music than Billy Taylor. From his days as the house pianist at Mintons, the seminal birthplace of bebop, to teaching jazz in the streets of New York with Jazzmobile—from professor at the University of Massachusetts at Amherst and author of books and articles to becoming the most articulate spokesperson in media on American jazz music (as he created the phrase), jazz is America's classical music—Billy Taylor is a legend.

From left: Krystal and me, Bill Brown, Louise Toppin, and Leon Bates.

Louise Toppin

One of our treasures, Dr. Louise Toppin has perfect pitch. She runs the only recording label in the world that exclusively records music by Black classical musicians. Her father was the great Black historian, Edgar Toppin. She is a coloratura soprano opera singer. She received her master's in classical piano and doctorate in voice performance from the University of Michigan. She is voice professor at University of Carolina, Chapel Hill.

Cornel West and me.

Dr. Cornel West

No one in our time has more beautifully, visibly, and profoundly represented a walking, connected prophet, and philosopher.

Charles Wilson and me.

Charles Wilson

My cousin makes more money than I could ever imagine a young musician making. He says his generation is the "beat generation," and they hear things differently. In the band as pianist for Justin Timberlake, Timbaland, Rihanna, and John Mayer, he is the current generation of musicians. He is truly representing.

Women Musicians

The ladies of my generation take their humanity, genius, artistry, and womanhood and represent in the most powerful way we have seen in history. They command their artistry and identity as artists with a power that has to do with mastery of music and meaning and never merchandising, selling perfume, purses, and makeup. In addition to Regina Carter, Patrice Rushen, Straight Ahead, and the ladies of Sweet Honey in the Rock, who I have already mentioned: Geri Allen, Teri Lyne Carrington, Maria Schneider, and the Uptown String Quartet.

With Teri Lyne Carrington.

With Maria Schneider.

The Uptown String Quartet.

With George Benson.

Kevin Eubanks and me.

With Mick Goodrick.

Earl Klugh.

Guitar Voices

George Benson, Kevin Eubanks, Mick Goodrick, Earl Klugh, Lionel Loueke, Pat Metheny, and Emily Remler. I am growing today to become a guitarist because of them. Each one changing the direction of modern guitar. For Emily Remler, Pat Metheny, and me, the master Mick Goodrick shaped us. Earl Klugh and Kenny Burrel are my big brothers from Detroit, both whom I check in with. George Benson and Pat Metheny always encouraging. The guitarists of my generation, Kevin Eubanks, Stanley Jordan, and Lionel Loueke, keep adding to the further innovative directions the guitar in jazz has taken, yet these masters are never torn from the traditions that the people mostly know. That is real important.

With Pat Metheny and Mark Ledford.

Emily Remler.

Back row (left to right): Dwight Andrews, Donal Fox, T. J. Anderson, unknown, Oliver Lake. Front row (left to right): Evan Thomas, Anthony Kelly, Trevor Weston, Alvin Singleton.

Black Beethovens

There are at least thirty Black American working classical composers here in these shots, a rarity if ever seen, and certainly never together at once. This group I know well. I literally wrote the book about their work and processes (*Landscapes in Color*, 1996). Here is one of the rarest group of Black artists, mostly invisible to the American public. These artists don't write jazz, popular, nor gospel music. Most of these artists only write for operas, symphony, chamber, or solo "classical music" works. These musicians are highly, highly trained, the most sophisticated musically, and write works that critics would call the work of "musical geniuses." But you will never, ever and more never hear about these musicians and their work on CNN, BET, MTV or see them on YouTube. Black Beethovens: Michael Abels, Leslie Adams, T.J. Anderson, Dwight Andrews, Lettie Bechon Alston, Regina Harris Biocchi, Noel Dacosta, Anthony Davis, Donal Fox, Adolphus Hailstork, Howard Harris, Augustus Hill, Jonathan Holland, Anthony Kelly, Oliver Lake, Tania Leon, Wendell Logan, Dorothy Rudd Moore, Jeffrey Mumford, Hannibal Peterson, Gary Nash Powell, Daniel Romain, Ralph Russell, Kevin Scott, Alvin Singleton, Hale Smith, Robert Tanner, Frederick Tillis, George Walker, Trevor Weston, Julius Williams, Kimo Williams, Olly Wilson, and Michael Woods.

Back row (left to right): Author, Regina Harris Biocchi, Kevin Scott, Ralph Russell, Leslie Dunner, Gary Nash Powell, Anthony Kelly, unknown, Augustus Hill, unknown, Stephen Newby. Front row (left to right): T. J. Anderson, Lettie Bechon Alston, Hale Smith, Adolphus Hailstork.

Clockwise from left front: Gary Nash Powell, Kevin Scott, Kaye George Roberts, Lettie Bechon Alston, Wendell Logan, Regina Harris Biocchi, Michael Abels.

From left to right: Alvin Singleton, Wendell Logan, Olly Wilson, Me, George Walker, T.J. Anderson, Dwight Andrews.

With Tania Leon.

From left to right: Hale Smith, Anthony Davis, T.J. Anderson.

Index

About the Author

The author performing at his fiftieth birthday celebration.

Dr. William (Bill) Banfield is a composer, jazz guitarist, author, and educator. He is professor of Africana studies/music and society in the Liberal Arts Department and director of the Africana Studies Center and Programming at Berklee College of Music. His work focuses on the aesthetic history of Black music culture and the power of music to hold, transfer, and sustain cultural value.

His other books include *Musical Landscapes in Color: Conversations with Black American Composers* (2003), *Black Notes: Essays of a Musician Writing in a Post-Album Age* (2004), and *Cultural Codes: Makings of a Black Music Philosophy, An Interpretive History from Spirituals to Hip Hop* (2010), all published by Scarecrow Press. He also serves as the editor of the African American Cultural Theory and Heritage series published by Scarecrow Press.